Transformers and a Flour Mill. These forthright simple forms are determined by their functions. At the same time we may see them as a group of cylinders of contrasting light and dark, rhythmically repeated. (Photograph of Charles Rain)

UNDERSTANDING
THE ARTS

BY

HELEN GARDNER, A.M.

ASSISTANT PROFESSOR OF HISTORY OF ART
IN THE SCHOOL OF THE ART INSTITUTE OF CHICAGO
AUTHOR OF "ART THROUGH THE AGES"

HARCOURT, BRACE AND COMPANY
NEW YORK · CHICAGO

PRINTED IN THE U·S·A

Preface

TODAY the arts are coming to the fore. Colleges and high schools are increasing their courses both in number and in content. Art appreciation programs, especially in music, are coming over the air. The layman is demanding better design in his car, in the furnishings of his home, in advertising. Thousands evince a healthy interest in art and a genuine desire to understand it. The purpose of this book, then, is to suggest an approach to an understanding of the arts; and while it is adapted primarily to high school and normal school art appreciation courses, it is the hope of the author that it will serve anyone who is eager for guidance.

Guidance, we say. For neither book nor instructor can teach true appreciation of art any more than a guide can climb the mountain for the traveler. The most that one can do is to offer guidance, to show a path which will help the student to do his own climbing, that is, to see, to feel, and to think for himself. How this guidance can be given will always be a matter for difference of opinion. There can be no *one* approach. For the subject is too complex and appreciation too personal to be reduced to catchwords. Dudley Scott is sensitive to rhythm; hence a work of art that is strongly rhythmic will appear to him as " great." James Ball, on the other hand, is sensitive to color, to certain harmonies and contrast; Sally Brown, to other color combinations; Lee Barnes, to austere symmetry; Marian Fischer to grace and charm. There is neither formula nor authority to judge dogmatically which among pictures is " the greatest." Art is broad enough to include many kinds of greatness. It matters little whether Dudley Scott and James Ball agree or disagree on this or that picture. But it matters much whether each knows *why* he likes one

picture better than another; that each can trace his preference in part, at least, to fundamental principles.

An appreciation of art, then, involves an understanding
of essential principles of art expression — balance, proportion, rhythm, variety, unity, harmony. Hence it is the aim
of the author so to present these principles that the student
can see them, feel them, and can think through the *whys*
of their operation, and can discern this operation not only
in great works of art but also in everyday life.

The approach suggested in this book is the result of
years of experience in teaching the introductory course in
the subject in the School of the Art Institute of Chicago,
with modifications to make the volume practicable for
classroom use. It recommends going to the best teachers
first, that is, to works of art of acknowledged high quality.
" I go to the Louvre," said Cézanne, " to find myself." Its
theory is this: show the student a building of the best
quality and explain *why* it is what it is and *why* it is good;
and show him, for contrast, a building that is not so good
and explain *why* it is not so good; then lead him to see that
his own home or school is good or not so good for the
same reasons. Answering this question " why " in the
case of a dozen buildings will bring out principles that
are common to them all and will reveal the fact that the
skyscraper, the Nebraska State Capitol, and the University
of Chicago Chapel are one in principle with the Colosseum, the Parthenon, Chartres, and the Taj Mahall. Thus
the student is given concrete evidence of the universality
of these principles; of their equal functioning in the cathedral and in the factory; and of their equal validity today
and two thousand years ago.

In the same way other arts are discussed — city-planning,
sculpture, painting, book-making, weaving, pottery — arts

which seem a little closer to the student's experiences than others. Etchings, lithographs, metal work, ivory carvings, glass, drama, the dance — these and others have been omitted for the obvious reason that all the arts cannot be included in one volume. The examples selected have been chosen not on grounds of age or nationality but because of their quality and because they lend themselves clearly and forcibly to the question " why "; so clearly, in fact, that the student is led easily and logically to see that the principles disclosed permeate all life and that the things of everyday life are good or bad for the same reasons as the master-works.

With the last objective in mind, projects are suggested in many of the chapters on the theory that understanding comes from doing, and that doing is applicable to a far wider range of daily activity than seems at first apparent. The last section, " Art in Everyday Life," aims to gather into a unit the suggestions on this point scattered through the book.

In building up this approach to understanding there has been a conscious emphasis, perhaps overemphasis, upon certain points at the expense of others: upon seeing, for example, seeing everything as a form created by nature or by man and re-created (not copied) by the artist according to such fundamental principles as balance, proportion, rhythm, variety, unity, harmony. The technical handling of the medium and the relation of the form to the medium is another point of emphasis. On the other hand biography and history are not touched upon and social background is not given its due.

This quest for understanding is an adventure, great but not easy. In its pursuance, however, the student has learned to appreciate a few of the more important art

forms; to become more observant; to look at things in a new way; he has been exposed, at least, to good taste, has laid a basis for sound judgment, and has opened up a world that will enrich his life immeasurably.

In writing a book of this type the author has drawn upon many sources, far too many to acknowledge individually. Ideas and germs of ideas have been reaped in the written page, in the class room, in discussion, in travel, now accepted *in toto,* now transformed by the writer's own mental and emotional processes, consciously and subconsciously. To whatever source of old and of today thanks are due, they are here given, genuine and hearty. More immediate and concrete has been invaluable constructive criticism on the part of some who are interested in art education to whom the author is sincerely grateful:

Miss Floy Dentler, Rockford High School; Miss Effie A. Gardner, Former Principal of Brooks Classical School, Chicago; Mrs. Kathryn D. Lee, University High School, University of Chicago; Miss Emma McCall, Supervisor of the Teaching of Art Education, University of California; Miss Elizabeth Mitchell, Supervisor of Art, Akron, Ohio; Miss Florence Newcomb, Haaren High School, New York City; Mr. William G. Whitford, Associate Professor of Art Education, University of Chicago; Mr. Leon L. Winslow, Director of Art, Baltimore; Mr. Joseph Wiseltier, Director of Art, State Board of Education, Hartford. To my colleague Kathleen Blackshear I owe a debt of gratitude for her companionship in a vigorous attack upon probems of art appreciation and also for some of the analytical drawings; to Electra Papadopoulos Cryer and Elizabeth M. Fisher for drawings; to individuals and firms for permission to reproduce, acknowledgment of which is noted with the specific illustration; to Marion F. Williams for assistance with proof and index; to the Ryerson Library of the Art Institute of Chicago for the use of photographs; and to the publishers for their generous coöperation.

HELEN GARDNER

Contents

PREFACE iii

I EYES TO SEE 1

II THE ART OF BUILDING 9
The Skyscraper, 16; The Colosseum, 25; The
Parthenon, 32; An Egyptian Temple, 43; The
Baths of Caracalla, 52; Santa Sophia, 59; Two
Early Christian Churches, 68; Chartres, 74;
Two Domes, 92; The Nebraska State Capitol,
101; The Taj Mahall, 106; A Colonial Home,
113; Some Interiors, 116

III THE ART OF THE GARDEN 125

IV THE ART OF CITY PLANNING 132

V THE ART OF SCULPTURE 141
The Columbus Memorial, 148; Khafre, 151;
The Tomb of a Prince, 154; Three Figures
from the Parthenon, 158; A Japanese Saint,
162; A Bronze Maiden, 165; Two Commemorative Statues, 168

VI THE ART OF SCULPTURE IN RELIEF 174

VII THE ART OF PAINTING 178
Some Masters of Line, 189; Some Masters
of Line and Color, 194; Some Masters of
Space, 214; Water and Rocks, 232; Three
Portraits, 236

VIII THE ART OF THE BOOK 243
A Book of Persian Romances, 253; Some
Printed Books, 256

CONTENTS

IX THE ART OF WEAVING 272
. Tapestries of Peru, 281; Silk Fabrics, 284;
A Persian Carpet, 287; A Navajo Blanket, 291

X THE ART OF POTTERY 296
A Persian Jar, 300; A Pitcher from Bokhara,
304; A Greek Cup, 306; A Hopi Jar, 309;
China and Today, 313

XI ART IN EVERYDAY LIFE 318

INDEX 329

Part One

EYES TO SEE

WHAT do eyes do? They are seeing all the time. Every waking hour they are carrying to the mind a picture of the world in which we live — our homes, our friends, our schools, cities, and the country. But a little reflection or a talk with an artist on the subject reveals the fact that this ordinary daily seeing is quite different from the artist's way of looking at things, though the objects seen are the same and the means of seeing — the human eyes — the same. Has the artist then a capacity of vision not granted average people?

Before answering this question, shall we discuss these two kinds of vision? Let us take, as an illustration, your week-end visit to the country. On your return you talked enthusiastically of your friend's summer home. The family began to ask questions. How near the lake was the house? What kind of trees were there in the yard? What color were the curtains? Your recollection of the visit seemed reduced to a blurred picture and a general feeling of pleasure, with certain impressive details standing out vividly. You say that you really did see everything; it is memory that has failed. Perhaps so. As a simple experiment take a house with which you are familiar. Look at it again and shut your eyes. How many questions can you ask about it that you cannot answer? "Every time I see it, I see something different" is a familiar saying. The more we think about it, the more does everyday seeing, for us average folk, seem a very imperfect sort of thing.

But is it seeing alone that is so makeshift? At the concert last evening you heard pleasurable sounds, sometimes

soothingly harmonious, sometimes stridently discordant and exciting. Now there was a low tranquil mood, now a thrilling outburst. Was that all? When you listened more closely, did you notice a repetition of a certain melody? Now you heard it in the major, now in the minor; now in one tempo, now in another; played now on the violin, now by the French horn, now by all the instruments in unison. And soon you began to realize that the composition was built up on the various things you could do with that melody.

It is the same with our sense of touch. We handle countless things mechanically. Do we follow with our fingers and palms the rounding surface of the tumbler or the flat surfaces of a square box and the edges where they meet? Do we consciously feel one object as soft or hard, rough or smooth, silky or woolly? What a soothing delight there is in the soft silkiness of velvet! How cool and smooth is polished marble! How rough is the bark of an oak tree! There is an irritating harshness in some kinds of stucco; a quieting pleasure in the pliancy of soft leather; a forbidding sternness in the rigidity of bronze.

Generally speaking, we do not see, hear, or feel more than a fraction of what the mechanism of our eyes, ears, and hands is capable of experiencing. Imperfect, however, as our ordinary seeing, hearing, and tactile sensation may be, still they serve us well for the practical purpose of getting around in the world. This is because the whole process is a much more complex thing than the matter of the actual image, sound, or feeling which the eye, the ear, or the hand sends to the mind. When the picture of a house, for example, travels from the eye to the brain, it does not rest there alone, isolated. It intermingles with countless other impressions of houses and of everything

associated with houses, impressions that we have been storing up from earliest babyhood. Another thing that the
message from the eye, ear, or hand to the brain does, is to
start action somewhere in the body. Touch something
hot and you start away. Hear a sudden crackling in the
woods, and your muscles tighten in suspense. See a red
light flash when you drive a car through a city and your
feet and hands work almost unconsciously to stop the car.

But what of the unused capacities of the eye, the ear,
and the hand? Can we isolate just seeing as the scientist
in his laboratory isolates a germ, a cell, oxygen, a ray of
light? Let us try, with a tree for our material.

The opening of my porch frames a patch of fairly thick
woods over which towers a fine large oak. How many
associations and meanings in the minds of my friends and
myself the sight of that oak can arouse because of the
thousand and one impressions of oak trees stored in our
minds! My friend the scientist sees the tree as an example
of a certain kind of oak, and is thinking of its life history.
The lumberman sees it as so much potential flooring and
wonders about its graining. The builder sees it as an
important feature in landscaping, and broods over the
possibilities of its place in a future garden. As for myself,
I am particularly interested just now in discovering what
I can really see. I observe that sun and shadow fleck the
warm gray of its rough trunk, and glossy green foliage
weaves dancing patterns on it. This trunk is a cylinder,
rough and irregular, to be sure. My eyes and fingers seem
to be working together, seeing and feeling the rough curving surfaces. At the base it spreads outward with a fine
sweep into the wintergreen carpet of the earth. It then
moves upward and sends forth warm-gray gnarled branches
to hold a dome of glossy green foliage which sweeps above

the rest of the woods. Near by is a small pine that shoots straight up out of the earth. Its horizontal branches are spaced at regular intervals and its dark spiky foliage masses itself into a cone. A storm is just retreating and a high wind from the lake is dappling the sky with swiftly moving patches of gray, silvery white, and intense blue. I look out to my oak and pine. What movement and what stability! What scintillating light and deep rich color! Over the ground runs the light movement of the bracken and the brush; the tree trunks are richly dark with wet; the great oak stands firmly in the wind, while the little pine sways elastically as if it would pull itself free from the earth and run off with the wind. The foliage is all aquiver. The oak leaves flash in the light and a diamond sparkles on the tip of each long pine leaf. Above race the clouds across the blue.

Let us look at another scene, this time at a city thoroughfare. As I emerge from my underground station I meet abruptly a great traffic artery. Huge buildings rear their masses sheer from the sidewalk. This one, not so large, is a warm note with its rough red brick. Next to it is the overpowering cliff of a lofty skyscraper, its gray stone as cold as its sheer, crushing façade. On up the avenue the eye is carried by the wall of buildings whence rise lofty towers which cut sharp angles boldly against the sky or emerge from the mists or recede into them. In rain, snow, or sunshine they create fantastic outlines, whose irregularity is balanced, down at the street level, by the receding line of the black lamp-posts, so sternly regular in spacing and so uniform in design, like an insistent rhythm in poetry or music that forcefully binds all variations into a unity. Along the base of the wall and by the motionless lamp-posts crowds of hurrying people surge backward and forward.

Automobiles glide swiftly by, accented and enlivened by the bright yellow of the taxis.

But it is difficult to separate our " just seeing" from the impressions and associations stored in the mind. Shape, color, space, movement, take on meaning; in the case of the city, the meaning of the city, its power and energy, its hurry and restlessness; in the country, the mean- ing of the forces of nature, as we see them typified in our oak. The cylindrical trunk, we said, spread with an out- ward curve at the base. Why? Because it thrusts roots downward and outward into the earth, both to give it a firm hold so that it can lift a heavy expanse of foliage without danger of falling over even when storms beat upon it, and also to reach far down for the vital water. The dome of foliage it spreads out to the sunlight to get material for making food. The trunk, with the branches and stems, not only supports this green leafy area, but also contains and protects with wood and bark the channels by which the water and salts are conducted up to the cells of the leaves. Marvelous factories, these leaf cells, where food is made and sent to all parts of the tree. Here then is an orderly organic life that explains the underlying reason for the two forms,[1] the cylinder and the dome. These forms are fundamentally the same in all trees, yet they vary in detail, as in the pine and the oak, and give each tree a de- cided personality. The forms alone have great capacity for giving us pleasure with their masses, lines, color, textures,

[1] Form is used not as a synonym for shape, but in a wider sense, including shape, proportions, contours, weight, material, texture, color — every element that enters into the composition of an object which can come to us through our senses. Everything has form; and this form is not unchangeable. Seen in the full sunshine, because of light, shadow, and color, it gives an illusion of depth; seen against the setting sun or in moonlight, it appears to flatten out into a silhouette; in varying lights its colors vary; at varying distances color, size, and other elements change.

and movement. But when form is infused with life and meaning, does it not then give us added delight?

There is another way in which our eyes are working as they see the tree and the life within it. Have you not observed that the more you see a landscape, the more details drop away? In the shore of a lake, minor irregularities disappear in the big sweep of line where sand and water meet. In a tree, twigs are lost in the big masses of trunk and branches, and single leaves, in the big masses of foliage. What matters most in seeing the tree is a feeling of strength in the cylindrical trunk that sends roots down into the earth to secure a firm hold, not the details of the bark; and a feeling of reaching out to the sun in the leafy dome, not the exact shape of each leaf. Trunk and spreading foliage — essentials of life; cylinder and dome — essentials of form; and both life and form gain in emphasis as tiresome details fade away.

Let the painting of a *Young Girl* illustrate this (PL. 1B). Place beside it the photograph of a girl (PL. 1A). In the photograph, the eye wanders from one detail to another. The flashing eyes, the tousled hair, the gay headdress, the elaborate necklace — each is a realistic detail with no clearly felt inner relationships. And soon the eye wearies of it all. In the painting, the details that we know actually exist have been submerged into a large simplicity in which there is unity and harmony because all the parts reveal a relationship one with another. Unbroken contours and surfaces form a pattern based on curves, with straight lines and angles in the loose end of the turban which contrast with the curves and bring the whole into harmony with the frame (Fig. 1). Details, such as the curves of the eyes, the mouth, the earring, and the folds of the turban, all relate to these large controlling lines and

PLATE I

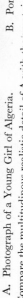

A. Photograph of a Young Girl of Algeria.   B. Portrait of a Young Girl.   Vermeer.

Compare the multitudinous realistic detail of A with the great simplification of B; and the pleasing relation of the head to the space that it occupies in B with the lack of such a relation in A.

PLATE 2

A Skyscraper. From a lithograph by T. E. Tallmadge. An expression of upward rhythmic movement of masses as inevitable as that of the plant form in Fig. 12. (Mr. Tallmadge)

surfaces. And this unified whole has a definite relation to the space that it occupies, defined by the frame, which is as much a part of the painting as the figure itself. The head is placed slightly to the right and the strong straight lines and the mass of the turban-end balance the unbroken ground on the left and emphasize the beauty of the contour of the head so firmly cut against it. The eye of the artist has seen these larger relationships and by emphasizing them has expressed not only an intrinsic harmony and balance that delight us but a more convincing characterization of the girl, because our eyes, undistracted by detail, are free to be guided easily through the picture to see what the painter wanted our eyes to see.

Fig. 1. Line Organization of PL. 1B. Note the repetition of the oval and the contrasting long straight lines of the turban end.

To return, then, to the question asked at the beginning of the chapter: Has the artist a capacity of vision not granted every one? If he lacks this capacity, he is not an artist. But who is the artist? Although we think of him as one who has built a skyscraper, composed a symphony, painted a picture, or written a drama, the potential artist exists in every one who, in his looking about the world, uses his eyes in the artist's way. He may well be yourself as you hang a picture in your room, select your clothes, or take your kodak pictures.

SUGGESTIONS

1. Observation from different points of view: Select a landscape, street, person, chair, room, in fact almost anything, and write the different ways in which different people might see it, one of which will be the artist's way of " just seeing."

2. Look at a view out of a window, or a print, or a lantern slide on the screen. (a) Look for five minutes. Write for five minutes what you see. (b) Look for five minutes. Remove the view and write from memory what you saw. Add another five minutes of observation. How many additions can you make to the first observation?

3. Observation of line: (a) What lines do you see: vertical, horizontal, diagonal, curved? (b) Are they continuous or broken? (c) Do any repeat?

4. Observation of light and dark: (a) Where is the highest light, that is, nearest white? (b) Where is the lowest light, that is, nearest black? (c) Is there more light or more dark?

5. Tactile sensation: (a) Handle objects with closed eyes. Follow the shapes with the fingers and the hands to feel curved surfaces, flat surfaces, change in direction of surface, edges, volumes, proportions. (b) Handle objects for quality of surface: rough, smooth, warm, cool, hard, soft; textiles, such as velvet, satin, wool, pile fabric; rough, smooth, and highly polished stones. Handle for varying degrees of resistance: stone, ivory, wood, metal, leather, and clay.

6. Select a landscape, a person, or any object. Observe it carefully and select what is most important, most essential, in it.

7. Find other examples, analogous to those in PL. 1, for a comparative study of a photograph and a work of art. Suggestions along this line will be found in M. H. Bulley, *Art and Counterfeit* (London, Methuen, 1925) ; in Pennell's etchings of American industrial centers; in Corot's paintings of the Italian cities; in Méryon's etchings of Paris; in El Greco's *View of Toledo*. See particularly " Cézanne's Country," by Erle Johnson, in *The Arts,* April, 1930, in which photographs and Cézanne's paintings of the same subjects are placed side by side.

Part Two
THE ART OF BUILDING

IN ALL lands there are buildings, isolated on mountain tops, crowded into the valleys, nestled on seacoasts, and scattered about in woods, on plains, and on hillsides. So common are they that it is difficult to imagine our world without them. Some seldom see clouds or rain and never snow; others stand now in the cold rain, now in warm sunshine, or lie partly buried in sand. Some shelter one race of people, some another; some the lowest savage, others the most cultivated peoples. In all lands, in all climates, in all ages, man has built for himself. The South Sea Islander's thatched roof on four posts squats by the shining Pacific; the mighty pyramids rise on the edge of the Nile; the Navajo's hut dots the Western desert; powerful skyscrapers loom above the shores of the Atlantic.

Look at the myriad buildings of man the world over and ask the questions: How many of these buildings really interest you? How many delight you? How many are just buildings to house somebody or something, and nothing more? Why do some buildings catch and hold your attention? Why does one bridge, which is an engineering feat, give you a sense of efficiency only, while another not only satisfies but thrills you? Why do you select one car in preference to another when the mechanical parts are equally satisfactory? To answer these and similar questions is the purpose of our course.

Picture again the whole world and you will note four things about every building: (1) that it has a specific purpose; (2) that it is a mass or volume [1] standing in light;

---

[1] When we say *mass* we are thinking about the bulk of the building without considering its form; when we say *volume* we are emphasizing the form of the mass and the surfaces that define it.

(3) that it is made of certain material; and (4) that it stands in a definite geographic and climatic setting. Let us discuss these four points.

First, every building has a purpose, a function to perform. Man has not built for the sake of building but because he wished to provide himself with a shelter, with a place of retirement or seclusion for private life or for worship; with places for amusement, for education, for the conduct of his government or his industry. Immediately the questions arise: Is the building well adapted to its use? Is there harmony between its appearance and its use? Does this building *look* like a factory? Does that *look* as if it could accommodate large crowds comfortably? Does another inspire the feeling of seclusion and friendliness that is the mark of a home?

Another question relating to function is: Why do certain people expend their best energy in erecting certain kinds of buildings? Why did the Egyptians build tombs and temples? Why the twentieth-century American, skyscrapers? Why cathedrals in Europe of the Middle Ages? Architecture touches everyday life very intimately. To understand the purpose of a building is to understand the life of the men who built it: how they lived, thought, believed, worked, governed.

Whatever its purpose, every building is a mass or volume set in the out-of-doors light — our second point. In other words it has width, height, and depth, is a volume made of the floor, the walls, and the roof. The parts of the volume which face the light are light and those away from it are in shadow, as is true of all volumes (Fig. 2). Few structures, however, are as simple as the cylinder or the pyramid. Buildings usually consist of a group of two or more masses made interesting by shape and proportion, by the way in

which they are combined, and by their projections and depressions which catch light and hold shadow. In this *Chapel* for instance (PL. 3 and Fig. 3),[2] one large rectangu-

Fig. 2.   Geometric Solids and Buildings Based upon Them.   *A*, cube;
B, pyramid; *C*, cylinder; *D*, sphere.

lar volume set on its long side forms the body of the building and another, set on end, the tower. From the view seen in PL. 3 these two main volumes are united and given variety and interest by the smaller volumes in the corner.

Fig. 3.   Mass Organization of the Chapel of the University of Chicago.

This interest results partly from the forms themselves and their relative proportions and partly from the masses of alternating light and shadow, which differ, however, every hour and every season. When the sun is intense and the

---

[2] *The Chapel of the University of Chicago.*   Bertram G. Goodhue and the Goodhue Associates, architects.   1929.

air clear the contrast of light and dark [3] is strong. In winter or on a gray day it is only the half-lights that play. In the dark or by moonlight the building seems to flatten out and reveals only the mass and its contours. Moreover, it can be seen from many angles. In our chapel, the two main rectangular volumes give a different appearance when seen from the front and from the other sides. But from all angles the volumes unite harmoniously in a feeling of rocklike strength and noble aspiration — strength, from large, simple masses, unbroken lines, and the strong rhythm of the great windows; aspiration, from the bold verticality and proportions of the tower.

Another source (our third point) contributes to this strength — the thick stone walls. Power through solidity could never have resulted from light material. Not only is stone strong but also it gives an appearance of enduring strength, which with its color and its texture are inescapable factors in the total effect of the building. The compelling force of some of our bridges (PL. 5) is due largely to the fine frank use of steel. Yet it is not only the material itself but also the way in which it is handled that makes a good or a bad building. A good building must stand firmly and present to the eye an appearance of stability. For with the rarest exceptions, the volumes which make buildings are not solid but hollow. Walls and pillars rise

[3] One needs to distinguish between light and shadow, and light and dark (light-dark, dark-light). The former is the natural result of illumination; the latter, an arbitrary breaking up of unbroken masses and surfaces which tend to be monotonous, for the eye can find nothing but the edges to catch its attention. Break them up ever so little by making some parts lighter and some darker (often lighter and darker color), and the attention is fixed and a rhythm started. Light and shadow often coincide with light and dark, as in Fig. 2A and Pl. 3, where the diagonals of the shadows create an effective light-and-dark pattern; and in Pl. 6, where the deep shadow of the open arches forms the same kind of a pattern as if one had painted dark arched areas on an unbroken cylindrical surface.

from the ground to support a roof, and even the flimsiest roof bears down heavily. Here is an engineering problem that must adjust the downward pressure and the upward thrust in such a way that there is no danger of col- lapse. How this is done depends upon the material of which the building is made and how that mate- rial is used, as we shall see later.

Fig. 4. Building in the Mountains of Switzerland.

A building, then, has a purpose; it is a mass or volume constructed of a certain material, stabilized by mechanical laws, and organized so as to give evi- dence of its purpose and to please the eye; that is, it is mass *designed*. And also (our fourth point) every building has a definite climatic and geographical setting which deter- mines certain elements of the design. In a hot dry coun-

Fig. 5. Adobes on a Mesa of the Southwest.

try protection is needed from the heat and glare, and a flat roof will suffice. In a northern country, on the contrary, the light and heat of the sun are wel- comed through ample openings; the walls are tight against the cold wind; and the roofs slope enough to shed rain and snow. Again, the location of a building calls for a harmony between the shape of the volume and itself. For example, the *Parthenon* (PL. 7) crowning a

cubical hill in a mountainous country; the *Nebraska State Capitol* on the Great Plains (PL. 24) ; the *Swiss Chalet* among the steep slopes of the Alps (Fig. 4) ; or the *Indian Adobe* on the Western mesa (Fig. 5) . Place each of these types in a different setting. For example, interchange the

Fig. 6.   An Early Automobile Model.

chalet and the adobe or set the *Parthenon* down in the midst of a crowded American city. Discord results and the original pleasure that we took in the building has vanished.

To return to our query: When is a building a work of art (which is architecture) in distinction from " just a building "? We have noted four fundamental qualities that are essential to architecture. Yet it is not the existence of these qualities as separate elements but the harmonious functioning of all together that distinguishes the art in building. Just as in an automobile. The smoothness and speed of the engine, the proportions and long curves of the low-swung body, suggest swift movement over the ground; the harmonious adjustment of lights, spare tire,

Fig. 7.   A 1930 Model.

and fittings are part of the general design. It is not one of these factors alone that constitutes the most desirable car but the harmonious unity of them all. This is why the design of the automobile has been so revolutionized since the early days when a car was a buggy with an engine (Figs. 6 and 7) . Notice how unfinished Fig. 6 appears without the horse. We have come to understand that a vehicle drawn by a horse calls for a very different design from one propelled by a motor. Function and design must harmonize. So in a fine building. The function, the

shape and proportions of the mass, the materials of which it is constructed, the manner in which the lights and shadows combine, the relation of the organized mass to its setting — all these elements must fit together harmoniously if the building is more than just a building.

When any building seems, for these reasons, to rise above the ordinary, have you noticed how its whole effect impresses you in a personal way? A person may be a stranger in language, dress, customs, religion, society, and yet have a power, a charm, a poise or verve, that is understood and appreciated universally. In the same way the *Taj Mahall* of India (PL. 25) impresses every one, Hindu or American, Moslem or Christian, with its tenderness and poetry; *Chartres Cathedral* (PLS. 17 and 18), with its aspiration; the *Skyscraper* (PLS. 2 and 4), with its self-assurance, boldness, and efficiency; the *Colonial Home* (PL. 26), with its comfort and cordiality.

Thus in a general way we have set up a method of looking at a building and a standard for judging its art quality. To test this method let us journey to various parts of the world and " see " buildings.

READING

BROWN, G. B., The Fine Arts, London, Murray, 4th ed., 1916.
FLACCUS, L. W., Spirit and Substance of Art, N. Y., Crofts, 1931.
HAMLIN, T. F., Enjoyment of Architecture, N. Y., Scribner, 1921.
MUMFORD, L., Architecture, Chicago, American Library Association, 1926.

SUGGESTIONS

1. Select some good building, a local building that can be studied in different lights and from several angles, and try changing the proportions of the main volumes. In the *Chapel*

of PL. 3, for example, lower the tower, shorten or lengthen the body, remove one or both of the corner volumes.

2. Select five or six local buildings. Study each for the relation of purpose, material, and design. Does the general aspect or personality harmonize with the function? If not, what changes would you make to secure this harmony?

3. A study of line, and of dark and light. Select a building and choose a point of view. At a time when the shadows are not too strong study the lines alone. What important vertical, horizontal, diagonal, and curved lines do you see? Are these more generally broken or unbroken? Does any one predominate? Make a sketch. From the same point of view but at a time when the light and shadow are strong, make a similar study of light and dark. Compare the sketches.

4. Select any geographic setting. Design a building to fit into it, the main volumes and lights and darks only. Do not go into detail. For illustrations of the progressive steps in the designing of the mass of a building, see R. W. Sexton, *The Logic of Modern Architecture,* N. Y., Architectural Book Publishing Co., 1929, pp. 35 and 62.

THE SKYSCRAPER

LET us begin our journey at home — in the America of today. Take an airplane trip across the country: Boston, New York, Detroit, St. Louis, Kansas City, Los Angeles, San Francisco. Wherever we stop, in the urban industrial sections we see towering buildings of bold simple masses which create a fantastic sky line above and cañon-like streets below. There is something thrilling in the sight.

Should our ancestors see today these cities which they founded but a century or two ago, how puzzled they would be! What are these gigantic piles, they would ask, rising twenty, thirty, forty stories, cutting the sky with bold angles (PLS. 2 and 4)? Why so huge and why so severe? How do they stand, so tall and so thin? How can you climb

to the top, and how many stoves does it take to heat them? No, it must be a fairyland of giants that we see.

Let us look at one of these buildings of " giants," to see what it really looks like. The *Daily News Building* (PL. 4) [4] will serve our purpose. We can see it best from across the narrow river. And what do we see? A huge mass, not heterogeneous and misshapen but organized into an orderly, powerful group of volumes that stands so firmly and soars so assuredly. The building is made up of rectangular volumes with exceptionally clean unbroken lines and angles. From the river there is a definite rhythmic movement upward and inward. · At the base, upward and inward in rapid succession and varying interval; then a great leap upward; then a repetition of the steplike upward and inward. The masses, the lines, the lights and darks, all move to this rhythm. These volumes seem to rise naturally one out from the other like a plant that pushes up from the earth and unfolds naturally, inevitably. Nor is this rhythm wavering or uncertain but bold and assertive, giving the building a forceful personality.

As the eye is being carried by this rhythm from the river to the top it is also noticing that the lights and darks are largely a matter of openings. There is as much window space as wall. The building seems to summon light and air from every direction. In a northern climate, with variable weather, it is adequately serving a great many people by providing efficiently for their needs. The impression of assertive strength that the building gives on first appearance means that it is expressive of some assertive force. And that force is the present-day highly organized industry. Our Colonial forbears knew nothing of central heating

[4] Chicago. The river front measures 394 ft. Holabird and Root, architects. 1929.

plants, electricity, elevators, telephones — all the things that make for efficient working quarters in a large complex city. Nor did they conceive of business on the scale that we know it. Hence, they would be puzzled at the sight of such a building as this, which to us is a clear expression of business efficiency on a colossal scale. So we take added delight in the design when we realize that the use of the building and its design harmonize.

Let us look at this relationship a little more in detail. First we must see the plan. For in any building, from the colossal *Skyscraper* to the summer cottage, the plan determines its salient features. A peculiar situation met the builders of this *Daily News Building* (Fig. 8). Here was a long, narrow plot of ground with railroad tracks and a river front on one long side. What was to be done? The need of widening the plot

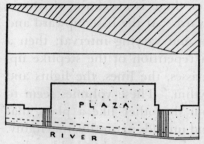

Fig. 8. Plan of the Daily News Building (PL. 4). The portion shaded by diagonals is the part resting on the building lot; the remainder is on air rights, easement (right of way) granted to the Union Station; and a dock.

and reaching the river led to the utilizing of air rights, that is, the space over the railroad tracks, without, however, interfering with their operation. What is the result? The main mass of the building covers the plot of ground. It is symmetrically balanced about a central axis marked by the fountain. Projecting wings form a plaza, which is in reality a roof over the tracks. At the river level the deep shadow in the evenly spaced openings adds variety to this base without detracting from its strength and strikes the first note in the upward rhythm

as it is carried by dark accents. At the same time these openings are amply wide for handling freight, for this lowest level is a dock. The plaza and the wings furnish unbroken surfaces restful to the eye and at the same time provide an open recreational spot. The large openings, with deep shade and unbroken wall between, play a vital part in furnishing solidity and shadow to the base of the design and in receiving and holding for a moment the rhythm of darks begun at the river. At the same time they suggest proper space and adequate lighting for the gigantic presses of a modern daily paper. Above, the many small windows evenly spaced give a quiet steady movement equally vertical and horizontal in contrast to the sheer verticals of the enframing projections at the sides. At the same time these numerous windows suggest a large number of small rooms, offices of all kinds. Near the top they are recessed and

Fig. 9. Rhythmic Movement in the Daily News Building.

grouped vertically to create tall slender areas of dark that again accent the movement started at the river. Two more rows of small windows, and again the dark motif appears to terminate the design (Fig. 9). Thus we find that every part of the design — and this can be carried out in far greater detail — echoes something functional in the building. Or, to put it the other way around, every phase of the use of the building reveals itself in harmony with the design.

But what of the construction? What do our eyes tell us of that? Do they see any relation between the way the building is constructed and the way it looks? We have already noted the insistence upon the vertical line held in restraint by horizontals. Our ancestors wondered how stone could be laid firmly to such a height and with so many openings. That was because they did not know about a great building material of today, steel. We see the beauty of its strength in some of our bridges (PL. 5) where riveted steel girders, slender, strong, and elastic, mark a definite rhythm within the fine sweep

Fig. 10. The Framework of a Skyscraper: Steel and Reinforced Concrete.

of the low-swung curves. It needs no mask. It frankly reveals its function of strong support and at the same time presents to the eye a beauty of proportion and of line.

The *Daily News Building* is constructed of steel girders riveted together. Their foundations of reinforced concrete reach far down, in places ninety feet, until they find a firm foothold on bed rock. In the building, however, the situation is different from that in the bridge. As the building cannot serve its function without a protective screen against the weather, it must have walls. And these are largely glass with thin stone between. The stone is really not a wall at all, as it is in the *Chapel* (PL. 3). The real structure that lifts and supports the building is the framework of steel (Fig. 10). A good builder usually wants his building to show how it is built. What can he do in this situation? Since he cannot leave the steel beams exposed, he uses the stone and glass to suggest the framework beneath. As its slender girders rise one directly above another, making an unbroken line with horizontals between, so the stone and glass repeat the verticals and horizontals. Is there a curve in the design? [5]

Thus we see how the purpose of the building, its material, its structure, and its design form a whole that is beautiful and forceful because all these elements work together in harmony. But why, you ask, are we building *Skyscrapers* today? Did two or three or even a whole society of builders get together and decide, " We will build skyscrapers " ? No. Things do not happen that way. A definite need in a definite situation determines what the builder shall do, and predestines certain factors in the result. What in our age predestined the *Skyscraper*?

[5] Note the present tendency to use glass alone to fill the spaces, making even more emphatic the idea of a steel frame. (See the designs of Frank Lloyd Wright in America and the buildings of Walter Gropius in Germany.)

When our ancestors founded the American colonies they were farmers, many on a small scale. It was not long, however, before they began to develop trade even across the Atlantic. Manufacturing followed. Trade required centers for making and distributing goods. So cities arose. Soon the colonists pushed across the mountain barrier at the call of the unbounded wealth of the prairies. Agriculture developed by leaps and bounds. Great natural resources such as lumber and minerals provided the raw materials for making articles of trade. The inevitable result has been the large city, growing larger and more complicated in proportion as industry has grown more and more complicated. To be manageable at all it must be efficiently organized. Large numbers of people must live near by. Crowded conditions make land expensive. Prices rise. Buildings must not cover much of this costly ground, even if larger plots were available. Hence the necessity of rising up into the air.

This great industrial development and the *Skyscraper* that symbolizes it were impossible without science, another dominating force in our lives today. Scientific discoveries have made possible structural steel, fireproof construction, elevators, and devices for heating and lighting. How difficult it is for us to realize that only within the last hundred years of the thousands and hundreds of thousands that man has lived on the earth has he had machinery, electricity, and all that these imply. Within the last fifty years have come the most marvelous and the most numerous scientific discoveries that man has ever made. While on the one hand these have made living more comfortable and in some respects easier, on the other they have brought great complexity.

It is a hurrying world in which we are living, with in-

PLATE 3

Chapel of the University of Chicago. The compact massing and proportioning of the body and tower and their clear definition in light and shadow; the solidity of the stone walls; the upward reach of the sturdy tower in a quick strongly accented rhythm (an allegro in stone) and the contrasting reposeful strength of the body with a slow stately rhythm through the use of a few large windows (an andante in stone) — all these elements contribute to an impression of power and aspiration. (Photo. R. W. Trowbridge)

PLATE 4

The Chicago Daily News Building. Rectangular masses with clean-cut un-broken lines and angles rise rhythmically from the river to the top. Their organization is determined by the function of the building which is to house a newspaper plant and many offices on many floors; and by its constructional material, steel. (Chicago Daily News)

dustry as a controlling factor. That is why it is the industrial building in which we see some of the most creative work. Huge scale in industry expresses itself in huge scale in building. Yet scale (quantity) of itself never created a work of art.

Another factor in our city situation has proved to be a great asset to the builder — the zoning law. The multiplication of *Skyscrapers* had begun to make the streets into cañons and the lower stories of the buildings too dark and airless for health. To meet this situation laws were passed which limit the height to which a building can rise without stepping back. What an illustration of how a necessary limitation may prove to be an Aladdin's lamp, artistically! In Fig. 11, how boldly powerful are the great masses of the *Telephone Building!* Would the builders have profited so much by this device had it not been forced upon them?

Fig. 11. Telephone Building, New York.

As one more example of the *Skyscraper,* we shall look at a design never carried out, a design of a European who saw the possibilities with great imagination (PL. 2).[6] Above the restless traffic at its base it rises majestically serene. Its mass is of extraordinary

[6] The design was submitted by Eliel Saarinen, of Helsingfors, Finland, and awarded the second prize in the international competition for the *Chicago Tribune Tower*, 1922. The lithograph reproduced in Pl. 2 is an imaginative rendering by T. E. Tallmadge.

compactness: a single rectangular volume set on end for the base, from which rise the other volumes with a feeling of controlled movement. Each grows out of the other, is not set one on top of another. The feeling of life growth is as inevitable as in nature (Fig. 12). The mass is firmly rooted in the soil. Decisive contours mark it off as an astonishingly coherent unit and also define the volumes of which it is composed as well as their proportions. But within these lucid, almost stern definitions of mass, volume, and contour, is a fluid rhythmic movement as the volumes interweave. Notice how the horizontal meeting of planes is softened by sculpture and by curves in the window openings.

Fig. 12. Winter Horsetail. One part seems to grow from another by some inevitable law of nature. (After Blossfeldt)

Each volume is a box of small boxes made of steel beams with tops, bottoms, and sides of tile, concrete, stone, and glass. This structural organization reveals itself in the appearance of the building, not with mechanical consistency but with sensitive variations, as in the ornament and the curves. Because of the geometric simplicity of form the shadows are bold and simple, with broken shadow at important points for the sake of accent.

READING

CHENEY, S. W., Primer of Modern Art, N. Y., Boni, 5th ed., 1930.
—— New World Architecture, N. Y., Longmans, 1930.
LE CORBUSIER (JEANNERET-GRIS, C. E.), Towards a New Architecture, N. Y., Payson and Clark, 1927.
MUMFORD, L., Sticks and Stones; a Study of American Architecture and Civilization, N. Y., Boni, 1926.

Park, E. A., New Backgrounds for a New Age, N. Y., Harcourt, 1927.

Tallmadge, T. E., Story of Architecture in America, N. Y. Norton, 1927.

SUGGESTIONS

1. Study any building of the *Skyscraper* type for (a) mass, (b) silhouette, (c) light and dark, (d) material and evidences of construction, (e) fenestration (window arrangement).

2. Fenestration. Find good and bad examples, explaining in each case why the arrangement is good or bad. Suggest changes for improvement. Make sketches or use a kodak to illustrate.

3. Design a *Skyscraper* in your immediate locality. If there is no zoning law, create an imaginary one. From the ground plan, determined by the use and the site, organize the mass.

THE COLOSSEUM

From the bold masses of the *Skyscraper*, angular, sky-reaching, the expression of colossal industry, we turn to an expression of colossal amusement, a huge cylinder reaching far out over the ground (Pl. 6). This building too is powerful; but its dominating curved lines produce a more undulating rhythm than do angles where verticals and horizontals meet. Our cylinder's surface, everywhere curving, is organized into uninterrupted arcades [7] which hold deep shadows and are firmly united by the unbroken sweep of shadow-making cornices.[8] Built on a valley floor in the midst of a crowded city, surrounded by low hills covered with houses, palaces, gardens, and temples — a broken variable setting — it takes its place assertively by the largeness and boldness of its design.

[7] A series of arches supported on piers or columns.
[8] A broad horizontal projection used chiefly to crown a design or an important part of the design. Note the absence of the cornice on most *Skyscrapers*.

" While stands the *Colosseum* Rome shall stand; when falls the *Colosseum* Rome too shall fall; and with it shall fall the world." Such was the impression that this amphitheater made upon the pious pilgrims who journeyed to Rome — a dangerous and difficult adventure in the chaotic days of the eighth century. Standing in the midst of silent ruins, it so impressed them with its power and grandeur that it became to them a symbol of the ultimate power of the universe. And notwithstanding the varied and tragic events through which it has lived — struck by lightning, shaken by earthquakes, now serving as an iron mine (for its stones are held by bits of iron), now as a stone quarry, a fortress in war, weathered by nature, and mutilated by man — notwithstanding all this, it still rises a silent, impressive ruin, symbolizing the grandeur and magnificence of pleasure-loving imperial Rome.[9] What circumstances led to its erection?

In the reign of Nero a great fire had destroyed a large part of Rome. In addition to this disaster the emperor had angered the people by his extravagances, especially by building a gorgeous palace and by appropriating for gardens and a lake public open places and even important

[9] Also called the *Flavian Amphitheater*. Built, on the exterior, of travertine held with iron cramps; on the interior, of tufa, brick-faced concrete, and some travertine. Greater diameter, 620 ft.; lesser, 513 ft.; height, 157 ft.; seating capacity, about 45,000. It was begun by Vespasian; continued and opened for use by Titus, 80 A.D.; completed by Domitian; repaired by later emperors; was used for shows until the sixth century; was struck by lightning in the third century and again in the fourteenth. In the earthquake of 1349 the western half collapsed; in the fifteenth and sixteenth centuries it lay a vast heap of ruins overgrown with shrubbery. From the time it ceased to be used as a place of amusement it has served builders as a quarry; in fact has contributed half its material to this end. The marble seats and all ornament have disappeared. Many of the marble seats were used as bishops' seats in the early Christian churches. It is only since the middle of the eighteenth century that the structure has been protected from demolition, has been excavated and the weak parts strengthened.

PLATE 5

Michigan Avenue Bridge, Chicago. A revelation of the beauty of naked constructional steel when its use is subject to proportion, line, rhythm. (Photo. W. C. Duncan)

PLATE 6

Colosseum. Rome. A cylinder whose sweeping curves unite rhythmically repeated arches. At the same time it adequately performs its function of enabling huge crowds to see the enclosed arena.

thoroughfares. What joy, then, ran through the city when Nero's successor, Vespasian, destroyed the palace, reclaimed the garden space, and began to build on the bottom of the drained lake a huge amphitheater for games and shows for the people! Slowly it rose, even with plenty of cheap labor, so huge was it. Finally it was opened in the reign of Titus, Vespasian's son, an event so important that a representation of the structure appeared on this emperor's coins, as it did on those of later emperors who repaired the building (Fig. 13) ; just as today events are commemorated with our stamps. Tickets were distributed free for the shows that continued a hundred days: gladiatorial fights, animal hunts, and, most exciting of all, an actual naval battle in the flooded arena.

Fig. 13. Coin of a Roman Emperor, Gordianus. Beside the Colosseum is seen a Colossus after which the amphitheater may have been named.

Thus the *Colosseum* served a definite function, as its name implies: *amphitheatrum,* a seeing from all sides. It provided seats for nearly fifty thousand spectators around an out-of-doors arena, with reasonably easy entrances and exits. These specific needs determined much of the design and the fundamental unit of the design — the arch. It is the heart of the construction and facilitates the use of the building. Let us study the *Colosseum,* then, from these points of view: stable construction, efficient functioning, satisfying appearance, and finally and most important, the harmonious unity of all these elements.

The construction is of stone masonry (stone or brick laid with cement or metal fastenings) and concrete used on the

arch principle.   Arch and arch principle — what do these mean?   In all building a vital mechanical problem is how to raise walls which have openings for doors and windows, and how to roof over the space enclosed by the walls, so that the structure is stable.   The simplest way is the method of the child playing with blocks: build the walls of blocks, place blocks over the space left for openings, then lay more blocks over the top from wall to wall (Fig. 14).   This method, known as the lintel method because the blocks are called *lintels,* has been successful in some of our finest buildings.   But they are usually on a small scale,

Fig. 14.   Two Systems of Building. *A,* the lintel system; *B,* the arch system. *C,* an arch under construction showing the centering (the wooden framework) which holds the arch until it is set by the keystone.

because the moment you increase the size of your building you meet the problem of where to obtain lintels long enough to span the space.   Timber is fairly long but not permanent.   Stone, though permanent, is costly, difficult to obtain except in comparatively short lengths, and very heavy.   The larger the building, the larger the roof, and the more heavily it weighs down upon the walls.   Additional supports may be added (Fig. 26) but they often mar the appearance as well as take up too much space. To be independent, then, of too many supports, and to be able to use small material — which is only too often necessary from an economic point of view — is the constructional problem solved by the arch.

An arch is made by building wedge-shaped blocks of
stone, brick, tile, or concrete from the supporting piers
along a curved line until they meet and are held securely
by the central wedge, called the *keystone* (Fig. 14) . There
are several advantages in the arch: its method of construction enables the builder to use small, easily obtainable material; the science of its construction enables it to carry
a heavier weight than a lintel because it throws this weight

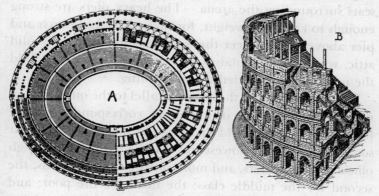

Fig. 15. *A*, Plan of the Colosseum. Lower right quarter, first or ground
story; upper right, second story; upper left, third story; lower left, top or
attic story. *B*, Section of the Colosseum.

away from the space beneath to the supporting piers and
the adjoining walls; its shape gives the builder an opportunity to use curved lines.

Let us return now to the *Colosseum* and see how this
arch principle dominates the building. Look at both the
exterior (PL. 6) and the section (Fig. 15B) . Everywhere
you see these arches with heavy piers for support. Italy
supplied the Roman with abundant material for building:
a fine hard stone called travertine, softer volcanic stones,
and small rock, gravel, and lime for concrete. Yet abundant as the supply was, and wealthy in money and labor as

Rome was, she could not quarry enough travertine for so gigantic a structure. So, while the exterior is made of travertine blocks, the interior is chiefly of other stones, and of concrete faced with brick. Of these materials the builders constructed a great system of arches both parallel to and at right angles to the outer circumference (Fig. 15A). These arches form three stories of the outer shell, the exterior corridors, and the supports for the sloping seats surrounding the arena. The heavy piers are strong enough to carry the weight, for arch rises above arch and pier above pier to meet the weight of the fourth or solid attic, whose walls contain closely placed brackets to hold the masts that supported a huge awning.

The seats surround the arena parallel to the outer wall of the building and rise in four tiers, corresponding to the four external stories and dividing the spectators into four social groups — the lowest tier for the royal family, high officials, ambassadors, and more distinguished citizens; the second for the middle class; the third for the poor; and the fourth for women. Access is easy, for each of the eighty arches on the ground story (except for two reserved for the emperor) form public entrances to the various corridors and stairways, providing free circulation of great crowds, and ample protection in all kinds of weather. Thus the framework of arches ensures both stable construction and adequate functioning. Can you think of a plan that would serve huge crowds better?

Let us look at the exterior design once more, and see if it relates to the construction and the function. This consists of three tiers of arches, arch exactly above arch, bound by a horizontal band with a projecting cornice. How these cornices follow and repeat the curving surface of the cylindrical shape! The rounding tops of the

arches, in rapid even rhythm, harmonize as no other line could. It is a design based upon curves, with contrasting horizontals in the cornices and verticals in the engaged columns.[10]

But it is not line alone upon which the builder is depending. The design of line is overlaid, as it were, with a similar design of light and shadow. The hollow arches hold deep shadows that suggest inward movement, and the projecting engaged columns advance to catch the light. Hence a movement is started in and out as well as around and upward, so that we have movement in three directions. Yet the piers rising from an inconspicuous two-step base seem rooted in the ground; the arches are bound firmly by the unbroken line and shadow of the cornices; and the solid attic finishes the design and marks it off from its surroundings. Thus, in spite of the vigorous movement within the limitations of its space, the structure gives the impression of quiet strength.

So we see that the organization of our volume — have you noticed that the *Colosseum* is one volume only? — by line and light and dark not only harmonizes with the purpose of the building and the arch construction but also reinforces them by its suggestion of movement and stability. Our study of the building from three points of view — stable construction, efficient functioning, satisfying appearance — has led us to a realization of the inseparable unity of the three, a unity which produces that total impression of power and domination, a symbol of the grandeur of imperial Rome, which even in ruin so impressed the early pilgrims.

[10] An *engaged*, in distinction from a *free-standing*, column is attached to a wall and projects only part of its diameter.

READING

ANDERSON, W. J., and SPIERS, R. R., Architecture of Ancient
Rome, rev. by Thomas Ashby, N. Y., Scribner, 1927.

BREASTED, J. H., Ancient Times, Boston, Ginn, 1916.

DAVIS, W. S., A Day in Old Rome, Boston, Allyn and Bacon,
1925.

SHOWERMAN, G., Eternal Rome, New Haven, Yale Press, 1924.

SUGGESTIONS

1. A relief map in sand or clay of ancient Rome will not
only serve to fix the sites in mind but will help to correlate
with history and Latin courses. See S. B. Platner, *Topography
and Monuments of Ancient Rome,* Boston, Allyn and Bacon,
1911. Such a map can also be used for medieval and Renaissance Rome.

2. Find examples, such as the modern stadium, in which the
architectural problem of function and design is the same as in
the *Colosseum.* Has the solution been the same?

THE PARTHENON

FROM the huge cylinder of the *Colosseum* set in the midst
of the capital of a great empire, with its spirit of grandeur
and domination, let us journey eastward to Greece and
look at a small rectangular structure (PL. 7) standing aloof
upon a hill overlooking a city (Figs. 16 and 17).[11]   Its

[11] *Parthenon,* Acropolis, Athens. Of Pentelic marble. The base, not including
the steps, 228 by 101 ft.   Begun in 447 B.C., dedicated in 438; work was still
going on as late as 432. It remained practically in its original condition until
it was converted, in the fourth or fifth century A.D., into a Christian church,
and in 1458 into a Mohammedan mosque. In 1687, when it was used as a
powder magazine during a war, it was wrecked by an explosion. Fortifications,
houses, and mosques were built in and around it. Until the nineteenth century
its stone served as a quarry and its sculpture fed the limekiln. In 1801–03 most
of what was left of the sculpture was taken to England by Lord Elgin and in 1816
was purchased for the British Museum. Since that time the foreign structures
have been removed from the Acropolis, which is now under the care of the Greek
Government. For fine plates showing the recent restoration, see W. Hege
and G. Rodenwaldt, *Die Akropolis* (Berlin, Deutscher Kunstverlag, 1930).

sides seem to continue those of the sheer cliff below; its base is a part of the level-topped hill; and its mass as a whole repeats the mass of the hill. Though it stands out clearly as something to demand attention against the intense blue sky or the broken grays of the storm clouds, still

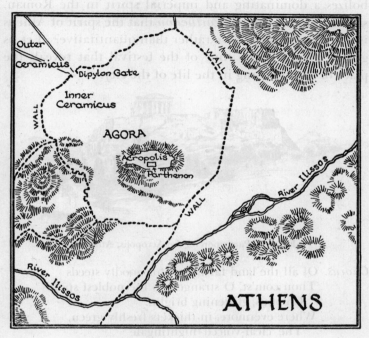

Fig. 16. Athens.

with the hill as its base, it takes its place in perfect unison with the varied mountainous landscape. Like the *Colosseum*, its exterior consists of alternating light and dark masses that suggest inward and outward movement. But these masses are rectangular, not arched, and are bound by a horizontal band into one large rectangular volume which meets the air and sky, not too abruptly, with a low-pitched

roof. Its whole personality is strikingly unlike that of the *Colosseum.* Apart from the difference in size and site, here is no striving aloft, no assertive power, but quietude and restraint.

If the *Colosseum* in size and dominating design symbolizes a dominating and imperial spirit in the Roman, shall we infer from the *Parthenon* that the spirit of Athens is serene, and qualitative rather than quantitative? Let us go to Athens, at the time of the festival that reveals the place of this building in the life of the city.

Fig. 17. Parthenon on the Acropolis, Athens.

Chorus. Of all the land far famed for goodly steeds
　　　Thou com'st, O stranger, to the noblest spot,
　　　　Colonus, glistening bright,
　　　Where evermore, in thickets freshly green,
　　　　The clear-voiced nightingale
　　　　Still haunts, and pours her song,
　　　　By purpling ivy hid,
　　And thick leafage sacred to the God . . .

　　　And in it grows a marvel such as ne'er
　　　　On Asia's soil I heard,
　　　Nor the great Dorian isle from Pelops named,
　　　　A plant self-sown, that knows
　　　　No touch of withering age,
　　　　Terror of hostile swords.

PLATE 7

Parthenon. Athens. A rectangular volume, strong yet reposeful because of the proportions and of the sensitive balance of vertical and horizontal. (Photo. H. Wagner, Athens)

PLATE 8

The Great Hall of an Egyptian Temple. Majestic in its massiveness and in the stately rhythm of its columns, an expression of enduring power. (G. Jéquier, *L'Architecture et la Decoration dans l'Ancienne Egypte*. Paris, Morancé)

Which here on this our ground
Its high perfection gains,
The grey-green foliage of the olive-tree,
Rearing a goodly race;
And never more shall man,
Or young, or bowed with years,
Give forth the fierce command
And lay it low in dust.
For lo! the eye of Zeus,
Zeus of our olive groves,
That sees eternally
Casteth its glance thereon,
And she, Athena, with the clear, grey eyes.[12]

Thus Agathocles quoted as he stood in the colonnade [13] of the temple on the hill and wrapped his woolen cloak about him more tightly. Day was dawning. The preparations for the festival were completed and soon he must join the procession that was already forming down in the city near the *Dipylon,* or *Double Gate* (Fig. 16).

Still he lingered, scanning the wide view before him. To the north and west swung a fringe of mountains. There were Parnes and Cithaeron, favorite haunts of Apollo and the Muses. To the south the vine- and olive-covered plain broke through the mountain circle to meet the sea, which deepened its blue as the sun rose above the eastern crests. Turning his eyes toward the hilltop where he was standing, Agathocles saw that the two bronze Athenas near by were reflecting the early sunshine. One was the colossal warlike champion of Athens with helmet, spear, and shield; the other was smaller, bareheaded, helmet in hand, gracious in appearance. Athena was both their champion and the guardian of their arts. And this

---

[12] Sophocles, *Oedipus at Colonos.* Translation of E. H. Plumptre.
[13] A series of columns connected by lintels.

was her very sanctuary where he was standing. Though Zeus was the king and father of all, Demeter gave them grain, Pan piped for their delight along the streams, as the dryads danced to his tunes; though Poseidon fought for their ships against the anger of the north wind, still dearest to their hearts was Athena, who had given them their olive trees and their name and had become their protector and patron. And this was her birthday.

For three days Athens had been celebrating with athletic and musical contests. How beautiful the torch race had been last night as the wind-blown torches danced across the plain in the hands of runners hidden by the dark! Agathocles' brother, though fifth at the goal, was winner of the race, for he alone had kept his flame burning. But Agathocles straightened with pride at the thought of his own prize in the flute contest — a wreath of olive and a jar of oil from the sacred trees of Athena. " Are we not fortunate," he thought as he moved away from the temple and looked up at the kindly Athena, " to be under the care of so strong and so gracious a goddess? "

Then down the steep path he hurried to meet the procession that was already winding through the narrow streets. Here were maidens with the embroidered robe; cows for the sacrifice; dignified elders with laurel branches; chariots rumbling over the cobblestones; and a long cavalcade, which Agathocles joined. As the throng reached the crest of the hill the temple was gleaming in the full light of the August sunshine. Conscious of the dignity of the occasion, they moved to the front of the temple through whose open door the colossal gold and ivory statue of Athena, filling the half-lighted room, gleamed majestically. After the robe had been presented all the people joined in the sacrifice at the altar in front of the temple, shared in

the ceremony with hymns and prayers; and after Athena's portion had been offered to her, all feasted and were joyous.

Throughout the day the festival continued until as the afternoon waned Agathocles again found himself alone at the corner of the colonnade. The great festival was over and not for four years would it be celebrated again. As the sun was sinking behind the ragged crests of the mountains everything stood out with crystalline clearness, saturated and quivering with color and gold.

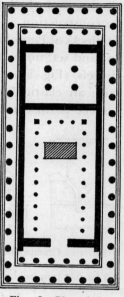

Fig. 18. Plan of the Parthenon.

The sun god himself seemed to be saying a joyous farewell, and soon the moon goddess would arrive in her chariot to close the festival by enveloping everything in her quiet light. Agathocles,

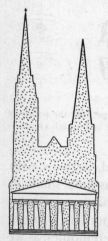

Fig. 19. Parthenon and Chartres Cathedral (PL. 17). (After Benoit)

young as he was, felt it all. The natural beauty of the land, the joyous harmony of a colorful nature, the pride in his city, and the love of a beneficent goddess were a part of the very fiber of his life.

First let us see the *Parthenon* as Agathocles did from his modest little home in the crowded city, standing clearly on the hill two hundred feet above — colorful, splendid, serene. Climb the steep path with this youth and study the temple close at hand. In

plan, construction, and size it is most simple. In
plan (Fig. 18) it is a rectangle, with a door at each
end, and surrounded by a colonnade doubled at the
ends. The columns support a superstructure with a
sloping roof which forms a gable, or pediment, at each end.
In construction, it is built on the lintel system (Fig. 14),
of blocks of Pentelic marble quarried in the mountain near
by, and set, not with mortar, but with bronze cramps and
dowels (Fig. 20), which hold the stones firmly and also
with an elasticity that is necessary in a land subject, as
Greece is, to earthquakes. Of what the roof was made,

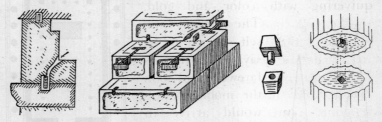

Fig. 20. Cramps and Dowels. Iron or bronze cramps hold the stones of
the same course; iron dowels, packed with lead poured in through channels
left for that purpose, hold the stones of different courses.

we are not certain. It was probably tiled, perhaps with
translucent marble. In size, the temple is very small in
comparison with many of the buildings that we are visiting on our journey. But what need was there for a larger
one? The Greek performed his religious ceremonies, as we
have seen, at an altar outside the temple where there was
ample space for all the people to participate. The only
need for the building was to house the statue, to protect
the gifts, to glorify the divinity and, indirectly, the city
which erected the temple.

Is not this fact illuminating, that the Greek in one of
his greatest works of art was content with, in fact pre-

ferred, small size, the simplest method of construction, and
an old well-known plan? It was not to something novel,
or colossal, or grandly splendid that he devoted his best
efforts, but toward refining and perfecting an old form
(Fig. 21) and expressing through it a quiet harmony that
was consistent
with the Greek
ideal of balance
and moderation.
Again, his ideal
was qualitative.

Long since
the Greek had
evolved a build-
ing that suited
his geographic
setting and his
religious needs,
and he felt no
need of changing
its essential ar-
rangement. In
these circum-
stances two things
can happen. The

Fig. 21. Similar Elements Combined in Different
Proportions. *D* is the Parthenon.

new building can be a copy of the old and, while adequate,
quite devoid of life and feeling. Or the new building,
while still retaining the old form, can present new proportions, new refinements of all detail, such an entirely new
way of putting together the old forms that it becomes filled
with life and vitality. That is originality. Return to
Fig. 21. The older Greek temples are superior buildings,
but their heaviness reveals a rugged age not yet trained to

the sensitive proportions of the *Parthenon*. The very fact
that the builders of the *Parthenon* refused to follow the
old exactly, though accepting the best of it, shows how
keenly they felt that their expression must be their own.

Like these prototypes, the *Parthenon* is a building of
quiet vigor and serenity. To realize this compare it with
Chartres Cathedral (PL. 17 and Fig. 19), a building filled

Fig. 22.   Design of
the Façade of the Par-
thenon.

with restless and eager aspiration. This
serenity results from the proportions,
variety, and balance of simple units of
mass, line, light and dark, and color.
Let us study these principles in the
façade. Long quiet horizontal lines
contrast in subtle proportion with active verticals, and with still more active
diagonals (Fig. 22A). The verticals
are long in the columns, and are emphasized by repetition because the columns are grooved or fluted. In the
frieze groups of short verticals are repeated twice as often as in the columns
below, thus affording a change in the
rhythm. But as the façade is made of
stones that project and recede, there
results a pattern of light and dark that
essentially repeats the pattern of line, and produces an inward and outward movement (Fig. 22B). Still the design
is not satisfactory until you add the sculptured ornament
and color in the frieze and gable, for these supply the
broken irregular masses of light and dark to give variety to
the regular rectangular areas below, and also provide
curved broken lines to soften the severity of vertical, horizontal, and right angle; while the diagonal of the sky line is

softened by the ornament and thereby better united with the sky (Fig. 22C).

Thus the sculptured ornament is far from being something added or applied as an afterthought. It is so integral a part of the organizing lines and lights and darks that without it, vitality is lost. On the other hand these sculptured forms are not abstract, in order to provide line and light and shadow only, but they represent subjects suitable for the temple: *The Birth of Athena,* the *Contest of Athena and Poseidon,* and other subjects that relate to gods and heroes; and finally, as evidence of the close harmony between humanity and divinity, inside the colonnade along the top of the solid wall of the temple runs a *Frieze* representing man's tribute to Athena, the great *Panathenaic Procession* (PL. 51). This same happy union of content and design we shall find in the mosaics, frescoes, and glass of the Christian churches and cathedrals, and in the carved ornament of the *Nebraska State Capitol.*

Color was necessary, the Greek felt, because of climatic conditions. The sunshine in Greece is brilliant, and when reflected by the glittering marble would efface the forms. So he differentiated them with color, not naturalistic but conventional. The ground of the *metopes* [14] is red, against which the sculpture can be seen; the adjoining *triglyphs* [14] are blue because red and blue are contrasting colors. Blue was also used as a ground for the sculpture in the *pediment,* [15] while a little green or gilding brought out a detail or furnished an accent. Strongly contrasted color stressed the decorative pattern of the upper cornices and the roof

[14] *Metopes* are the "between places," the squares between the *triglyphs* or grooved parts of the frieze (border) which runs around Greek temples of the *Parthenon* type just beneath the cornice (Pl. 7 and Fig. 23). There is now no color on the *Parthenon.*

[15] The gable at the end of a building made by the sloping roof (Fig. 23).

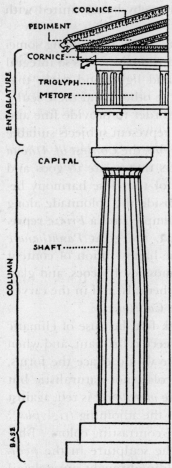

CORNICE

PEDIMENT

CORNICE

TRIGLYPH

METOPE

ENTABLATURE

CAPITAL

SHAFT

COLUMN

BASE

Fig. 23. Corner of a Greek Building. Notice that it consists of a base and columns which support the upper parts weighing down upon them. The balance between these two parts is most important in the general effect of the building (see Fig. 21). The technical terms are not specifically Greek but are common architectural terms.

ornaments. Color is found in the upper parts of the building only. This is significant. There was no need of it below, where the base, the column, and the wall were clearly distinguished. Furthermore, if color is judiciously and conventionally used it enlivens the white marble and by contrast enhances the beauty of the stone, just as black iron brings out the richness of colored glass (see page 90).

But there is another factor that plays an important part in the art of the *Parthenon*. All through our discussion we have been speaking of the temple as a rectangle. Rectangular, vertical, horizontal, serve our purpose in a general way, but are really inaccurate, for in this building there is literally not one straight line. The corners standing strong against the light (PL. 7) show how the columns slope inward as they rise. Careful measurements added to sensitive vision disclose the fact that the entire volume slopes inward, that

the contours of the columns are ever so slightly curved; that the stone base, too, curves upward from the corners to the center. The columns stand considerably closer together at the corners than in the central parts of the colonnade. Go wherever you will about the building and you will find these deviations from regularity, slight, sensitive, powerful. For the *Parthenon* has life, vitality, power; but power that is quite different from the power of the *Skyscraper,* which is the product of the Machine Age. Each is " right " in its own way, consistent with the age out of which it grew.

READING

ANDERSON, W. J., and SPIERS, R. R., Architecture of Ancient Greece, rev. by W. B. Dinsmoor, N. Y., Scribner, 1927.

DAVIS, W., A Day in Old Athens, Boston, Allyn and Bacon, 1914.

DICKINSON, G. L., The Greek View of Life, Garden City, Doubleday, 7th ed., 1925.

Any readings, in translation, of Greek literature.

SUGGESTIONS

1. A relief map of Attica showing the relation of Athens and the Acropolis to the surrounding country. See E. A. Gardner, *Ancient Athens,* N. Y., Macmillan, 1907, or C. H. Weller, *Athens and its Monuments,* N. Y., Macmillan, 1913.

2. Find examples of slight variations from regularity in colonnades or arcades, spacing of windows and doors, etc. Compare with examples of mechanical regularity.

3. Find examples of buildings designed after the *Parthenon.* Observe the site and the purpose. Do you think the design in each case is well adapted to the use?

AN EGYPTIAN TEMPLE

" STILL another rectangular building," you say as our boat ties at the landing at Thebes, far up the Nile River

Fig. 24. Egypt.

(Fig. 24). Through the palms appears a long low mass of stone terminating at one end in a high wall with sloping sides (Fig. 25). Solidly massive, it suggests neither the upward reach of the *Skyscraper* nor the inward movement of the *Colosseum* and the *Parthenon*. Its great windowless walls make it appear to close in upon itself, disdainful of the outside world. Yet these surfaces are not monotonous, for they are broken by masses of red, blue, yellow; and the general austerity of the *Temple* is softened by the flags floating above the high façade,[16] by flashes of metal, and by the enfolding greenery of palms and of grain fields. Beyond, the distant barren cliffs with horizontal crests repeat the sheer walls and their unbroken level tops.

Is this impression that the *Temple* makes on us the same that it made on the Egyptian of old, who understood it infinitely better than we can? We are already in Thebes. But let us go back to the Thebes of long ago.

[16] This façade is known as the *pylon*, a Greek word for a gateway. Hence this type of temple is called the *pylon temple*.

Even in the chill of early morning Nakht felt the approaching heat as the sun rose fiercely brilliant into a cloudless sky. He was standing on the bank of the Nile, this young noble (Fig. 26) who for the first time was visiting Thebes for the festival of the sun god. "The Nile," he mused, "the gift of the gods. Yes, only through the power of the gods can it perform its yearly miracle of bringing down a great flood of life-giving water and fresh soil." The long line of barren cliffs on both sides of the river valley, he well knew, offered open portals to vast deserts. Only

Fig. 25. An Egyptian Pylon Temple.

in the narrow valley between the long even line of their menacing brows could life exist. It was a luxuriantly rich valley, this gift of the gods, with its grain fields, groves of palms, cities, and villages, and barges with their wares sailing up and down. "Yes, the gods are good in this their greatest gift."

Thus pondering he turned toward the *Temple,* the abiding-place of these gods. The building was but a short distance from the river, and as Nakht looked, he stood in wonderment. A broad avenue flanked by solemn recumbent animals carried his eye to the huge mass as it rose sternly simple, bold, and colorful in the midst of the surrounding palms. Flags floated lazily above the high façade, and two lofty obelisks lifted their pointed metal tips to catch and reflect the sunshine. Stern giant statues looking straight forward sat in solemn silence at the small doorway through which he could see far into the *Temple;* first a

flash of sunshine, then dimness, and in the far distance mysterious darkness. How majestic! How filled with the spirit of worshipful awe of the gods who gave the sun and the wonderful river! Through the trees he caught a glimpse of the bordering cliffs, suggesting the sterile deserts so vast and so close that they almost seemed to choke, in their jealousy, the luxuriant valley between. How the temple's vastness and sternly simple lines on the one hand and the vivacious color, gleaming metal, strong light and shade, and enshrining greenery on the other, just exactly fitted! And as he looked at the only entrance, a small door in the great façade guarded by the seated statues, he felt how effectively the world was shut out and how secure the sacred dwelling-place was from profane eyes.

Fig. 26. Costume of an Egyptian of the Time of Nakht. It consists of a tunic with loose plaited sleeves; a plaited skirt, tight in the back and held by a sash with one end fringed and the other, pointed, hanging down in front. The dress is white linen. Accessories are important in Egyptian costume: armlets, bracelets, chains with pendants, and a bead collar. (Metropolitan Museum)

As he slowly approached along the avenue he loitered behind the gathering crowds to look at the reposeful rams with statues of the pharaoh between their paws and between their horns polished metal discs that flashed brilliantly. And here were the two famous obelisks, single granite shafts nearly a hundred feet high. Every one in Egypt knew their story: how they had been quarried at the cataract far up the Nile (Fig. 24) and when the river was high had been loaded on a barge, a load so great that it took thirty galleys and nearly a thousand oarsmen to tow it down to Thebes. And there the

pharaoh had them carved with inscriptions telling of his
exploits and set them up in front of the temple to cele-
brate his jubilee.   As they rose high into the air they
tapered finely, and their simple shape and unbroken line
were as grandly monumental as the *Temple* itself.   Behind the obelisks rose the majestic façade with sloping
sides, its sheer wall vibrating with carvings painted in large
flat areas of intense color but softened by the brilliant light

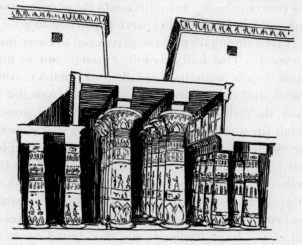

Fig. 27.   Section of the Great Hall of an Egyptian Pylon
Temple.   The pylon (gateway) is the lofty entrance.

and finished at the top by a cornice whose broad outward
sweep cast a deep horizontal shadow that gave a definite
finish to the façade so that the blue of the painted carvings
would not be lost in the blue of the sky.

Music in the distance reminded Nakht that he must
hurry to the *Temple*.   For was not the festival the very
purpose of his visit?   This was the day when the pharaoh
alone, closest of all people to the sun god, entered the
mysterious dark sanctuary.   As Nakht passed the solemn

statues guarding the doorway he noticed that the great cedar doors with silver inlay, swung back to admit the crowd, were gleaming dully in the shadow. "These are suitable doors," he thought, "for the house of Amon, Amon-Re the mighty sun god."

Through the doorway, and he was in the sunshine of a large open court (Fig. 28), along the sides of which ran a covered colonnade whose shade afforded a welcome protection from the heat. Into this court the people crowded, waiting. It was as far as they were permitted to go. Only a few, Nakht among them, were privileged to enter the dim hall beyond. This hall was lofty, though not so high as the great façade with its flagstaffs and obelisks, and was dim, cool, and mysteriously quiet. Apart from the small doorway, the only light filtered through narrow stone gratings high up under the roof, so high that it was soon lost in the shadows (PL. 8 and Fig. 27). The people too seemed lost in the enormous space, if not hidden by the columns. A double row of majestic shafts, higher than the rest, formed a central aisle. Near the top they spread out in great curves as if stretching out their arms to receive the weight of the huge roofing-stones that rested upon them. At first Nakht felt as if he were back in that forest of Lebanon where his father once took him on a journey to buy timber.

The music was sounding nearer as the procession crossed the open court. The insistent clatter of a rattle was keeping away the evil spirits. A priest with a censer headed the procession, followed by musicians and dancers, and a military escort, above whom appeared the king seated, carried high on a palanquin. He wore a lofty crown with the serpent, the emblem of royalty, on his forehead, a collar necklace and other jewels, and carried a flail and a crosier,

the royal insignia. His officials bore his standards, fans, and sunshades, and his servants followed with his sandals, his bow and quiver. Brilliant in gold and color the procession passed through the crowded court into the shaded hall and disappeared in the dim distance, where, Nakht knew, the pharaoh, after he had been anointed, robed, and ornamented, entered the sanctuary alone to perform the rites and to entreat the favor of the gods.

. . . Thou shalt give me high and plenteous Niles in order to supply thy divine offerings and to supply the divine offerings of all the gods and goddesses of South and North; . . . in order to preserve alive the people of all thy lands, their cattle and their groves which thy hand has made. For thou art he who has made them all and thou canst not forsake them to carry out other designs with them; for that is not right.[17]

Without in the court, the people stood silent.

Thus the *Temple's* function was to provide a dwelling-place for the divinity, secluded from the world, and so constructed as to impress with awe and mystery. For the Egyptian's religious belief centered about majestic power and its mystery. The mass of people could approach only at a distance; hence the large open court, beyond which they could see only into the great columned hall, dim and majestic, and thence toward unfathomable darkness, the dwelling-place of the god. This vista was the reason for the *Temple's* being built along an axis (Fig. 28). The lofty hall of stone columns and the still loftier stone façade added to the feeling of majesty, an austere kind of majesty, to be sure, yet powerful and enduring.[18]

[17] J. H. Breasted, *History of Egypt*, N. Y., Scribner, 1912, p. 458.

[18] The conservative Egyptian, when once he had evolved a temple plan that met his needs, continued to build for centuries on this plan; and ambitious pharaohs kept adding to the original temple; for, as the site was sacred, a new location could not be chosen. Hence the huge temples at *Luxor* and *Karnak*

To build a temple that would serve this function, his country afforded the Egyptian an abundance of stone and his social system provided almost unlimited slave labor. He understood how to make arches but preferred not to use them except in inconspicuous places. Massive solidity and great scale he could well secure by the lintel system. It was a simple matter to build great walls with no open-

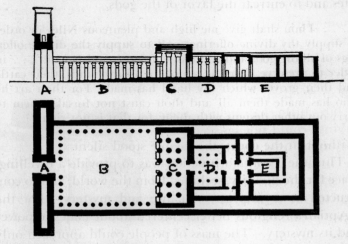

Fig. 28. Plan and Section of an Egyptian Temple. *A*, entrance through the pylon; *B*, open court; *C*, great hall; *D*, vestibule to the sanctuary; *E*, sanctuary.

ings. But how could he roof a spacious hall with lintels? This problem he solved by adding more and more supports (Fig. 27). By seeing how many rows of roofing stones

(ancient Thebes) are but elaborations of the simple pylon type (Fig. 28), are aggregations of pylons, courts, halls, and small additional complete temples. *Karnak* represents two thousand years of such building. The *Great Hall* (Fig. 27) was erected by Seti I and Rameses II of the nineteenth dynasty (1350–1205 B.C.). Study these temples as colossal expressions of enduring power through the simple organization of mass. The *Great Hall* of Pl. 8 is from the *Ramesseum*, a temple at Thebes built by Rameses II.

there are we can tell how many rows of columns stand beneath. The great size of the columns is due largely to the weight of the huge stone lintels that form the roof. In this case the filling of the space with columns mattered little, as but few were admitted to the hall and the vista through it was enhanced by the repetition of the vertical lines.

To break the monotonous stretches of surface and to add a note of vivacity, low reliefs cover the walls and the columns; on the interior, scenes and inscriptions relating to the gods; on the exterior, to the pharaoh. In the brilliant light and in the deep shadow — there is but little half-light — these carvings could not be seen were not color used to differentiate the figures. Rich though they are, these colorful carvings are kept sternly subject to the main surfaces and lines. They enhance; they never obtrude.

Fig. 29. View from the Back of the Temple toward the Pylon. For simplicity and power of mass compare with the skyscraper.

The design of the *Temple* as a whole — bold geometric volumes and unbroken lines, with light and dark and color used in large units, with detail kept rigidly subordinate (Fig. 29) — recalls that of the *Skyscraper*. Yet in the *Skyscraper* the mass is pierced by many openings; the stone is a thin protective curtain; the steel beams that construct the building rise with dynamic force. In the *Temple* the mass is only lightly broken by carvings and color; the stone walls function as supports, are solid, inert, enduring. Hence, though similar in some respects, the buildings are quite opposite in effect, because

differences in function, material, and geography are destined to produce different results.

BREASTED, J. H., Ancient Times, Boston, Ginn, 1916.
BAIKIE, J., Life in the Ancient East, N. Y., Macmillan, 1923.
NATIONAL GEOGRAPHIC MAGAZINE, March and September 1926.
For color in Egyptian architecture, see under *The Tomb of Nakht and Tawi*, p. 194.

SUGGESTION

Make a model of a pylon temple. Ivory soap is good because it will take color. Cut the soap into blocks for the masonry and carve the statues out of the same material. Place the temple in a proper setting, which can be made of sand or clay.

THE BATHS OF CARACALLA

A Roman Clubhouse

THE *Great Hall* of the *Egyptian Temple* (PL. 8 and Fig. 27), with its deep vista through avenues of lofty columns, refreshingly dim and mysteriously quiet, adequately served a favored few as a vestibule to the dwelling-place of the god. Its majestic impressiveness not only befitted the house of a god but also attuned the spirit of the worshiper to an attitude of reverence.

There are circumstances, however, when it is necessary to accommodate large numbers of people in an enclosed space where columns would both break the view and encumber the floor. It then becomes a problem of how to free an enclosed space of supports other than the walls. It was the demands of the luxury-loving Romans that stimulated the builders to solve the problem successfully.

Compare the *Hall* of this Roman club (PL. 9) with the *Great Hall* of the *Egyptian Temple* (PL. 8). The latter

conveys an impression of sheer bulk and enduring power. Yet only here and there can you catch a vista of the length or width, much less grasp a conception of its mass as a unit. The former enables your eye with one sweep to take in the entire space enclosed. Within the unencumbered interior of a great volume you are standing, yourself serving as a scale by which to perceive its size. This interior space is molded into a design by the walls and the roof; thick sturdy walls, though broken with openings, and gigantic columns from which springs a roof of varyingly curved surfaces. Nothing obstructs. Hundreds of people can move about easily. The polished colored marbles of floor, columns, and walls, and the gilded and painted ceiling glittering in the light from the large high windows, give an air of wealth and luxury. Yet this hall could no more serve the *Egyptian Temple* than the latter the Roman club, because each fittingly expresses its function.

What was the Rome of Caracalla, and what function in its life did such a club play? Rome at this time did not exist for herself alone. She was the proud capital of a great empire, just now peaceful and prosperous. Literally and figuratively all roads led to Rome (Fig. 30), on land and on sea, good roads and well-charted sea lanes safe from bandits and pirates. From all parts of this vast empire and even from beyond her boundaries these routes brought grain from Egypt, silk from China, tin from Britain, cotton goods from India, marbles from Greece, Asia, and Africa. Was it not natural and even necessary that the leading city of such an empire should present an appearance befitting her station? And so Rome was magnificent, outwardly perhaps the most magnificent capital that the world has known. Her material power found expression in lavish display. Fringing this city of a million people was a green

ring of parks, gardens, and fountains. Within the walls little oases of gardens and fountains dotted the crowded city of fine homes, broad streets, splendid public buildings, and temples around open squares. Sumptuous places

Fig. 30. Rome under the Emperors.

of amusement and miles of covered porticoes offered protection from sun and rain.

The populace was cosmopolitan. Many foreigners — traders, provincials, soldiers, ambassadors — could be seen at any time. As for the Romans themselves, the stern discipline of Vespasian in the days of the building of the *Colosseum* was gone. The wealthy upper classes idled in luxury. The masses found both their bread and their pleasure during long indolent days in the patronizing dole and free

PLATE 9

Baths of Caracalla, Central Hall (restored). Rome. The entire interior space is grasped as a unit for the roof curves up from the sides with no intermediate supports. (Anderson and Spiers, *Architecture of Greece and Rome*, London, Batsford)

PLATE 10

Santa Sophia. Istanbul. Spherical masses, compactly grouped, rise rhythmically to the climax of the dome. (© Pub. Photo. Service)

tickets of weak emperors who by these means sought political support.

It was for this Rome that the great clubhouses were built. As the city was large, the emperors wealthy, and the masses to be entertained ever growing in number, so the baths became correspondingly huge and magnificently luxurious. Their purpose was not simply to provide a place for the daily bath, a necessity to the Roman, but also to furnish a place where one could find association with friends and the great of the day. More than sixteen hundred people at a time could be comfortably cared for by the great corps of slaves at the

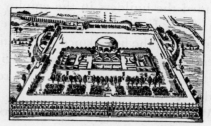

Fig. 31. A Roman Club, or Baths.

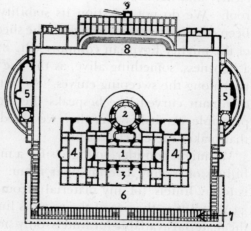

Fig. 32. Plan of the Baths of Caracalla. 1, tepidarium (warm lounge); 2, calidarium (hot room); 3, frigidarium (cooling room); 4, open peristyle; 5, lecture rooms and libraries; 6, promenade and gardens; 7, shops; 8, stadium; 9, reservoirs.

baths proper, and many more in the gardens, athletic grounds, libraries, concert halls, and dining-rooms (Figs. 31 and 32). Whatever the Roman's inclination in

the matter of exercise and leisure, there he could indulge it.

To build on a large scale,[19] with magnificence and also with practical conveniences, was the problem that confronted the builders in the employ of the rich emperors. That they built well and magnificently might not be inferred from the first glance at the ruins today, mightily impressive though they are even in their gauntness. To form an adequate conception, we must rebuild the fallen roofs and restore the marbles.

We have already formed our first impression — a volume of uninterrupted interior space, great in scale, molded clearly and held firmly by the enclosing floor, walls, and roof. We do not question its stability. Yet how has it been done? In comparison with the sheer bulk and weight of the mighty Egyptian columns (PL. 8), here is a spring, a lightness, something alive, as the eye is caught and carried along the sweeping curves. As in the *Colosseum,* the dominant curved line bespeaks the arch. It is the arch principle, carried farther than we noted in the *Colosseum,* that makes the effect possible.

We might consider, to digress for a moment, some possibilities of roofing a rectangular room. The simplest way is to lay lintels (of any material) from wall to wall (Fig. 33A). But as the size of the room is limited by the size of the material available for lintels, only small-scale rooms can use this method unless additional supports are added between the walls (Fig. 33B). If the lintels are heavy, as when made of stone, the walls must be proportionly thick enough to carry the weight. The interior space thus en-

---

[19] *The Baths of Caracalla.* The entire establishment has a frontage of about 1200 ft. The central hall, the *tepidarium* or warm lounge, is 183 ft. by 79 ft., and 108 ft. high. The *Baths* contained many Greek and Roman statues, so that the ruins have yielded important examples of these. 212–16 A.D.

closed is rectangular, of small dimensions, and most suitable for seclusion and privacy. Most of the rooms in our
homes are built thus. But add to this rectangular volume
a sloping roof (Fig. 33C),
and you have a much more
interesting exterior because
of the diagonal line and
the gabled ends, as well as
additional height on the interior. This is the basic design of many buildings the
world over.

So far we have kept to
straight lines and used lintels only. Let us now em-
ploy the arch and introduce
the curved surface and
curved line. Fig. 33D
shows our volume covered
with continuous arches
forming a barrel vault.
Built of stone, brick, or concrete, it is very heavy and
so demands thick walls to
support it and walls not
broken by doors and win-
dows enough to endanger
their carrying power. On

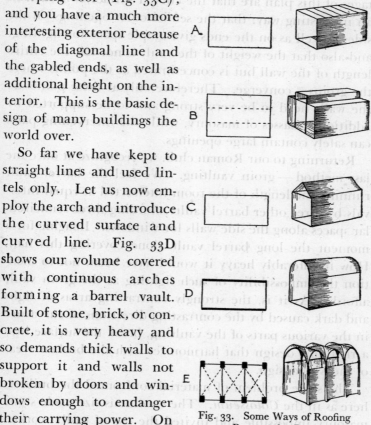

Fig. 33. Some Ways of Roofing
a Rectangular Room.

a small scale, where dim
light is desirable, a barrel vault may be used with impressive result. But if too large, its unbroken uniformly curved
ceiling may prove monotonous.

To obviate the limitations of the barrel vault — that is,

to secure size, lighting, variety — the Romans conceived the idea of crossing the barrel vault at right angles with one or more other barrel vaults (Fig. 33E). The advantages of this plan are that the curved surface is broken in an interesting way; that the semicircular openings on the sides as well as on the ends give ample space for lighting; and also that the weight of the vault is not felt the entire length of the wall but is concentrated at the points where the groins [20] converge. Therefore only at these points do the walls need to be very strong and to be supported by additional masses of masonry, while the intervening parts can safely contain large openings.

Returning to our Roman club, we recognize at once the last method — groin vaulting. We feel the barrel vault running the length of the room intersected at equal intervals by three other barrel vaults affording three semicircular spaces along the side walls for windows. Imagine for a moment the long barrel vault alone covering this hall. How insufferably heavy it would have been, not to mention the impossibility of such lighting as the groin vault affords. As it is, the strongly contrasting areas of light and dark caused by the contrasting directions of curvature in the various parts of the vaulting, break the surface into a rhythmic design that harmonizes with the broken areas of the wall design.

The same problem of material confronted the builders here as in the *Colosseum*. The enormous size made stone masonry impossible and invited the use of easily worked concrete. A dislike of the plain concrete surface, however, led the builders to sheathe it with colored marbles, which, together with the supporting columns of red, green, and other colored stones, ships brought from the ends of the

[20] A vault formed by the intersection of barrel vaults is called a *groin vault* for the curving edge where the vaults meet is known as a *groin*.

PLATE 11

Santa Sophia, Interior. As the exterior suggests, arches and half domes rise in increasing rhythmic volume to the crowning dome. No intermediate supports hinder the eye from apprehending the unity of the interior space organization. (Drawing by J. B. Fulton, in the *Architectural Review*)

PLATE 12

Mosaic Portrait of Theodora. Detail of a group in San Vitale, Ravenna.
The technical demands of mosaic lead to great simplification of form while
the flatness and gold ground add to the decorative effect.

empire. Added to these were the gilded and painted coffers (sunken panels) of the vaulting and the large number of bronze and marble statues, many of them Greek masterpieces, which Roman conquerors had brought to Rome.

Return from our imaginative sojourn in third-century Rome to the Rome of today to wander among these quiet majestic ruins. What builders these Romans were! If the taste of their day demanded too much colored marble and gilding, at least in the structure itself the artist's soul could find expression. And now, with the marbles and gilding gone, how impressive is the impelling sweep of arches and of vaults!

READING

See under THE COLOSSEUM, p. 32.

SUGGESTIONS

1. The *Baths of Diocletian* may also be studied in this connection. They are even larger than those of Caracalla and more of the structure remains today because Michelangelo made part of it into a convent and the central hall into the church of Santa Maria degli Angeli (Saint Mary of the Angels).

2. Note the influence of the Roman baths upon the design of some of our larger railroad terminals (such as the *Pennsylvania Station* in New York). Is the modern builder using the same materials in the same way that the Roman did? Is the function (that of housing large crowds of people) the same?

3. Make models to illustrate the different ways of roofing a space, as suggested in Fig. 33.

SANTA SOPHIA

ON the headland that thrusts the old part of Istanbul (Constantinople) out into the sea (Fig. 34), by the side of

an open square rises a compact pile of masonry, a closely knit group of volumes that rise rhythmically to the culminating dome whose contours suggest the contours of the sky (PL. 10 and Fig. 2C) .[21]   Imagine away the four corner towers, later incongruous additions, and the heterogeneous

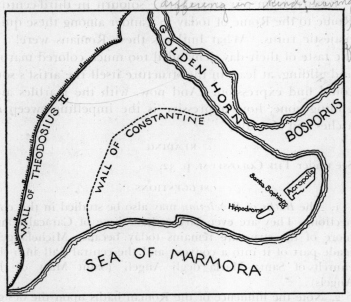

Fig. 34. Istanbul (Constantinople). The heart of the city, in the time of Justinian, was about the Acropolis.

encumbrances about the base.   Volumes with curved surfaces and curving contours dominate the mass but are sta-

[21] *Church of Santa Sophia.* Of brick set with thick joints of mortar. Probably part of the exterior was sheathed in marble; the domes are lead-covered, the windows of carved marble lattice. On the interior the constructional brickwork is entirely covered with rare marbles and mosaics. 235 by 250 ft., exclusive of the court; diameter of the dome, 107 ft. Built by Justinian (527–65 A.D.) on the site of an older church of *Santa Sophia* (Church of the Holy Wisdom); consecrated, 537; reconsecrated, after damage by an earthquake, 563; pilfered of its finest furnishings by the Crusaders, 1204; converted into a Mohammedan mosque and many of the mosaics covered, 1453; minarets built between 1453

bilized by rectangular volumes with straight angular contours. Together they form a unit of singular harmony and
quiet strength. The red brick set in thick layers of mortar
and the dull gray lead covering of the domes offer no display and hint at no magnificence. It is the volumes alone
that hold the attention, catching light and holding shadow,
speaking clearly of an inclosed space.

Let us step within (PL. 11). You stop a moment to catch
your breath in surprise and then to breathe deeply as if in
a newly discovered great out-of-doors, more insistently real
than in nature itself. Arches swell into greater arches,
and half-domes into greater half-domes. Everywhere is
rhythmic movement upward in a great crescendo to the
culminating dome. Light from many windows, softened
by the stone lattice, reveals the splendid interior of the
drab inclosing shell, an interior entirely incrusted with
the richest of colored marbles, gold-ground mosaics, lacy
carving, polished metal. Every inch of the surface gleams
with color and gold, splendid but not glittering; quite
subordinate to the powerful sweep of the arches and domes,
yet enriching them with contrasting delicacy.[22]

What building is this? What purpose is met by an interior that impresses one with a feeling of reserved magnificence and serene exaltation? Your guide in Istanbul
tells you that it is a mosque (a Mohammedan, or Muham-
madan, church). To understand its original purpose,
however, we must go to the Istanbul (then known as Con-

---

and 1574; some of the mosaics uncovered and some restoration, 1847. *Santa
Sophia*, in fact all the culture and art expression of Constantinople and her
empire is called Byzantine after the older name of the city whose several
names it is well to keep in mind: Byzantium (about the seventh century B.C.
–330 A.D.); Constantinople (330–1929); Istanbul (1929–).

[22] This was the original effect. Today the church is shabby and marred
by the Mohammedan additions. Parts of the mosaic surfaces are covered
with paint or whitewash and all the lavish equipment is pilfered or lost.

stantinople) of the sixth century A.D., the city which had superseded Rome as the capital of the Roman Empire.

In 527 Justinian and Theodora had been crowned emperor and empress. Theodora was an extraordinary woman who had risen to this high station from a lower social rank through ambition, daring, and intelligence, qualities which sometimes made her, as empress, a wiser statesman than Justinian.[23] Together with affairs of state Justinian encouraged and liberally patronized the arts, especially that of building. A sedition in which he had nearly lost his crown furnished him an opportunity, for the old *Santa Sophia* in which he and Theodora had been crowned was burned during the rioting. Hardly a month passed before he began to rebuild the church in a manner that should be worthy not only of the Christian faith, for Justinian was a devout Christian, but also of leadership in the faith. For the emperor's aim was to restore the rapidly disintegrating Roman Empire and to make *Santa Sophia* not only the mother church but the symbol of a restored Christianized empire. Furthermore, his great wealth enabled him to build on a grand scale, with the richest materials, and to indulge his love and that of Theodora for costly splendor, as we infer from a sentence in his dedicatory prayer, " I have surpassed thee, O Solomon."

What were the problems involved? The Christian Church has always been congregational, that is, all followers of the faith have free access to the church, witness the ceremonies and participate in them, quite in contrast to the Egyptian faith, where the pharaoh or the priest alone entered the sanctuary. Thus a Christian church must provide a space large enough to contain all its membership and

[23] For a vivid picture of Theodora see C. Diehl, *Byzantine Portraits*, N. Y., Knopf, 1927.

make its sanctuary visible to all. To Justinian then fell
the problem of providing an interior of spacious proportions and sumptuous appearance, an interior that would
symbolize a great faith and a great empire. As for the
plan, there was no desire to create something novel but
rather, as in the case of the *Parthenon,* to refine a well-
known design. For centuries builders in eastern Mediterranean lands had been experimenting on the problem of
how to cover a square area with a dome and had succeeded,
on a small scale. Now came the summons from an emperor to build in the greatest city in the East on an un-
precedented scale. This was stimulation to great endeavor.
For nearly six years they labored, Justinian and Theodora
constantly consulting and advising.[24] Then early one
Christmas morning Justinian and all the people dedicated
the church as together they " hymned their songs of prayer
and praise."

Let us picture *Santa Sophia* as Justinian and Theodora
built it. It stood on a rocky hill (Fig. 34) with an open
square on the south, across which stood the emperor's
palace. At the foot of the hill lay the *Hippodrome,* the
great racecourse and a center of activity for political fac-
tions.[25] This part of the city was indeed its heart. In front
of the church lay its own open court (Fig. 35), above whose
walls towered cypress trees. Within, around the marble-
faced walls ran covered passages with marble columns;
marble walks wound through the gardens; and in the center stood a fountain for the customary ablutions before
entering a place of worship, a symbol, in the eyes of these
early Christians, of the purification of sin by the blood of

[24] Many of the royal monograms carved on the capitals of the columns contain the names of both Justinian and Theodora.

[25] For an air view of Istanbul showing *Santa Sophia,* the square and the
Hippodrome, see *The National Geographic Magazine,* Dec. 1928, p. 720.

Christ. Thus was the worshiper prepared to enter, both physically and spiritually.

The impression upon entering, according to writers of Justinian's day,[26] was one of being caught up into a mood of exaltation, particularly by the dome that " standing upon a circle does not appear to rest upon solid foundation but to cover the place beneath as though it were suspended by the fabled golden chain " — an impression similar to

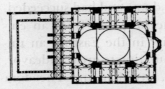

Fig. 35. Plan of Santa Sophia.

our own today, only more intense because of the accessories, now lost, and of the greater harmony which the Mohammedan additions and demolitions have marred. Even the Mohammedan conqueror of Istanbul found himself subject to its power.[26]

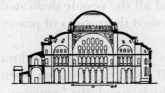

Fig. 36. Section of Santa Sophia without the Court.

What is the source of this power? It is due to the daring and masterly way in which the interior space is organized and to the richness of detail that enhances but never interferes with the clear enunciation of the big elements of the design (PL. 11). The space is enclosed with no other supports than the walls, and the walls and roof are so organized that all the lines and surfaces lead rhythmically to the focal point,[27] the dome. As the poet says, the dome seems to hang in the air and the

[26] There is a large amount of detailed description of *Santa Sophia* in the work of Justinian's court poet, quoted in W. R. Lethaby and H. Swaimson, *The Church of Sancta Sophia*, London, Macmillan, 1916. For the story of the Mohammedan conqueror, see *Ibid.*, p. 126.

[27] A *focal point* (center of interest, climax) is that point in a design (a drama, symphony, painting, building, city) where the artist wishes to concentrate emphasis.

light coming in through the windows that fringe its base seems to half-separate it from its supports.

Here the arch principle of construction has produced a different effect, based upon a different method of roofing a rectangular volume from any that we have noted so far (Fig. 33). Let us see how it is done. Both the exterior view and the plan show a square area covered with a dome flanked on two sides by rectangular areas with half-domes and on the other two by vaulted aisles. The problem involved is how, in covering a cube with a hemisphere, to handle the upper corners of the cube so that there will be a pleasing transition from the angular form to the spherical form, and how to secure a cir-cular base for the dome. The builder solves these problems by raising arches on the four walls of the cube, con-necting their crowns (highest parts) with an imaginary circle and filling the

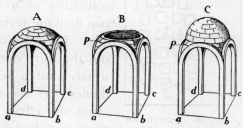

Fig. 37. A Dome on Pendentives. *abcd* is a square area to be covered with a dome. *A* illus-trates one method which, however, produces the feeling that four sections have been sliced off the sides of the dome to make it fit the square base. To secure a circular base the builder throws arches from pier to pier as in *A*, fills in the corners with masonry up to the crowns of the arches (*B*). On the circular base so secured he erects a dome with no sliced off sides (*C*). At the same time he has made a pleasing transition from the square to the circular base. The triangular surfaces which make this transition are called pendentives (*P*) and a dome so erected is known as a dome on penden-tives.

spaces between with masonry (Fig. 37). In this way, start-ing with a square base he has worked up with his arches and curved surfaces to a great circle and has supplanted the an-gular corners with upward curving surfaces that make a

transition between the vertical surfaces within the arches and the curved surface of the dome. The weight of the dome is carried toward the corners of the cube by the arches which are met there by heavy masonry. The walls then are quite unnecessary as supporting members and so can be omitted, thus enlarging the space as they do on two of the sides, or they can be filled with arcades and light walls largely broken by windows as they are on the other two sides. But the problem is more complicated in *Santa Sophia,* where the area to be covered is a rectangle consisting of a central square and two flanking rectangles (Figs. 35 and 36). The solution consisted of erecting the lofty dome over the central square and a series of lower half-domes over the rectangles, thus creating the effect of rhythmic movement of volumes and surfaces that is the most marked characteristic of the building.

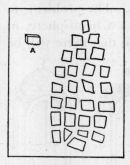

Fig. 38. Tesserae for Making Mosaic. These squarish pieces of glass and stone average one-fourth inch in size and are roughened on the under side (*A*) so as to adhere more firmly to the cement. (After Lethaby)

To this rhythmic space design a wealth of detail — colored and carved marbles, gold-ground mosaics, bronze, gold and silver — lent color, flash of metal, and contrasting textures. All this richness enhanced the effect because nothing obtruded itself at the expense of the basic space design. Marbles covered the floors and sheathed the walls; columns, door frames, and window lattice were of marble: dull red, emerald-green, soft green with dark veining, rose-red, rich red on white, warm yellow, startling black on white, all laid to bring out the harmonies, gradations, and contrasts of color and vein-

PLATE 13

Cloister of Saint Paul's Without the Walls. Rome. Long sweeps of cornice and frieze bind the arches together and by contrast accent their sweeping rhythm. The proportions, in all details, are peculiarly fitting for an interior court.

PLATE 14

Saint Paul's Without the Walls. Rome. In this rectangular interior the lines and lights and darks lead the eye in a horizontal direction to the altar framed by the great arch, instead of upward as in Santa Sophia.

ing. As these marbles were handsawn, their surfaces were pleasantly, not mechanically smooth and, finished with wax, reflected softly the gold of the mosaics.

These mosaics covered all the upper surfaces. By *mosaic* we mean a surface incrusted with a design made by laying tiny pieces of colored glass or stone, called *tesserae*, in cement. The tesserae are roughly square in shape, averaging less than half an inch in the Theodora mosaic (PL. 12), though many are triangular. They are usually roughened on the under side so as to adhere more firmly to the cement (Fig. 38). Set irregularly so as to produce an uneven surface, they catch and reflect the light, thus creating a vibrant effect. Gold tesserae were often used for the background against which the figures stood out in dull reds, ivory-whites, blues, and greens, for the colors used were few. The portrayal of the human figure in mosaic demands, one can see, a highly simplified treatment. Not naturalistic appearance but an almost abstract pattern of line and color derived from the figure becomes the aim of the artist.

Mosaic is highly decorative and of solemn splendor, most impressive in a half-light. But it was not to the decorative effect alone that these mosaics contributed; their subject matter was carefully determined by the Church. In this age, we must remember, when the mass of the people was illiterate, the Church taught the Christian story and the Christian faith by the decorations in its meeting-places. So, just as the lines and volumes rise to the climax of the dome, the subject matter of the mosaics rises from the angels, saints, prophets, and doctors on the lower walls through the four great cherubim of the pendentives to the sternly majestic colossal figure of Christ as Judge and Redeemer in the crown of the dome.

READING

BYRON, R., The Byzantine Achievement, London, Routledge, 1929.

TWO EARLY CHRISTIAN CHURCHES
Saint Paul's Without the Walls
Santa Maria in Cosmedin

FROM the exaltation of *Santa Sophia's* dome we turn to another early Christian church to find ourselves in an atmosphere of serene calm (PL. 14 and Fig. 40). The rectangular volume with a flat wooden ceiling is so organized that the rhythmically repeated arcades, silhouetted against shadow, the cornices, the patterning of the floor, the coffering of the ceiling — all the lines and lights and darks — carry the eye to the great central arch which frames and emphasizes the canopied altar. Here too, as in *Santa Sophia,* is richness of marble and mosaic. The dominant note is a cool blue seen in the floor, the columns, and the mosaics, through which plays the yellow of alabaster, mellow light from the high windows, and the gilded carvings of the ceiling, which shines " like a sea of gold."

There is an enfolding peace about this interior close to the earth. And one feels it the more as he steps outside and looks at the plain exterior (Fig. 39). Perhaps we may see in this contrast a symbol of life as the early Christian saw it — the meanness and roughness of external life contrasting with the rare beauty of the inward spirit. For life was rough and chaotic in the Rome that built *Saint Paul's,*[28] a very different Rome from the one that lifted the great

[28] *Saint Paul's Without the Walls (San Paolo fuori le Mura).* On the road to Ostia, about three miles from Rome. The site of the tomb of Saint Paul had been marked by a church since the days of Constantine. The present church was first erected in 390; was enlarged and embellished frequently; was largely destroyed by fire in 1823; and was rebuilt in 1854 on the same plan and dimensions but with more gorgeous decoration. *The Cloister,* 1205–41 A.D.

vaults of the *Baths of Caracalla*. Then there was order, peace and prosperity, wealth and magnificence. Now there was no central power to maintain order. The city was falling in ruin, overwhelmed as it was with warfare, poverty, squalor, beggars. Why the change? Rome's earlier splendor, cloaking inward decay, had no strength to withstand the rugged northern invaders who for centuries had been battering the frontiers. Again and again they swept in upon the city, sacking, plundering, looting. The emperor himself lived at Constantinople in the peaceful East, and though he sent governors to Italy he could not prevent chaos.

But a new power was gradually growing into the place of old Rome — the Christian Church. The vigor of the new faith, however, could not always rise above despair. A governor sent out from

Fig. 39. Saint Paul's Without the Walls Before the Fire of 1823. The side wall of the court is omitted to show the façade. The windows are filled with stone lattice.

Constantinople writes to the Emperor Justinian that Rome was " a vast empty mass of tumbling ruins among which dwelt in misery the merest handful of despairing men." A pope sends to France for clothes and money. Gregory the Great thus addressed the Roman people: ". . . the world grows old and hoary and through a sea of troubles hastens to an approaching death."

And yet the city did not lose its power. On the whole the Church was gaining strength. The barbarians were becoming a little less barbarous. Here in this pitiable city were the sacred places, sites made memorable by martyrdom, by the burial of saints, by relics. Among the

most sacred were the tombs of Saint Peter and Saint Paul.
To these shrines came pilgrims from all parts of Europe.
We see them, in a great throng, making their way along

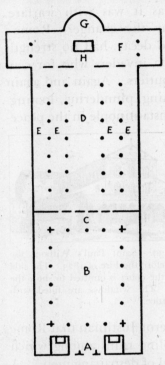

Fig. 40. Plan of an Early
Christian Church of the Type of
Saint Paul's (a Basilica). *A*, en-
trance; *B*, open court (atrium);
C, vestibule (narthex); *D*, nave;
E, aisles; *F*, transverse aisle; *G*,
apse; *H*, altar. Notice that the
plan as a whole is T shape.

shaded porticoes — for the
northerners are not ac-
customed to the hot sun of
Italy — past the silent ruins
that so impressed these
strangers, out through the city
gate toward the church that
covers the burial place of
Saint Paul. Here are all kinds
and all classes of people —
kings, criminals, the learned,
the adventurer, the knight in
coat of mail, and the bare-
footed monk in woolen cas-
sock.

Hence a memorial church
in Rome needed not only to
provide a suitable shrine for
the sacred spot and for local
needs of worship but also to
care for these great throngs of
pilgrims. And this was not so
simple a matter as for the
builders of *Santa Sophia*, difficult as their problem had
been. For in these dark days
in Rome the building craft

had suffered and was so well-nigh lost that it was necessary
to send to Constantinople for craftsmen. Nor was the lavish wealth of Justinian at their disposal. Materials were

PLATE 15

Santa Maria in Cosmedin. Rome. A similar design to that of Pl. 14 but more direct and emphatic. The difference in feeling is due to the greater simplicity, to different proportions, and to a different rhythm in the arcades because of their interruption by the walls. The walls were formerly covered with frescoes.

PLATE 16

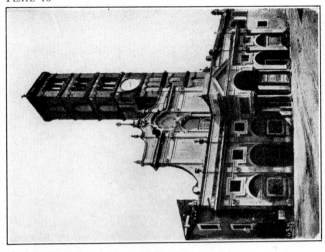

Santa Maria in Cosmedin.

A. Restored to its original condition.   B. As remodeled in XVI–XVIII century.
The clear unity of harmonious masses in A is quite lost by the inharmonious additions in B.

difficult to obtain, for robbers lurked outside the city walls. The " Roman peace " no longer protected the old highways. Yet materials were at hand within the walls in abundance. Great quarries of finely cut travertine, columns, marbles of all colors and sizes, existed in a vast number of ruins such as the *Colosseum* and the *Baths of Caracalla.* Inscribed stone and marble could be used by turning the inscription to the wall or the under side of the floor; columns could be set up intact for interior arcades and if one ruin did not supply enough for a long arcade, more could be taken from another and it mattered little if they did not match in style or even in size, for additional bases could prop them up to the required height. Furthermore, the great Roman shafts of varicolored marble could be sawn into discs for flooring, pulpit, and altar decorations, and the small pieces made into encircling borders.

Because of the importance of the site, *Saint Paul's* became the center of a settlement. Monasteries, chapels, porticoes, clustered about it, all within a protecting wall; and round about were farms and orchards. Though much of this settlement has disappeared, one of its most charming parts, a *Cloister,* remains (PL. 13). It is a square open court with grass and flowers and in the center a fountain. Around its sides runs a spacious arcaded portico. Looking through the arches in the foreground to the side seen in the background, the movement, variety, and unity of the design appear. What the eye sees first is the regular repetition of arches, holding deep shadow, united by a long quiet horizontal — movement under control. Was this not the basis of the design of the *Colosseum* (PL. 6)? In the cloister these same elements are used with a lightness and an elasticity that are suitable for this light one-story arcade and which would be unsuitable for a massive struc-

ture like the *Colosseum*. Having caught the two main factors of the design, the eye begins to see details. Just above
the swinging arches runs a frieze of round and rectangular
pieces of red and green marble interlaced and set in white
stone. How beautifully the round of the arch and the
horizontal of the cornice are here combined! And what
a pleasing touch the color adds! Bring your eye back to
the columns in the foreground. Many are twisted, some
straight. A twisted column does not impress one as sufficiently strong to support anything. Should you see it in
the *Colosseum* you would run away from the building.
But here in the cloister the small scale, the lightness, the
single story, justify its use. Many of the columns are fluted
and the flutings filled with bands made of bits of colored
marble and gilded glass, thus carrying out the color scheme
of the frieze. Though grouped in pairs — more often
than not, the two of a pair are unlike — there is a refreshing charm in these minor irregularities and in the vivacity
of the color with its occasional flash of gold, because the
whole is dominated by the steady rhythm of the arcades and
the sustained horizontals.

To see the same design as that of *Saint Paul's* creating a
different effect, let us return within the city and make our
way to a small church near the Tiber, *Santa Maria in Cosmedin* (PLS. 15 and 16).[29] As we enter we see a rectangular volume whose side walls are cut by groups of arcades.
The end is nearly filled with the arch of the apse, whose
shadow brings out so definitely the center of interest, the
canopy-covered altar. Reaching out into the nave in front

[29] Erected in the fifth century A.D. on the site of an ancient corn exchange,
it utilized in its structure some of the columns of an ancient portico. Built for a
Greek brotherhood, it was first called *Santa Maria in Schola Graeca;* later the
name was changed to *Santa Maria in Cosmedin* after a square in Constantinople.
Campanile, twelfth century. Remodeled in Renaissance style, sixteenth to
eighteenth century; restored, 1884–99.

of the altar and shut off by a low marble rail is the choir, the space occupied by the clergy who participate in the service. Here are the two pulpits from which are read respectively the gospel and the epistle. About the sanctuary and the choir is concentrated the decoration — carving, marble inlay, mosaic.

Compare this interior with that of *Saint Paul's*. The latter is sumptuous throughout, which perhaps detracts from a trenchant emphasis upon the sanctuary. Its proportions create a peaceful spaciousness and majesty, and the columns, set at regular intervals, a quiet rhythm. *Santa Maria* is plain. Its clearly defined parts with the help of the concentrated decoration impel the eye to the focal point of the design. Its proportions accent the vertical, the line of aspiration; and the walls, rising from the floor where they break the arcades, strengthen the unity and vary the rhythm.

In *Santa Maria in Cosmedin* one sees how the materials of older Rome were used. The first column at the left is fluted and carries an elaborate capital carved with figures. The others are plain, all of different sizes with varying capitals and bases. These incongruous details, however, do not interfere with the clear strong design.

Seen from the outside (PL. 16A), simple unadorned volumes, sensitively proportioned and coördinated, make the exterior as effective as the interior: first, the nave with *clerestory* [30] and sloping roof; then an arcaded vestibule set at right angles, with a roof of the same angle of slope; next, a central projecting portico with an arch and a sloping roof, the arch linking it with the vestibule and the line of the roof repeating the line of the nave roof. Finally,

---

[30] The *clerestory* is the part of a building which rises, like an additional story, above the roof of the rest of the building and contains openings for lighting.

the tower standing in the angle of the nave and the vestibule, though later in date and broken by arched openings, offers a fourth rectangular volume. What a clear coördination of these parts! Clean-cut in light and shadow! Contrast for a moment a later remodeling (PL. 16B). The eye no longer sees clear interrelations. The church has flattened out because the lofty façade masks the clerestory, the roof, and part of the tower, thus concealing its conjunction with the building. The gable over the portico finds no answering gable above. The square windows over the arches are related to nothing. It is a jumble of forms where everything jars. How restful to return to the quiet harmony of the original church!

READING

LOWRIE, W., Monuments of the Early Church, N. Y., Macmillan, 1923.
SHOWERMAN, G., Eternal Rome, New Haven, Yale Press, 1924.

THE CATHEDRAL OF OUR LADY OF CHARTRES

FROM almost any part of the old French city of Chartres you can see rising boldly on the hilltop the big mass of a church with two tall spires (Fig. 41). Close about it huddles the city, low and compact. Once, danger from robbers and warring lords forced the city to protect itself with heavy walls, a moat, and drawbridges, and the farmers to build their homes within this wall. That is why the houses are so crowded and the streets so narrow.

Let us climb up one of those streets toward the hill, a street so steep that part of the way it rises by steps, and turn into Shoemakers' Lane. Here the houses, projecting over the street as they rise, leave but a slit of the sky visible and then draw back as if to disclose a partial view, a hint

PLATE 17

Cathedral of Chartres. An expression of lofty aspiration through the insistence upon vertical lines and the upward reach. Compare Pl. 7 for an opposite expression of restraint through different proportions and a greater emphasis upon the horizontal.

PLATE 18

Cathedral of Chartres. The organization of this interior space by proportions, insistent verticals, the pointed arch, and rich color creates an impression
of unfulfilled aspiration. Compare Pl. 11 where a greater width for the
height and unbroken round curves express a more completely fulfilled exaltation. Chartres is restless; Santa Sophia, serene.

as it were, of the majestic building (Fig. 42). The houses, so small by comparison, cluster very closely as if clinging to a strong protector. From the tiny square in front a great precipice of wall rises sheerly and parting, reaches by its two lofty spires far up into the sky (PL. 17). Everywhere is the upward-moving line, so insistently repeated that you feel as if you too would like to reach up, far above the earth.

Step inside a moment. After the sunshine of the open square you can hardly see, and you have no desire to speak.

Fig. 41. View of the City of Chartres.

When your eyes have become adjusted to the light you begin to notice that the space, though very large, is so narrow and high that although the eye impulsively looks upward for the ceiling it finds only curved surfaces and pointed arches disappearing into violet shadow. And then it is carried down a long vista, like a straight narrow road through the woods, at the end of which the eye is caught and held by masses of intense blue and red like gigantic clusters of rubies and sapphires. Look to the right and to the left, through the columns, and high up on the walls. There are the same glowing masses warming the

cold gray stone with splashes of red, blue, and violet.
When to the spirit of uplift that comes from the lines and
proportions are added this ecstatic color and stately music,
the outside world is forgotten as you are carried into another world that we may call the realm of religion.   What-

ever one's belief or creed, here is a
building that catches one up into that
searching, that aspiration, that mystery, which underlie all religious belief.   To return to the little square
outside involves a readjustment not
only of the eyes to the ordinary light
but of the feelings to matter-of-fact
existence.

Shall we sit down on this bench in
the little square and while looking at
the façade recall the tale of the building of this lofty church? [31]   For, way-
farers though we may be from distant
lands, of different customs and beliefs,
it needs no proof of words to convince
us that a great spirit lies back of the

Fig. 42.   A Street in
Chartres, Showing the
South Porch of the Ca-
thedral in the Distance.

building of this church and has infused into its stone and
glass as strong a personality as that of any human personality.

It was in June of the year 1194.   The people of Chartres

[31] *The Cathedral of Chartres.*   Built of local limestone, which is rather coarse
but hard and very pleasing in texture and color.   Exterior length, 506 ft.;
width of western façade, 156 ft.   Interior, nave, 426 by 53½ ft.;   height, 122 ft.
The site appears to have been associated with Christianity from its introduction,
each successive church suffering from fire and pillage of war.   The present
cathedral dates from the fire of 1194 A.D., which destroyed all except the
western end, and was dedicated in 1260.   The north and south porches were
added in the thirteenth century.   The northern spire, of wood, was destroyed by
lightning in 1506 and reërected of stone in 1506–12.   The windows, removed
in 1918 for safety during the Great War, were cleaned and replaced in 1919–23.

were weeping over the smoking ruins of their church. "But weeping will do us no good," young Jacques the weaver was saying. "Surely the Virgin will show us a way to build for her another church, perhaps a finer one, said the cardinal yesterday, all of stone so that we shall have no more fires. Fires enough we have had. Well I remember the stories my father used to tell us of the big one sixty years ago that burned everything, church and town. But see what they did. You've all seen old Mother Marchand point out her stones in the church over there near the bottom of the tower. Though only twenty years old then, she pulled on the same cart as Prince Jean, Father Louis, and Pierre the pastry cook. Of all the carts that covered the five miles from the quarries theirs reached Chartres before any one else's, though young Sir Gaspard, who had just returned from a Crusade, nearly passed them as he carried one huge block alone on his shoulder. Back and forth that five miles they dragged their loads. It seemed like a miracle. Can't we do what our fathers did? We've got something to begin on. The fire is all out and the towers are not hurt. The doorway is left and the three windows above it. And, too, our Belle Verrière, our Beautiful Window, is safe. That is a good omen. For when that part of the church was catching fire Our Lady herself seemed to help us as we worked, we don't know how, so frantically did we struggle to get the window from the frame; and, heavy as it was, it seemed light as we carried it through the smoke down into a safe stone cellar."

Jacques stopped for a moment as if overcome by the recollection. "Yes," he continued, "Our Lady will help us. How clearly she shows us the way! Not much is left of my house or my shop. But I can give a piece of silver that escaped, and time and labor. And you know the car-

dinal told us yesterday that the fathers are giving the income from their farm lands for three years. Our rich fields and gardens just outside the walls and our shops inside that make us famous for our shoes, our wines, our pastry — what are all these things without Our Lady enshrined on the hill? ''

The youthful enthusiasm of the weaver became contagious. Old and young began to plan what they could give: what treasure, what labor. Years passed, five, ten, twenty. The cathedral rose steadily behind the old towers. It was slow work cutting each stone to fit its place. For, as the cardinal had said, it was all of stone, inside and roof as well as outside. Jacques's hair was turning gray. When he was not at his loom he was around the big church with his boys and girls, watching the walls

Fig. 43. Stone Carvers Working on Statues with Hammer and Chisel. From a window.

and the stone roof gradually close in the interior. The places they loved best were the quarters of the stone-carvers and the glass-makers. The sculptors with mallet and chisel (Fig. 43) were carving hundreds of statues large and small for the big side portals which the king and royal family had contributed. They were especially fond of the beautiful Christ so full of tenderness that was to stand on the pillar in the center of the doorway, and of Saint George and Saint Theodore. Never did they tire of hearing how Saint George saved the princess by killing the dragon and how

Saint Theodore pretended to worship an idol in order that he might get it into his hands to break it to pieces, for which he was beheaded. One day they found a jovial carver chuckling over his work. For on the block of stone he had carved a picture of his best friend the farmer, with his dress tucked up, a plaited straw cap on his head, standing in the ripe grain that he was cutting with his sickle (Fig. 44). How proud he will be, the old carver thought, when he learns that he represents July on the big church!

Fig. 44. Month of July. On the arch above the left entrance of the Western Portal of Chartres (PL. 19).

Perhaps it was the glass-makers' shop that they loved the most. Jacques's oldest son Pierre, who had been apprenticed to this shop, was now one of the master workmen and was very busy directing the work, for there were many large windows needed to fill the great openings of the walls. What excitement ran through the city when a new order came in! Now it was from the Guild of the Bakers, now from the Shoemakers, now from the Furriers. Jacques's own Guild of the Weavers had already commissioned two windows and was planning a third. What fun it was to stand by the big benches on which the design of the window was drawn and watch the men build up pictures of the story of Charlemagne and Roland by leading together tiny bits of red, blue, yellow, and green glass! At the bottom of the window Pierre put a little picture of a

furrier selling a cloak as a signature (Fig. 52), for the
Guild of the Furriers donated this window. Then in medallion after medallion they pictured the incidents of
Charlemagne's adventures in fighting the Saracens and of
Roland's brave fight and death at Roncevaux. And when
the window was finished and lifted into its place in the
church and the sun streamed through they almost cried for
joy, so like a cluster of jewels did each little story become.

And so the years went by. When the walls and the great
stone roof were finished they could worship in the church.
Still there were many things to be done: the sculpture at
the doorways, more windows, the wood carvings in the
choir and in the sanctuary, the vessels for the altar. At
last the great day came, in October of 1260. The cathedral
was ready, though not completed. It remained unfinished: the towers planned for the side portals and over the
crossing were never built. The king and the royal family,
cardinals and bishops, nobles and people, crowded into
the spacious church. For now they could dedicate their
labors to the Virgin. Near the front row sat Jacques. He
was nearly ninety years old and long since his eyes had been
unable to guide his shuttle through the warp of his loom.
In the fall sunshine the windows gleamed and warmed
the stone with color. The robes of the king and the vest-
ments of the clergy shone with gold and jewels. All this
Jacques saw, though dimly. He had not realized before,
how beautiful it was. Tears came to his eyes as he remembered that his father, he himself, his sons, and his grand-
sons had all helped to create this beauty; and he uttered a
prayer of gratitude that he had lived to see this day.

That *Chartres* is an expression of faith and aspiration
was suggested by our first impression. What do our eyes
see to arouse this impression? From an air view — there

is no building in Chartres high enough for us to look down
on the cathedral — the mass looks like a thick Latin cross
laid on the ground (Fig. 45). Do you remember the interior, long, narrow, and lofty? The cross is curved at the
top, flanked by two towers at the bottom, and covered
with a steep roof. Around it, except at the towers and
across the front, are low masses like crouching or kneeling
figures that seem to be lifting up arches of stone to the
walls like hands and arms braced up against them. Look

Fig. 45. Air View of Chartres Cathedral.

directly at the façade (PL. 17). Everywhere the accent is
on the vertical line, restrained, at intervals, by horizontals.
The openings in the wall of stone, generally high and narrow, some topped with round arch and some with pointed,
hold shadows which make a pattern of dark or half-dark
against the light of the stone (Fig. 46). This design of
light and dark is balanced on each side of a central axis,
although marked differences occur in the towers, partly in
the lower stories but especially in the spires. One is
plainer and more robust, harmonizing with the lower
parts; the other, more slender and more ornate and, though

beautiful in itself, less harmonious. Yet this difference does not disturb the balance because mass balances mass, not detail, detail.

This pattern, however, is not perfectly flat for it is made of projecting and receding masses which, beside forming the general composition sketched in Fig. 46, cast shadows over the surface, like overtones, making it vibrate now strongly, now lightly, according to the hour and the kind

Fig. 46. Light and Dark Pattern of the Façade of Chartres Cathedral.

of weather. The triple portal, on the one hand, accents the doorway and suggests entrance within; on the other, creates a mass of dark between the towers that strengthens the base. It is not a solid, uninterrupted dark, however, but is broken; for it is elaborately carved, and its richness is enhanced by the plainness of the surrounding stone. Come nearer and you see that these carvings are figures, hundreds of them (PL. 19). The larger ones are curiously stiff and elongated, and seem to hang in the air. But stand back at a little distance and see how harmoniously they fit the shafts.

Their garments hang in vertical folds and their arms cling tightly to the body, so that there is almost no break in the contour of the figure as its mass shapes a column which stands out against the carved surface behind it. With what orderliness everything takes its place! This sculpture does for the portal at *Chartres* what the *Parthenon* sculpture does for the pediment of that temple: by creating contrasts of broken and unbroken surface it not only accents the entrance but gives variety and, therefore, unity to the entire façade.

PLATE 19

The Western Portal of Chartres. Both masonry and sculpture are of the same limestone, an important element of unity. One is aware of the figures, primarily, as integral parts of the building, and yet not without significance as Kings and Queens.

PLATE 20

The Southern Portal of Chartres. Here the figures are more naturalistic than in the Western Portal and, though still decorative, impress one more as figures.

There is another purpose, however, besides architectural decoration. To compare it again with the *Parthenon,* there is a meaning in the figures that strikes deep into the life of the people who built it. Columnar though their bodies may appear, look into their faces — eager, happy, and earnest — and you begin to feel that these are real people and the imagination easily enough transforms the columns into bodies, if you wish to be more literal. This portal is known as the *Royal Portal,* that is, the portal of *Christ* as King of Kings. His figure is carved over the doorway, tenderly stern, for he is the Last Judge, and at the same time a forgiving Father, as his hand, uplifted in blessing, signifies. All the figures on the portal relate to this central one, the columnar ones being *Christ's* ancestors, the *Kings and Queens of Judah.* But more than that. Look up at the smaller figures in the arches above the *Kings and Queens* at the extreme

Fig. 47.   The Goat, a Sign of the Zodiac.   Western Portal, Chartres.   See how beautifully the goat with wings and serpent tail intertwines with the conventional shrubs to fill the space.

right of PL. 19. They are not columnar like the figures below. There was no need for it. Here is the neighbor cutting his grain in July (Fig. 44), the figure which Jacques and his children watched the stonecutter chuckling over. Follow the arches around and you will find the characteristic labor for each month with its sign of the zodiac (Fig. 47) — a real calendar. And why a calendar on a church? Because man has sinned and needs to be

redeemed, Jacques would have told you, and by consistently doing the everyday things of life, month by month as the occasion demands, he helps himself to salvation. Thus all the sculpture of the portal, and of the side portals as well, is bound into a literary unity, as it pictures both literally and symbolically the Christian story and the Christian faith. And do not forget that while it is presenting this story it is at the same time fulfilling its architectural function. What harmony of content, form, and function!

Before going inside again, shall we look at one of the side portals which the king gave (PL. 20)? A broad flight of steps and a delicately carved portico lead to the triple doorway. Here are hundreds of figures. The larger ones, comparable in position and size with the *Kings and Queens* of the *Royal Portal,* are no longer stiff. They stand firmly on their feet and turn slightly to the left or to the right. Altogether they look more like human figures. How did this happen? All over Europe, in this thirteenth century, men were beginning to observe more accurately what people and things looked like, and the work of the painters and sculptors shows this. " Why shouldn't we paint and carve our figures to look more like real people? " they asked. And that is what they began to do. At the same time they did not forget the column.

Let us go inside. Again we must wait a few minutes for the eyes to adjust themselves. Everything is stone and glass and everywhere are arches that are pointed, not round-topped like those in the *Colosseum* and *Santa Sophia.* Strong pillars made of a group of columns and half-columns rise from the floor and support stone arches, or *ribs,* as they are called, that reach out in great curves to meet in a point those that curve up from the opposite pillar. Thus you have a strong stone framework of sup-

porting pillars and ribs; and it is not a difficult matter to fill the spaces between the ribs with masonry (Fig. 48), making what is called *rib vaulting*.

What do you suppose a vault like this weighs? It must be many, many tons. And we begin to wonder if the columns, heavy as they are, are strong enough to hold it so high in the air. Is there anything about the cathedral that tells us how the builders met this problem? Yes. Do you remember the arches that we noticed from our air view (Fig. 45), which seemed to reach up as if to brace the

walls? Builders had learned by experience that the pressure of such a vault must be counter-balanced by an equal amount of support. So they gave the pillars added strength by building masses of strong masonry along the outside of the walls in line with the

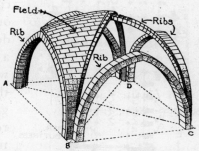

Fig. 48. Stone Ribs with the Field Partly Filled in.

pier (Fig. 49) and by throwing thence arches, or *flying buttresses,* up to meet the wall at the points where the heavy vault tries to push out and to weigh down. So that if you should cut the cathedral in two, vertically, it would look like Fig. 50. The stability of the building, then, depends upon the balance between the vault on the one hand, and the supporting piers and buttresses on the other.

Here then is an additional way, difficult but impressive, of roofing a rectangular space (Fig. 33). Its method shows why the inside of the cathedral, with the exception of the roof, is all open arches and glass. The structural part is an open skeleton framework of stone that has no need of walls

(Fig. 51). But to keep out the weather and to make the interior quiet and secluded, the builders filled in the wall spaces with light masonry and largely with rich glass. This was fortunate. For with no wall space for fresco or mosaic, the stone interior would have been cold indeed had not the windows provided the necessary warm note with their color. Their effect differs very much with the weather. Though always intense in color whenever there is any outside light at all, a window produces one effect on a cloudy day and another when the sun streaming through makes the glass gleam like jewels. But it reaches its finest effect when newly fallen snow still further intensifies this jewel-like radiance. Is he not a hopelessly stolid soul who comes away from *Chartres* without having lost himself for a few moments at least in a feeling of exaltation? It is not only the color that so impresses one but the

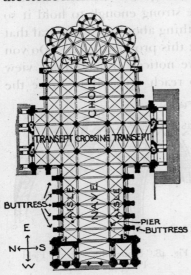

Fig. 49. Plan of Chartres Cathedral. Compare this with Fig. 40 of which this is an elaboration. The transept has moved down the nave making the plan cross-shape. The simple apse, still the sanctuary, has been surrounded by aisles and chapels. Notice in Fig. 45 that the apse, which terminates the nave, is high while the surrounding aisles are low.

harmony of the windows with the whole interior space. The flat decorative areas of glass in shape and proportion form an integral part of this interior design, and furnish the needed contrast. For their sparkling color acts as a foil to the cold stone and caresses it into warmth.

This wonderful decoration was the gift of the faithful of all classes. Kings and princes contributed, as did church-men. But it was the people themselves through their guilds who gave many of the finest windows. In the Mid-dle Ages the trades were organized into trade guilds, each with its patron saint. So what could be more fitting than for a guild to contribute a window to a chapel dedicated to its saint? These guild windows carry at the base little pictures illus-trative of the trade as a guild signature (Fig. 52).

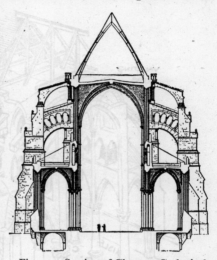

In making these win-dows, as in carving the sculpture, two things must be kept in mind and harmonized: deco-ration and illustration. They were at the same

Fig. 50. Section of Chartres Cathedral. Note the lofty nave with its protecting roof and the low aisles over which the flying buttress sweeps.

time to decorate the interior and to furnish an illustrated edition, we might call it, of the Golden Legend, the most popular book of the Middle Ages. How did the glass-workers do it?

First and last they strove to keep their colors harmoni-ously massed and contrasted, irrespective of whether the colors used were those of naturalistic appearance or not. They did not paint these colors on the glass but added the color to the *pot metal,* that is, the molten glass. When it was cool they cut it into small pieces, which they put to-

gether with strips of lead because that metal is strong but
pliable.   The only painting done was the detail of the face,
the hair, or the drapery, in a brown enamel paint which
was fired before the piece was leaded into its place.   If you
examine the glass closely you will find that it is rough,

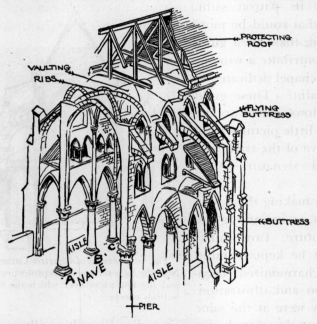

Fig. 51.   Stone Framework of a Gothic Cathedral.   In the
bay $A-B$ the ribs only are shown; in $B-C$ the field of the
vaulting has been added.

streaked, and bubbly; thick or thin.   This was intentional,
to give a vibration and an intensity that could not be
obtained in glass of even texture and thickness.   The
chief colors used were red (ruby) ; blue (sapphire) ; green
(emerald) .   In fact the names of the jewels were used in
speaking of the colors.   Now when you use intense color
in this way you need some contrasting element to set off its

brilliance. This is furnished by the opaque leads and iron frame. The iron performs another function. A large area of leaded glass is pliant and if it is not held by strong bars will soon give way to the pressure of the winds.

One more consideration is important in the decorative element. Light and distance act differently with different colors. Blue expands and red contracts. So when you look at some of the windows at a great distance they seem to be vibrating masses of blue only.

With the limitation of keeping the area of glass decorative, how could the window-makers take into consideration the narrative element? Let us look at the *Window of the Virgin* given by the Shoemakers (See page 90). It is what is called a medallion window, because the iron framework has been molded into medallion shapes, each containing a picture. These windows always read from the bottom to the top. At the

Fig. 52. Furrier Showing a Fur-lined Cloak to a Customer. This scene serves as the guild signature of a window given by the Guild of the Furriers. Chartres.

base is a half-medallion containing a picture of a shoemaker at his bench, with a high boot hanging behind him. Above the shoemaker are represented the Death of the Virgin, the Funeral, the Assumption, and the Coronation. How simple the drawing is! There is no attempt to make a naturalistic picture with buildings and landscape. Nor is there any use of light and shade. Yet how adequately is the story told! Notice the beauty of the grouping about the recumbent figure. Three groups are so massed that they fill the space and the lines of the

figures and the draperies curve toward the head of the
Virgin and at the same time harmonize with the curving
frame of the medallion, while here and there one head
turns away, giving just the amount of opposing direction
of line that is necessary for contrast. A beautiful sensitive
piece of decoration and a beautiful sensitive way of telling
the story, with nothing to detract from the heart of the
incident, no background but flat scintillating blue. While
blue and red are the chief colors used, see how strong areas
of green and yellow play through the design, and how a
large mass of green on the right is balanced by smaller
masses of the same hue on the left.

Thus we see that the glass is as necessary to the interior
design as the sculpture is to the exterior; and that it combines, as does the sculpture, decoration and meaning. Together they form a great book filled with the affairs of
everyday life and with the deepest mysteries of life, one
and inseparable. From this book we have read but a few
paragraphs. Read the rest and you will learn all of the
life, the thought, the fancy, the fun, and the beliefs of the
people who wrote it. And nowhere will you find a more
beautifully illustrated book.

And how was this accomplished? By a great corps of
craftsmen, generations of them, thoroughly trained in the
principles of their crafts, intensely living their own life,
working harmoniously toward one end — to erect a building that was a symbol of their faith and their life.

Compare the interior of *Chartres* (PL. 18) with that of
Santa Sophia (PL. 11). Both are Christian churches and
in both a large unimpeded space is organized by proportions, line, light and dark, and color. Yet how different
are the results! In *Santa Sophia* the proportions are broad
for their height, with a quiet balance of vertical, horizon-

Detail of a Window in Chartres Cathedral. Masses of blue, red, green, and yellow create a flat pattern of jewel-like color which warms the stone and provides a radiantly beautiful wall decoration. Lower half medallion: a shoemaker at his bench, a signature of the Shoemakers Guild, the donor of the window. Circular medallion: the Death of the Virgin. (E. Houvet)

tal, and curve. At *Chartres* the width is very narrow for the height, with an insistence upon vertical lines. In *Santa Sophia* the flowing rounding arches and uninterrupted curves carry the eye to the light radiant gold of the mosaic-lined dome and the spirit to joyous exaltation, then easily back again to the earth. In *Chartres* the emphatic verticals and staccato pointed arches take the eye and the feelings rapidly upward and hold them in the mysterious shadows, or down the long vista of the nave and hold them in the scintillating color. In *Santa Sophia* there is confidence and something definite and complete. In *Chartres* there is mystery, something indefinite and aspiring.

Thus two quite opposite effects were secured, though the elements were the same. The difference is due to the fact that the raw materials of life, that is, the immediate life of the builders, determined whether they should build a *Santa Sophia* or a *Chartres*.

READING

ADAMS, H., Mont-Saint-Michel and Chartres, Boston, Houghton, 1913.

HOUVET, E., Monographie de la Cathédral de Chartres, Chelles, Faucheux, n. d.

MÂLE, E., Religious Art in France, XIII Century, N. Y., Dutton, 1913.

MARRIAGE, M. and E., Sculpture of Chartres Cathedral, Cambridge, University Press, 1909.

SUGGESTIONS

1. Supplementary study. An understanding of *Chartres* means an understanding of all French Gothic cathedrals. Study in particular *Notre Dame of Paris, Amiens,* and *Reims.* Note likenesses and differences. The University Prints, Newton, Mass., and postcards furnish good material.

2. Gothic glass: a study of windows. Find examples of fine Gothic windows. Compare with these, in effect and in prin-

ciples of design, the pictures in glass found in many churches.
Find examples of modern windows designed according to the
principles of those at *Chartres,* of which color reproductions
and transparencies are published by E. Houvet, guardian of
the cathedral. See also Y. Delaporte and E. Houvet, *Les
Vitraux de la Cathédral de Chartres,* Chartres, 1926; and
H. Arnold and L. B. Saint, *Stained Glass of the Middle Ages,*
N. Y., Macmillan, 1926.

   3. Design a window for a definite place in the style of the
Chartres windows.

   4. Find examples of French Gothic in America.

   5. Make a model of a French medieval town with the cathedral as the center. This could be a group project in collabora-
tion with a history course. Also a model of the home of
Jacques the weaver: how it was furnished; how the people
dressed.

TWO DOMES

Saint Mary of the Flower, Florence
Saint Peter's, Vatican City

FROM the hills that encircle the city of Florence [32] spread
out in the valley of the Arno River (Figs. 53 and 96) you
look down upon a choppy sea of red-tiled roofs, above
which soars a massive dome (PL. 22). Let us go down
the crooked streets until we emerge upon a small open
square. From its pavement a tower, rose, ivory and green-
black, lifts itself with proud strength into the intense, blue
of the Italian sky; beside it, the façade of a church of
the same colors; and behind both, the curved surfaces of
the dome. In front of the church stands a low octagonal
structure of black and white marble with a low-pitched
roof.

Here is the very heart of Florence: *Santa Maria del Fiore,*

   [32] There is a large amount of interesting material on Florence and life in
Florence which is essential to the understanding of any artist of this city.
See H. Gardner, *Art Through the Ages,* N. Y., Harcourt, 1926, Chap. XV, and
the books there listed.

Fig. 53.   Florence about 1490 A.D.   From a woodcut in Berlin.

Saint Mary of the Flower [33] (Florence is the city of the lily), with its bell tower and *Baptistery*. Look at the tower once more (Fig. 54). It rises quietly story by story, for

the horizontal *moldings* [34] keep the upward movement in restraint. Compare with it the southern tower of *Chartres* (PL. 17), with its more rugged power of unbroken stone and its greater insistence upon the upward reach. The Florentine tower is solidly strong in its lower stories, breaks into slender arched openings as it rises, and harmonizes in design with the body of the cathedral. But the boldly simple mass and surface of the dome seem inharmonious and disjointed with the long rectangular mass and

Fig. 54. Cathedral of Florence (Santa Maria del Fiore) and Baptistery.

horizontal surfaces. It is only as, turning down a side street, we see the dome segregated from the rest of the

[33] Also called *Il Duomo* or the *Cathedral of Florence*. Length, 555 ft.; height, with lantern, 352 ft.; height of tower, 276 ft. From 1128 A.D. there had been a church on the site. In 1294 it was decided, by popular vote, to erect a cathedral. Various architects were employed, among them Giotto, who in 1334–36 designed the tower, which was completed in 1387 on his plan except for a spire. In the fourteenth century the original plan of the cathedral was expanded; in 1418 a public competition was announced for the dome, which was won by Brunelleschi, and the dome was erected 1420–34. The cathedral was dedicated March 25, 1436; the façade was not finished until 1857–87.

[34] A continuous narrow surface, either projecting or recessed, plain or ornamented, whose purpose is to break up a surface, to accent, or to decorate by means of the light and shade that it produces.

PLATE 21

A Scene in Florence about 1401 A.D. Before the door of the Baptistry a group is gathered discussing the competition for a new pair of doors. (Lorado Taft and the Art Institute of Chicago)

PLATE 22

Cathedral of Florence. The dome with its simple mass and unbroken sweep of line and surface dominate the city, symbolizing the power of the Church and the pride of Florence. It does not, however, harmonize with the body of the church.

PLATE 23

Saint Peter's. Vatican City. Here the dome rises from a base designed for it so that the entire mass of the church (with the exception of the later nave and main façade) is unified and harmonious.

PLATE 24

Nebraska State Capitol. Lincoln. Simple volumes with unbroken contours form a compact mass whose unity seems inevitable and at the same time dynamic because of the movement that carries the eye, by mass, line, and light and dark from the broad strong base through the mass of the portal to the upward reaching tower. (Goodhue Associates)

building, that we feel its real power.   Here then we have
a group of inconsistent elements, each fine in its own way
but not as a unit.   What is the reason?

To seek the reason we will go to Florence in the year
1401 A.D., when the youth Brunelleschi was defeated in the
competition for a new pair of bronze doors for the *Baptistery* (PL. 21).[35]   Eventually his defeat proved fortunate.
For with his young friend Donatello, later to become one
of Florence's greatest sculptors, he decided to carry out a
dream — to visit Rome.   When the two youths reached
the city, Brunelleschi seemed to have lost his wits, so the
story says, over the impressiveness of the ruins: the *Colosseum,* much of whose stone lay round about in heaps; the
Baths of Caracalla, from whose wreckage Greek and Roman statues were being excavated; and particularly the
Pantheon, the size of whose dome captured his imagination and fired his ambition.   For, though he had lost in
the competition for the bronze doors, might he not win in
a greater competition — to build a dome on *Saint Mary of
the Flower?*

Win he did.   The dream that was developing in Rome
became a reality, in spite of a doubting council and jealous
aspirants, and the dome soared above the cathedral and
dominated the city.[36]

Why does the dome not fit into the design of the cathedral?   Because, with its quiet, simple mass, its unbroken
curving surfaces and contours, it does not harmonize with
the restless Gothic, the style of *Chartres,* with its vertical

[35] *Scene in Florence, 1401.*   A model given to the Art Institute of Chicago by
Lorado Taft, under whose direction it was made.   Before the doors of the
Baptistery stand Ghiberti, Donatello, Brunelleschi, and Jacopo della Quercia of
Bologna, discussing the competition.   The door in the model is 32 in. high.
This model suggests an infinite number of projects to make the study of the arts
more vivid.

[36] For the story see Vasari's *Life of Brunelleschi* and *Life of Donato (Donatello).*

lines, pointed arches, and deep lofty nave. Several times
the ambitious Florentines had changed the plan of their
cathedral. Its final form (Fig. 55) is similar to that of
Chartres (Fig. 49), strongly modified by the Italian early
Christian church (Fig. 40). Gothic does not belong to
Italy because, in a general way, great areas of glass, suppression of walls, and pitched
roofs belong to the north; small
windows, dim interiors, thick
walls, flatter roofs, open shaded
arcades, to the south. Spires belong to Gothic. Yet a dome the
Florentines must have.

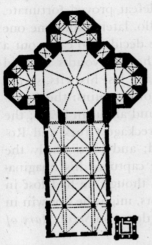

Isolated or seen from the hills
surrounding the city, Brunelleschi's dome is powerful because of
the simplicity and proportions of
the mass. Eight stone ribs and
eight surfaces rise unbroken from
its base to its crowning lantern,
and the dome which they form
soars free above the roof of the

Fig. 55. Plan of the Cathedral of Florence.

church, proclaiming by its form the sovereignty of the
City and of the Church.

Look once more at *Santa Sophia* (PL. 10). From the
exterior this dome is inconspicuous, half hidden by the
walls; only on the interior does one really grasp its power.
The interior of Brunelleschi's, on the other hand, counts
for little. The long nave leading to it gives no hint of its
vastness, while in *Santa Sophia,* as you step into the church
the full effect of the dome bursts upon you (compare the
plans of these two churches, Figs. 35 and 55).

If Brunelleschi's dome, though satisfying in itself, lacks

a harmonious base, can we point to an example that has one? Let a hundred years pass. One day Michelangelo,[37] riding his horse slowly over the hills above Florence, stopped to look back at the city and with his eyes fixed on Brunelleschi's dome remarked that he could not do a thing more beautiful. He was on his way to Rome, where he was to work on the new cathedral of Saint Peter.[38]

The problem involved in this new cathedral was the erection, on the site of the old *Saint Peter's,* of a great new structure that should worthily serve as the mother church of Christendom and that should symbolize, in its appearance, the power and grandeur of the Church. The project had already been begun on a plan which partly coincided with Michelangelo's ideas. This plan called for a dome, whose form as an expression of power Michelangelo realized. Brunelleschi's dome had taught him that. But it had also shown him, by its own lack, the need of a fitting base if there was to be harmony in the building. Finally, could not a dome with a fitting base mold an interior that would be as effective as the exterior?

What did he do with the problem? His plan (Fig. 56) shows an extraordinary compactness: a circle enclosed in a Greek cross, the arms of the cross terminating in apses, and the right angles made by the arms filled in. A portico with steps forms the entrance and the entire mass is set in a large

[37] Michelangelo Buonarroti, a Florentine sculptor, painter, and architect. 1475–1564 A.D.

[38] *Saint Peter's (San Pietro in Vaticano).* Vatican City. Interior length, 615 ft.; height of dome to summit of cross, 435 ft.; diameter, 138 ft. From early Christian times a church here marked the site of the burial place of Saint Peter. The present cathedral dates from the fifteenth century. At least ten architects worked on the plans and the construction. In 1546 Michelangelo was made architect and at the time of his death in 1564 he had brought the building to the top of the drum. The dome was completed according to his drawings. Between 1606 and 1626 the nave was lengthened and the façade built; in 1656–63 the colonnades were added.

open square. What we expect from this plan we see in a sketch (Fig. 58A) and in the cathedral itself if we look at it from the back (PL. 23), although the houses cut off the view and thus destroy the proportions. In the drawing particularly we grasp the design of the unified mass and realize how the dome is the culmination, just as the circle that represented it is the heart of the plan. The rest of the building exists for it. And now is evident the reason for the apses. The dome rises from a rectangular base and the eye is carried much more easily from one to the other if there is some means of softening the sharp contrast. In PL. 23 see how the curving contours of the cylindrical apse prepare the eye for the similar curve of the base of the dome. From every point of view these curved lines and curved surfaces affect this transition. In this view notice too the effectiveness of filling in the corners. Were the right angles left unfilled, the outline would have been so irregular that it would have weakened the solidity of the mass.

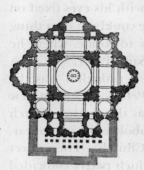

Fig. 56. Michelangelo's Plan for Saint Peter's.

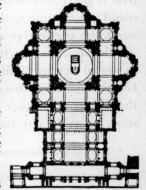

Fig. 57. Present Plan of Saint Peter's.

Thus the whole structure becomes a skillful unification of geometric volumes — cube, cylinder, and sphere — modulated and harmonized by line and by light and dark. The body of the building is broken by *pilasters* (vertical rectangular projections from the wall), cornices,

and windows. The pilasters furnish the soaring vertical lines that are halted by an insistent horizontal in the row of carved capitals, and especially in the deep shadow cast by the cornice, which also serves to bind the parts together, as

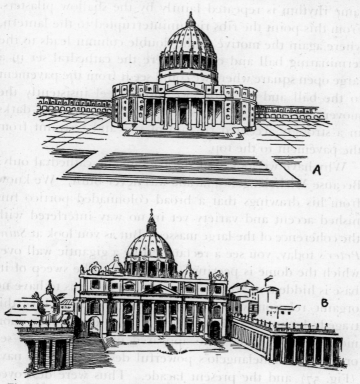

Fig. 58. *A.* Michelangelo's Design for Saint Peter's. *B.* Saint Peter's Today.

do the cornices of the *Colosseum* (PL. 6), and to emphasize the curves of the apses, thus bringing them into harmony with the curves of the dome. Above the cornice the pilasters again take up the vertical line and with the curves of the apses lead directly into the base of the dome. Here col-

umns, grouped by twos and projecting far out, catch the light and cast deep shadows, setting up a rhythm around the base. At the same time, with their emphasis upon the vertical line, they lead into the border above, where the same rhythm is repeated faintly by the shallow pilasters. From this point the ribs rise uninterrupted to the lantern, where again the motive of the double column leads to the terminating ball and cross. Were the cathedral set in a large open square where we could see it from the pavement to the ball and the cross, we should feel insistently the movement of the great masses and of the lights and darks in a strongly accented rhythm of rise and restraint from the pavement to the top.

Why have we looked at the back of the cathedral only? Because Michelangelo's façade was never built. We know from his drawings that a broad colonnaded portico furnished accent and variety yet in no way interfered with the coherence of the large masses. But as you look at *Saint Peter's* today, you see a rectangle like a gigantic wall over which the dome is peering (Fig. 58B). The sweep of its base is hidden, as are the apses, so that it seems to have no organic relation with the lower part. You ask how this tragedy happened? Desire for size, for even more enormous size, led those who appeared unable either to see or to feel Michelangelo's powerful design to add a nave (Fig. 57) and the present façade. Thus were destroyed both the unity of mass from the exterior and any hope of an interior space design dominated by the dome.

READING

GIBSON, K., The Goldsmith of Florence, N. Y., Macmillan, 1929.

HOLROYD, C., Life of Michael Angelo Buonarroti, London, Duckworth, 1903.

ROLLAND, R., Michelangelo, N. Y., Boni, 1915.
VASARI, G., Lives of the Most Eminent Painters, Sculptors, and
Architects, translated by Blashfield and Hopkins, N. Y.
Scribner, 1909. Also in Everyman's Library.

SUGGESTION

A study of domes. Find examples of domed buildings and
study the relation of the dome to the base. In each case note
why it is or is not harmonious. What change could be made
to bring in greater harmony? To what extent is the effect
marred by lack of proper setting?

THE NEBRASKA STATE CAPITOL

FROM the heart of the old Italian city we journey far toward the other side of the earth, to the broad plains of
the United States. But we have not left the principles
of architecture in Rome, although we have come to a part
of the world not far removed in time from pioneer days.
Here these same principles have produced as powerful a
form as *Saint Peter's* and equally filled with symbolic
meaning (PL. 24).[39]

This *Capitol* has a compelling dignity because of its
simplicity — three primary masses, with almost unbroken
contours, clearly expressed and harmoniously united. One
is long and low; one is lofty and soaring; and one, partak-
ing of the qualities of the other two, binds them together.
These masses present a clear, bold silhouette and a striking
rhythm that moves inward and upward from balustrade
to portal to tower, but halted and interwoven with the
quiet stately rhythm of the low façade (Fig. 59).

The long low mass is a rectangular volume, slightly pyramidal (see the contour at the left), of two stories. The

[39] *Nebraska State Capitol*, Lincoln. Base, 437 ft. square; tower, 400 ft. high.
Begun 1922; nearing completion, 1931. Architect, Bertram G. Goodhue
sculptor, Lee Lawrie.

lower is of beveled stone, which gives an appearance of
strength to the base, with small windows closely spaced; the
second is of closely joined stone, with large windows whose
spacing marks a slow rhythm in contrast to that of the
small openings below. A slightly projecting band finishes
this part of the design and binds the windows together, as
does the cornice on the *Colosseum* and on the *Parthenon,*

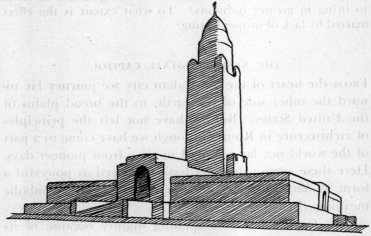

Fig. 59. Main Masses of the Nebraska State Capitol.

and provides an unbroken horizontal line that gives the
design much quiet strength and dignity.

The tower mass, by contrast, insists upon verticality. At
the corners, unbroken lines and surfaces rise with impressive simplicity and frame slender vertical areas of strongly
contrasted light and dark, like flutings in a column, which
by repetition lay emphasis upon the upward movement.
The corners terminate in masses which serve as a transition
to the octagonal drum, whose design repeats on a different
scale that of the main body of the tower. From this drum
rises the dome.

Given a volume that is emphatically lofty and vertical and a volume that is equally low and horizontal, how can you unite them without producing a feeling of abruptness? This problem is solved by the intermediate volume at the portal. Cover this part in the illustration and you will see the difference. It partakes of the horizontality of the one and the verticality of the other in very happy proportions; its door repeats the rectangular windows in shape and alignment; and its lofty arch, a strong accent of shadow, sounds here below the motif of the dome above. The profile of the portal's top, suggesting setbacks, is repeated in the small masses at the base of the tower. How sensitively here has the designer put in this wavering between vertical and horizontal before the ever-active verticals leap upward, while at the corners of the tower the clean-cut lines and surfaces rise from the very base! Thus two strongly contrasting volumes are brought into harmonious unity without compromising their own individuality and their contrast becomes pleasing instead of harsh.

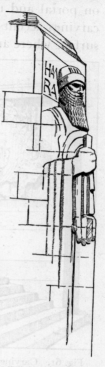

Fig. 60. A Law-Giver. A decorative figure at one corner of the Nebraska State Capitol. Note how the figure and the wall are one inseparable unity.

This unity and proportion of simple volumes give a feeling of " solidity with poise; stability with vitality." No detail is allowed to interfere. Although at a distance there seems to be no decoration, at certain points a broken light and dark hints at sculpture. Come near and you see gigantic figures of *Law-Givers* (Fig. 60) grow-

ing out of the stone at the corners to soften a sharp angle. *Buffalo and Maize,* in low relief, conventionally treated (Fig. 61), break the plain balustrades of the stairway. So on portal and tower and on the corners of the building carvings accent where an accent is needed and break the surface where an unbroken surface is too severe.

IN BEAUTY I WALK
WITH BEAUTY BEFORE ME I WALK
WITH BEAUTY BEHIND ME I WALK
WITH BEAUTY ABOVE AND ABOUT ME I WALK

Fig. 61. Carving on the Balustrade of the Entrance to the Nebraska State Capitol.

The subject matter of this sculpture, you will notice, relates to the life of which the building is an expression and to the function that it is to perform — the life of the plains, of the Indians, and of the pioneers; and the figures of Wisdom, Power, Justice, and Mercy, together with those of historical law-givers.

As a design the building has power. But is it design alone that gives it its quality? Does the structure stand as an abstract monument to the State or does it serve those who are carrying on the functions of the State as well? Its plan (Fig. 62) shows that it is square. In distinction from the *Daily News Building* (PL. 4 and Fig. 8), it spreads out over a large area of ground and, with the exception of the tower, is low. How can it, then, supply adequate light and air for the large number of offices that it must contain for the conduct

of the State's business? Look again at the plan and you
will see the answer. It is built around four large open
courts, possible only in a low building spreading over the
ground rather than rising up into the air.

As for its geographical setting, what more fitting design
for the illimitable reaches of prairie arched over by the
dome of the sky? And in this thought its symbolism begins.

The new capitol symbolizes
the inherent power of the State
of Nebraska and the purpose of
its citizens. The base in the form
of a rectangle four hundred and
thirty-seven feet square and two
stories high, typifies the wide-
spread, fertile Nebraska plains.
The central tower . . . expresses
the aspirations and ideals of the
citizens, leading upward to the
highest and noblest in civilization. . . . The capitol forms a
monument not only of the out-

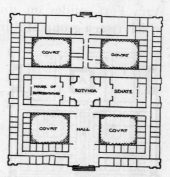

Fig. 62. Plan of the Nebraska
State Capitol.

door life of an agricultural state but also of the aspiration of a
pioneer community which broke its material sods in order to
sow its more splendid cultural future.[40]

Does not the abstract form of the building express the same
idea — growth from the soil?

Here then we see a building which in plan, in organization of mass, and in all details, functions adequately, delights the eye, and symbolizes a noble idea. So do *Santa
Sophia, Chartres,* and Michelangelo's *Saint Peter's.*

SUGGESTION

Make a study of state or county capitol buildings. How
many reflect the influence of the *Capitol* at Washington?

[40] *Report of the Nebraska State Capitol Commission.*

Study each for its general design. Does this design fit the surroundings? Does the building adequately fulfill its function and also express the dignity and sovereignty of the government?

THE TAJ MAHALL

LAZILY the Jumna River winds through the sun-baked plains of India and, washing the red sandstone walls of the Agra Fort, glides on toward a mass of greenery from which rises a group of shimmering domes and minarets, so

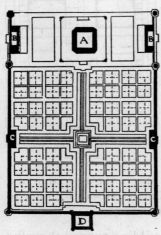

Fig. 63. Plan of the Taj Mahall and its Garden. *A*, Taj; *B*, mosques; *C*, pavilions for the keepers; *D*, entrance. *B*, *C*, and *D* are of red sandstone.

delicate that they seem to float and dissolve in the air. Or from the land approach (PL. 25), above the greenery the silver-white mass rises to its culminating dome.

Again a dome. One thinks of *Saint Peter's* (PL. 23). But here in India a kinder fate has preserved the *Taj* as its builders left it, in a spacious garden (Fig. 63) that serves it as Michelangelo planned a great open square should serve *Saint Peter's* (Fig. 58A). So far the comparison holds. Almost immediately, however, a sharp contrast presents itself. *Saint Peter's* is definitely powerful, restless, heroic, assertive. Its masses move with sharply defined lights and darks. The *Taj* rises with indefinite grace and delicacy, is reposeful, and exquisitely lyric. The rhythm of its masses moves quietly to its climax, for the lights and darks shift gently. Nowhere is there deep shadow or strong contrast. Both

PLATE 25

Taj Mahall. Agra, India. White marble delicately carved and inlaid; the avoidance of deep shadow; proportions that produce a feeling of serenity; the contrast of trees, bright flowers, and the red sandstone buildings at the side — all these elements create an impression of lightness, grace, and tenderness. Compare the strength and assertiveness of Saint Peter's (Pl. 23). (W. E. Clark)

PLATE 26

The Craigie House. The formality of the house is softened by the spacious grounds and the fine trees so that the balanced unity creates an atmosphere of well-being. (© Detroit Publishing Co.)

buildings stir the imagination, but they guide it into far different channels. Both are superbly designed volumes consisting of a compact base supporting a dominating dome. Yet the effect of each is almost at opposite poles. We have seen what *Saint Peter's* is. What is the *Taj?*

It was the year 1631. Shah Jahan was seated on his throne, haggard and broken, detached in his grief but stern in his rule. For weeks he had been very ill and wished only to die and thus to rejoin his inseparable companion, his beautiful young wife, Mumtaz-i-Mahall. It was not alone her beauty that won the affection of all nor alone her grace and charm, though these she possessed in unusual measure. Nor her queenly dignity. Above all, it was a rare loveliness of spirit in this " Crown of the Palace " that " inclined all hearts to love her."

With obvious effort the Shah straightened and addressed the silent council. A tomb was to be built, in a garden, as was the custom. He had already procured the site a mile down the river in view of the fort, where was his palace. As Mumtaz-i-Mahall had surpassed all women in loveliness and tenderness, so must her tomb exceed all wonders of the world. No portrait of her in stone could he erect. His religion forbade that. The building itself must be her portrait, breathe her spirit, and symbolize her tenderness.

The council stirred. Though they feared the cruel severity and avarice of a Shah, every one had loved the Crown of the Palace and it was almost enthusiasm that ran through the council as the Shah continued. They were to search the world for the greatest builders. They were to seek out the richest materials and most skillful craftsmen. This, they knew, was possible, for the Shah had stupendous wealth. So the command went forth. From far

and wide the designs came to be laid before the Shah. At
last one was accepted, that of a Persian. Again the commands went forth for the brilliant white marble of Jaipur;
for jade and crystal from China; turquoise from Tibet;
lapis lazuli and sapphires from Ceylon; coral and car-
nelian from Arabia; jasper, onyx, amethyst, pearls, and
diamonds from equally distant lands.

For seventeen years Shah Jahan watched from his palace
in the Fort or from his pavilion in the garden of the tomb.
The rank growth began to take on form. Here masses of
bright flowers, symbols of life; there, pinnacles of somber
cypresses, symbols of death and eternity. The building
rose slowly. For the rich detail required time: the inlay
of the marble with precious stones and the carving of it
into delicate tracery; the silver doors; and the cenotaph
itself, of white marble so inlaid with precious stones that
it resembled the bright flower gardens outside. At last
the building was ready and the body was placed in the
crypt beneath the cenotaph. On every Friday, the Mohammedan Sunday, a pall of pearls was placed over the cenotaph, the Koran was chanted, and soft melodies floated
clear and distinct in the dome above.

Today we approach the *Taj* [41] by the gateway of red
sandstone on which is inscribed in black marble a passage
from the Koran inviting the pure of heart to enter the
Garden of Paradise. From a window of this gateway where

[41] *Taj Mahall.* The garden is 971 ft. square; the platform, 313 ft. square;
the tomb, 186 ft. square and 187 ft. to the crown of the dome. 1632–57 A.D. A
few years after the completion of the *Taj* the serious illness of Shah Jahan gave
his sons the opportunity they were seeking to usurp his throne. For nearly ten
years he was cared for by a faithful daughter but was unable to build for himself
a companion tomb, as he had planned, across the river from the *Taj* and connected with it by a marble bridge. So he was buried beside Mumtaz-i-Mahall
in the *Taj.* This unfulfilled plan explains the position of the *Taj* along the
river bank.

we are standing a long sheet of water flanked by cypresses [42] and geometric masses of gay flowers arrest the eye and retard its movement to the silvery white arches, domes, and minarets. The rounding masses of foliage seem to withdraw to the sides so as not to obstruct the vista and at the same time to guard the tomb and to provide a dense greenery to enhance its delicacy.

Here is imagination that has been seeking the world over the most suitable concrete form in which to express itself. And where does it find it? In its own immediate life. It was not something novel or accidental that the builder's vision fixed upon, but the old traditional type of Mohammedan tomb. Under the stimulation of a convincing idea — the personality of Mumtaz-i-Mahall — the imagination molded these traditional elements — a platform, pointed arches, a dome, minarets, a garden, no element is new — into something that in turn stirs our imagination and arouses our profoundest feelings. That is originality and that is art. It was just so in *Saint Peter's,* a traditional design — the Greek cross covered with a dome — made vital by a convincing idea: the power and majesty of the Church.

The *Taj* consists of three parts — the platform, the four towers or minarets, and the central mass — balanced about a central vertical axis, and so proportioned and interrelated that the alteration or omission of one detail would be ruinous. Try covering one part after another and watch the result. Together they occupy an imaginary rectangular volume terminating in a low pyramid (Fig. 64). Beyond the boundaries of this volume nothing projects. That is one reason for the great unity in the group. It

[42] The newly planted cypresses have not yet attained the proper size to play their part in the design adequately.

was conceived as a unit and everything was subordinated to that unit. It is as if the builder had started with a gigantic block of marble and carved away enough to leave the central group and the towers. And in this respect it is very close to sculpture. The three parts consist of rectangular, cylindrical, and domical volumes. In the rectangular parts the corners are softened to avoid sharp

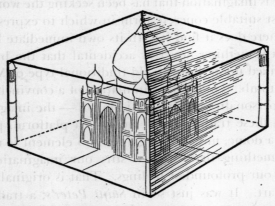

Fig. 64. As a piece of stone sculpture is determined by the block of stone from which it is carved, so the Taj and its minarets (towers) form a unit determined by a square block which terminates in a low pyramid.

angles and sharp cutting of light and dark, and thus to form a more harmonious base for the rounding parts.

The focal point of the design is the dome, slightly bulbous in shape, which rises with an exquisite contour from a compact group of small domes. Compare the assertive strength of *Saint Peter's* dome with the restrained delicacy of that of the *Taj*. Its base is fringed with a border of lotus petals and its apex is an inverted lotus, which, in the East, is the symbol of purity because it opens its fair flowers above the mud and slime in which it is rooted.

The line organization is very much like that in the

Parthenon: vertical, horizontal, and curved, with an emphasis upon the horizontal (Fig. 65). Yet it is a subtle emphasis. The unbroken lines of the platform are repeated again and again but in broken, suggested lines. For example, see how the accent which the slightly projecting balcony makes on the minarets carries over to the lower edges of the small niches, thence on to meet the opposite balcony. Every accent, every contour, every point, seems determined by these organizing lines.

Equally sensitive is the light-and-dark organization. The lowest darks are not found in the building itself but in the garden. Purposely

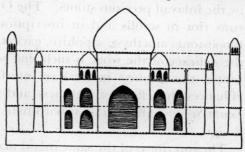

Fig. 65. Organizing Horizontals in the Taj. These horizontals are the edges of organizing planes which cut through the entire mass and determine important points in the design.

the building is kept in light and half-light. Everywhere the dark is avoided by making the projections just high enough to cast a light shadow. The large area of shadow in the lofty center niche containing the doorway gives a feeling of strength to the base of the dome. On each side a similar dark shape is repeated in the smaller niches, one to each story, thus quickening a rhythm that rises to the smaller domes. The shadow of the balconies on the minarets arrests the eye as it moves up the cylindrical surface, and unites the minarets with the central mass. Beside these almost constant lights and shadows are the wavering irregular lights and darks cast by the domes and minarets playing differently every hour, still further soften-

ing lines and unifying the parts. Through the openings of the minarets and the small domes the light and the blue of the sky play — another means of uniting the building with the surrounding air and sky.

To give vibration to the surface, the builders depended partly upon these changing lights and darks and partly upon the rich decoration. For the smooth glossy texture of the marble is softened and enriched by low carvings and by the inlay of precious stones. The Oriental love of color runs riot in scrolls and in inscriptions of crystal, topaz, bloodstone, amethyst, sapphire, garnet, jasper, agate. Yet the delicacy of the work is such that while the surface vibrates, the richness in no way interferes with but only enhances the effect of lightness and grace. And, as in *Santa Sophia,* all detail is subordinate to a simple forceful design.

The interior is of the same inlaid marble as the exterior, but is seen in the soft light that filters through carved marble windows. The mellow light, the soft echo and reëcho of the music played in the surrounding chambers beneath the smaller domes, and that of the chanting of the Koran all contribute to produce, in perhaps more chastened form, that effect of exquisiteness and tenderness which characterizes the exterior.

Unified and personal as is this total impression, still it needs a fitting setting. Take from it its gardens, its red sandstone gateway, and its red sandstone flanking mosques, and it would be incomplete. Dark foliage, strong color, and rough texture serve to bring out its beauty, as velvet does for a pearl. All these contrasting elements are integral parts of the unified form which " like a fairy vision of silver-white . . . seems to rest so lightly, so tenderly on the earth . . . as if it would soar into the sky."

Again a convincing idea has found appropriate form.

READING

COOMARASWAMY, A. K., Arts and Crafts of India and Ceylon, London, Foulis, 1913.

GROUSSET, R., The Civilizations of the East, vol. 2, " India," N. Y., Knopf, 1931.

HAVELL, E. B., Handbook of Indian Art, London, Murray, 1920.

A COLONIAL HOME

The Craigie House (*Longfellow's Home*)

THE buildings that we have visited so far have been public buildings, often on a large or a magnificent scale. We have done this because in them we can see clearly and forcibly the art qualities in building and the fundamental principles that control the art of building.

What of small structures? you ask. What of summer cottages, of garages? What of our homes? Of our bridges, our factories? Shall we expect to find in these the same art qualities, dependent upon the use of the same fundamental principles? Yes. The small inconspicuous building, in the city or in the country, is good or bad for the same reasons that the large building is good or bad. Your garage is good because you can see by its appearance, that it does what it is built to do and that it uses its material in a straightforward manner. At the same time its proportions and the balance of its mass are pleasing and it takes its place in the corner of the grounds, not as " just another shed " but with a direct relationship to the grounds and to the house.

As for factories, look how the *Cahokia Power Plant* (Fig. 66) functions adequately and thrills with the power of its design! See what an artist has accomplished with rooms for machinery and smokestacks. What organiza-

tion of masses! Rectangular volumes, long and low, with unbroken horizontals and regularly repeated verticals; slender cylinders grouped by twos. How these masses are coördinated, by line and by light and dark, into a unity that is harmonious, balanced, and boldly rhythmic!

The *Bridge* in PL. 5 is good because it gives one an impression of strong and elastic support by means of riveted steel and at the same time a pleasing sensation of proportion, line, and rhythm.

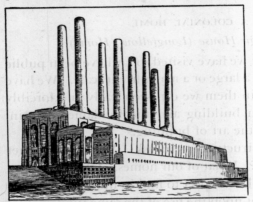

Fig. 66. Power Station. Cahokia, Illinois.

To be sure we shall not feel, in the modest house, the exaltation of *Santa Sophia*, the heroic power of *Saint Peter's*, nor the almost defiant assurance of the *Skyscraper*. Such qualities do not belong to a home, whose significance lies in its expression of friendliness, comfort, seclusion.

Shall we visit, for an example, one of our *Colonial* homes (PL. 26), the house in which the poet Longfellow was a lodger at the time he purchased it and in which he lived until his death? [43] Most appealing is the unity and harmony of all that we see. The house and its setting complement each other. On the one hand, spacious lawns and majestic trees relieve the quiet simplicity of the house,

[43] Vassall-Craigie-Longfellow House. Cambridge, Mass. Built by John Vassall, 1759; used by General Washington as his headquarters, 1775–76; enlarged by Andrew Craigie, 1793; purchased by Henry Wadsworth Longfellow, 1843.

PLATE 27

Colonial Room. Efficiency, refined taste, and consistency mark this room. (Metropolitan Museum)

PLATE 28

A. Stairway in a House of the Eighties. (Ryerson Library of the Art Institute of Chicago)

B. Colonial Stairway. The charm, restraint, and a clear grasp of the parts in B contrast with the wearying profusion, in A, which obscures the structural features.
(L. French, Jr., *Colonial Interiors*. N.Y., Helburn)

whose angularity, on the other hand, enhances the sweeping lines and masses of the trees. And in the matter of color, the repetition of the dark of the foliage in the blinds of the house contributes to greater unity.

The quiet reserve of the house is due to the same use of elements that we found in other quiet buildings. The repose of the *Parthenon* (PL. 7) is the result of a certain proportion of vertical and horizontal, as the restlessness of *Chartres* (PL. 17) and the *Sky-scraper* (PLS. 2 and 4) is due to another. The *Longfellow House* belongs to the *Parthenon* type. The vertical lines in the pilasters and in the placing of one window above another are balanced by horizontal rows of door and windows, cornice, the balustrade of the cut-off roof; and virility is secured by the play upon diagonals in the roof, gable, and dormers. The central part carries strong by its projection, by the steps leading to it, by the

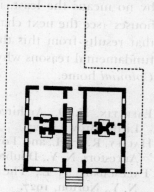

Fig. 67. Plan of the Vassall-Craigie-Longfellow House. The solid lines indicate the plan of the Vassall house; the dotted, later additions.

enframing pilasters, and by the gable. On each side is a symmetrical balancing of all parts. The result of such a design is a feeling of repose and dignity.

Such an exterior results from a symmetrical plan (Fig. 67). The door admits to a hall running the width of the house, with rooms balanced on the two sides as symmetrically as the windows are balanced on the outside. An important feature of the hall is the stairway (similar to that in PL. 28B), whose dignity and fine sweep of line break the regularity of the hall and give a tone to the interior.

Contrast the stairway seen in PL. 28A. The multiplicity of detail that overloads all the space conceals any basic design that may exist and reveals a taste that is far removed from the fine quality seen in the *Colonial House.*

Dignity and fine taste, a little austere in some cases, is what one feels in these Colonial homes, a taste that is consistently carried out in the grounds and gardens, the exterior, the interior, the furniture, the silver and glass, and, by no means the least, in the people who lived in these houses (see the next chapter and PL. 27). The harmony that results from this thorough consistency is one of the fundamental reasons why most people enjoy the *American Colonial* home.

READING

EBERLEIN, H. D., Architecture of Colonial America, Boston, Little, Brown, 1927.

HALSEY, R. T. H., and TOWER, E., The Homes of Our Colonial Ancestors, N. Y., Doubleday, 1925.

TALLMADGE, T. E., The Story of Architecture in America, N. Y., Norton, 1927.

SOME INTERIORS

THE art of interior architecture is no other than the art of building.[44] There is a definite relation between the exterior and the interior of a good building. One determines the other; and the resulting consistency is a primary factor in a building that is thoroughly satisfying. If the appearance of a house suggests spaciousness and you enter a stuffy, cramped room, there is an irritating dissonance; if the appearance suggests coziness and you enter a great barnlike room, the result is the same. Consistency of

---

[44] The current term *interior decoration* places too much emphasis on the decorative element, as if the decoration made the room, whereas decoration is but one of several factors in the design of any room.

scale and style, then, is necessary for success. How the type of hall in PL. 28B harmonizes in these respects with the type of exterior in PL. 26! Put into this hall the men and women of Colonial days. Everything just fits.

Consistency in an interior is also a matter of details. A successful room is a unit of several factors. There is its permanent background — the floor, walls, openings, ceiling — and there are the movable and changeable furnishings of all kinds. Still the room is incomplete. People using it complete the design. No room was built and furnished to be looked at, but to be lived in. Hence the successful room reveals a harmony among all these factors.

With this observation in mind, shall we look at several interiors? First, another *American Colonial* (PL. 27) from the home of Samuel Powel of Philadelphia, well known in Revolutionary days.[45] The house was an imposing building of red brick, with fine gardens at the back. Samuel Powel was a young man of sufficient means to travel extensively in Europe and with sufficient culture and influence to associate with well-known writers and artists and to be presented at the court of George III. Life in Europe appears to have inspired him to build a house in the colonies as fine as those in which he had been a guest abroad. But the growing intensity of feeling, in the colonies, over the stamp tax hindered him from importing the furnishings, though he appears to have brought

[45] The *Powel House* was built in 1768, sold to Samuel Powel in 1769, and is still standing at 244 South Third Street, Philadelphia. The room reproduced in Pl. 28, which faced the garden at the back, has been removed to the American Wing of the Metropolitan Museum in New York. For an account of Samuel Powel and his house, see R. T. H. Halsey, and E. Tower, *The Homes of Our Ancestors*, N. Y., Doubleday, 1925; and R. T. H. Halsey, and C. O. Cornelius, *A Handbook of the American Wing*, N. Y., Metropolitan Museum, 1928.

statues with him for the garden. It was possible to furnish the house, however, with Colonial furnishings which
quite equaled the European both in workmanship and
in design.[46]

In the important months during which the Constitu-
tion was being drawn up, Washington and his friends fre-
quented the *Powel House*. We can see them having tea
in this very room (PL. 27) as they earnestly discussed the
points involved in the framing of the government. And
we can also see them in the stately minuet when Benjamin
Franklin's daughter danced with Colonel Washington; or
scurrying in a panic at a reception when a lofty plumed
headdress came too near the lighted candles of the crystal
chandelier.

The rigors of a valiant life tempered by the amenities
of a cultivated society, good taste with no superficialities
— that is what we feel in such a room. It conveys an impression of efficiency and solidity without heaviness. Light
wood paneling fills one end of the room, with the fireplace
and overmantel as an accent, partly because of the dark
spot made by the picture and partly because of the strong
moldings, and the carving. In the rest of the wall the moldings are so low that they make but a faint inconspicuous
pattern except in the cornice, where again a dark shadow
unifies and finishes the wall area. The light note is continued in the stucco ceiling, the doors, and the tan Chinese
paper. Contrasting warmth of color is furnished by the
mahogany furniture, the damask upholstering and curtains, the fireplace, and the portrait; and a touch of
vivacity and gayety, by the sparkling glass lustre with

[46] A demand from the prosperous colonists for fine furniture had led to the
establishment of shops whose advertisements suggest versatile proprietors.
For interesting examples of these advertisements see Halsey and Cornelius,
op. cit.

candles, the silver [47] on the tea table, and the brightly colored statuettes on the mantel.

In the furnishings is shown the same desire for efficiency, good line, proportion, and a moderate use of ornament. The furniture is of mahogany, except the walnut clock, and is the product of the skilled cabinetmakers of Philadelphia. In the Chippendale style (based upon the design of Thomas Chippendale, a well-known English cabinetmaker of this time), it has the solid construction characteristic of that style and at the same time restrained, well-placed carving. The sofa has straight legs; the chairs and tables, curved — an influence from a current French style.

This *French Style* (PL. 29) [48] reveals a form and reflects a life quite in contrast to the *American Colonial*. Here is lightness, and a movement that flows rapidly and smoothly throughout the design, uninterrupted by right angles and sharp contrasts. Everywhere the eye is guided by this light rhythm and the feelings are attuned to its key. Light color, touched with gold, contributes to the impression, and mirrors repeat the dancing rhythms. Look at the paintings of Watteau, Nattier, or Fragonard and you will see the kind of people who lived in this room. The lustrous satins, ribbons, and brocades of their costumes and their grace of manner harmonize with the charm and grace of the slender panels, the delicate moldings, the curved lines, the light color, and with the sparkle of gilding and reflec-

[47] Early American silver furnishes an interesting subject from the point of view of both art and economics. For, with no banks, silver coin was made into cake baskets, sugar bowls, tankards, tea and coffee pots, and other articles, which constituted much of the family's wealth and at the same time reached a high level artistically. Paul Revere was a silversmith of fine taste and workmanship. See C. L. Avery, *American Silver of the XVII and XVIII Centuries*, N. Y., Metropolitan Museum, 1920.

[48] A French salon of the period of Louis XV. Ancien Hôtel de Carondelet, Aix-en-Provence, France.

tions. Everything speaks of gayety and wit, and of exquisite taste, superficial though it may be.

The furniture is in keeping with the background, with the same slender proportions and the same constantly moving line, particularly noticeable in the console, mirror, and candle-holders at the side. Though the straight line appears in some of the pieces, it is the curved line that dominates even in the brocaded damask of the upholstery. Some of the pieces are delightful trifles, but all reveal great craftsmanship. Inlays of tulip and other woods cover the surface with charming designs, which, however, do not relate to the structure of the object. When you open a drawer, for example, you break the design.

To keep everything consistently in the same key — the key of gayety, repartee, light movement — for a people whose lives are keyed to gayety, wit, frivolity, who had an exquisite taste for externals — this has been the objective of the designer; and he has succeeded.

For utmost simplicity and fine taste in interiors we go to the other side of the world — to Japan. Leaving your shoes at the door, step within a *Japanese House* (PL. 30).[49] To a Westerner the first impression suggests an unfurnished house. It is a large, airy room. Gray-green matting covers the floor, evenly and solidly. Wood forms the framework of the room, with sliding paper screens for the walls, and wood paneling for the ceiling. There is a conspicuous absence of doors and windows yet there is no dingy darkness, for the transparent rice-paper screens give a mellow light. As the eye sweeps about the room it is caught and held by an alcove at the end, in which hangs a painting mounted on a piece of brocade, with neither

[49] A room in a typical middle-class home. See R. A. Cram, *Impressions of Japanese Architecture*, Boston, Marshall Jones, 1930; and Okakura-Kakuzo, *Book of Tea*, N. Y., Duffield, 1925.

frame nor glass; and near by stands a bronze vase, with one spray of blossoming plum.

How quiet and refreshing! No one hurries. The servants glide noiselessly. Where do we sit? you ask. On these silk cushions on the floor. Where do we dine? In the same place, still seated on the silk cushions, from little traylike tables of red or black lacquer, a few inches high. Where do we sleep? In this same place. From a closet is brought forth the bedding, which is spread on the floor. The paper screens are drawn and the dining-room has become a bedroom. In the morning, the day being fine, the screens slide back and the entire side of the room opens on an outside corridor that overlooks a garden, a miniature landscape, with pine trees and rocks, a waterfall, a bridge spanning a tiny lake fringed with a sandy shore, and a clump of bamboo which the night before in the moonlight decorated the drawn screens with silhouettes of its gently waving sprays.

Out of the simplest materials, provided abundantly by their country, the Japanese have evolved this type of home that functions so adequately and at the same time reaches, unostentatiously, so lofty a quality of artistic excellence. The house is framed of wood. Wood, plaster, and rice paper form the walls and partitions, and thatch or tile, the roof. These materials and the elastic method of construction enable the buildings to withstand the shocks of frequent earthquakes. All the materials are used for their own intrinsic qualities. Wood is never painted, nor plaster covered. The wood is most carefully selected for its color and graining and is polished until all its capacity for color and texture is brought out. Likewise the plaster of various subtle tints and velvety texture, and the creamy translucent rice paper, sometimes with a light decoration,

contribute by subtle harmonies and contrasts to the effect of a restrained, reposeful unity.

Nothing is superfluous. A chest of drawers may be more or less permanent. The other furniture — the cushions, tables, bedding — is brought in and taken out as the occasion requires. The painting, the bronze or porcelain, the flowers in the alcove, are changed frequently, often in order to relate to something in the life of the day. If a festival is to be celebrated, objects that directly or symbolically relate to it are brought from the treasure house.

Into this simple reposeful background and mellow light the people fit, with their silk garments, their quiet voices. Their dignity and courtliness, the very fiber of life, is the result of age-long codes of etiquette, a rich inheritance, not suddenly acquired. Restraint, inherent in the room and in the people, is a stimulation to imagination. For true beauty, says Mr. Okakura,[50] can be discovered only by one who can mentally complete the incomplete. The essentials are there. Let each one add or not as his own personal feelings dictate. How free and imaginative is this attitude in comparison with the attitude revealed by the cluttered room of PL. 29A! [51]

READING

GILMAN, R., Great Styles of Interior Architecture, N. Y., Harper, 1924.

[50] Okakura-Kakuzo, *Book of Tea*, which is a very sensitive presentation, by a Japanese, of the Japanese tea ceremony.

[51] Some of our best interior architects today are working in the spirit of (not copying) the Japanese, with the result that we are seeing more and more rooms every year that are simple, free from overloading with furnishings. Also woods, stucco, metals, textiles, and other materials are used for their own color and texture. See examples in D. Todd, and R. Mortimer, *The New Interior Decoration*, London, Batsford, 1929; and in the current art periodicals.

PLATE 29

A French Salon. All curves and rapid movement, slender proportions, a gay dancing quality. (L. Deshairs, *Aix-en-Provence*. Paris, Librairie des Arts Décoratifs)

PLATE 30

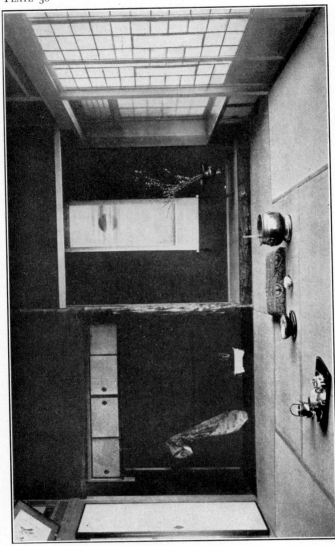

A Room in a Japanese Home. Simplicity and repose through the use of the fewest essentials and through the sensitive use of materials — wood, stucco, paper, silk, lacquer, matting — each for its own peculiar beauty yet all harmoniously combined. (Helen Gunsaulus)

SUGGESTIONS

1. Perhaps nothing is so intimately eloquent of any people as the people themselves in their homes. Make a collection of people of both the present and the past. Costume them properly and place them in their houses with the proper furnishings. This is a good subject for group projects and correlates well with other courses.

2. A study of furniture in its relation to the design of the room as a whole.

3. The relation of any interior to climate and geography. Why, for example, are tiles used in Spain and southern California? Why wood paneling in England?

4. Select actual rooms and design or redesign them. See the last chapter of this book.

GENERAL PROJECTS ON THE ART OF BUILDING

1. Make models of the buildings studied, or parts of them, with the general location, showing the relation of the building to it. This can be done in sand, clay, soap, plaster, boards of various kinds. Use one or two figures in each case, properly costumed. This could easily be made a group project, several groups working on the building, and one on the costumes.

2. Design original buildings in clay, soap, or some material in which the model is actually three-dimensional, not on paper. Determine first the purpose and the site. Work out the large elements: shape and proportions, balance, large masses of light and dark. Use an electric bulb at various angles to get the effect of the changing position of the sun. Avoid detail.

3. Construct a building, or part of one, on the lintel system and one on the arch system. Soap serves well, for it cuts easily into building blocks. It shrinks, however, in drying, and so is not satisfactory for anything permanent.

4. Find as many ways as possible of roofing a building. Illustrate each by a drawing or a picture of an actual building.

5. Find as many examples as possible of interior space organization of unusual quality, such as *Santa Sophia* and *Chartres*.

6. Find as many ways as possible of decorating a wall, such as the painted carvings of the *Egyptian Temple,* the marble facing of the Roman buildings, mosaics, the glass of *Chartres,* fresco (see sections on painting). In each case give the effect of the method, its suitability, its advantages and disadvantages.

7. Architectural sculpture. Find examples to illustrate harmony between the sculpture and the building and vice versa.

8. Find copies or adaptations of the buildings studied. Discuss the suitability of these to their purpose and to their setting.

Note: In finding examples, use actual buildings as far as possible rather than photographs or prints. See how many interesting points of view you can find. Use your kodak for a series of pictures of each building, taken from all sides.

Part Three

THE ART OF THE GARDEN

UNITY and variety are underlying forces in life and in art. No building exists in a universe of its own, but is an integral part of a larger whole, its setting. To secure unity with its environment and pleasing contrasts of texture and color many a building depends upon the garden. What would the *Taj* be without its garden (PL. 25), or the *Craigie House* (PL. 26)?

"To complete the incomplete," says the Japanese. To him a house or temple is incomplete without a garden. This is the result partly of his sensitivity to a broadly harmonious design and partly of his great love of nature. Hills with streams and waterfalls, lakes, pines, bamboo, varicolored stones, white sand — nature has endowed his land with all this richness and its enjoyment is a spiritual necessity in his daily life. Instead of hanging pictures of landscape on the walls of his house he slides back the screens and sees laid out before him a real landscape, however small, which he can enjoy in rain, in sunshine, or in snow — a whole panorama of which he and his house are an integral part. If he has no garden space in the crowded city, he satisfies his desire with a miniature box-garden or with a tiny gnarled pine tree in a pot. Every detail, whether of the large country estate or of the tiny city garden, reveals an unusual capacity to raise commonplace things to the level of art (Fig. 69).

Fig. 68 shows us a typical *Japanese Garden*. From a clump of bamboo near the house, stones mark a path toward a tiny lake with a white pebbly shore. The eye, in following this path, is arrested for a moment by a stone lantern before it pursues its way to a bridge which

crosses the lake. Here a picturesque gnarled pine, symbol
of longevity, forms a center of interest for the entire garden.   Just behind it a waterfall, partly concealed by a
branch of the pine, dashes over a cliff, contributing, with
its contrasting movement and silvery color, to the emphasis
at this point.   Near by a willow — another contrast with
the pine — droops gracefully over an arm of the lake.

Fig. 68.   Lay-out of a Japanese Garden Taken from a Japanese
Treatise on Gardens. Hills, ponds, islands, a stream with cascades, a
bridge, large and small stones and stone lanterns — all are arranged
with seeming informality but actually according to strict rules.
(J. Harada, *Gardens of Japan*, London, The Studio)

It seems so natural; yet the garden sketched in Fig. 68 is
taken from a manual which specifies the layout of a typical hill garden.   Underlying the apparent naturalism and
the asymmetrical balance is a set of strict conventions, a
pattern which determines just how the parts shall be composed.   Water, stones, pines, bamboo, willow, Crypto-
meria, box and various shrubs, sand and pebbles, stone or
bronze lanterns — with these, each selected for its shape,

color, and texture the Japanese gardener builds up, in accordance with the conventional pattern, a unified balanced whole that is related sensitively to the house. Flowers, you will notice, have almost no part in the design.

In PL. 31, for example, what a beautiful harmony results from the perfect unity of diverse elements! The magnificent sweep and fine angles of the roof and the expanse of its tiled surface emerge from and sweep into masses of varied foliage. The restful stucco surfaces contrast with the rocks and plants below and with the pine at the corner, reflect in the placid lake, and echo in the large smooth stones that form the bridge. Line, surface, texture, color — every detail exists in relation to the unity of the whole.

Fig. 69. Japanese Method of Wrapping Shrubs in Straw for the Winter. (After Morse)

The studied informality of the *Japanese Garden,* based upon strict conventions, is quite different from the unstudied informality of gardens which use materials at hand. In our *Colonial* homes (PL. 27) the plan was often informal, reflecting the English manor, where the natural landscape — great masses of fine trees, streams, open moors — formed the basis of the entire plan and determined the site of the buildings so that they would be one element in the large unity of the entire estate.

In *Italy,* on the other hand, formality and symmetry prevail in the gardens. As an example, let us visit the *Villa d'Este,* at Tivoli, in the Sabine Hills about twenty miles northeast of Rome. The villa, of stone, stands on the crest of the hill and its stone balcony commands a fine view out over the country as far as Rome itself; or down into the

rich shadows of the cypresses of its gardens (PL. 32).   The
plan of the estate (Fig. 70) shows how the building and
gardens are laid out along an axis which forms a broad
path from the villa down the hill.   How insistent is the

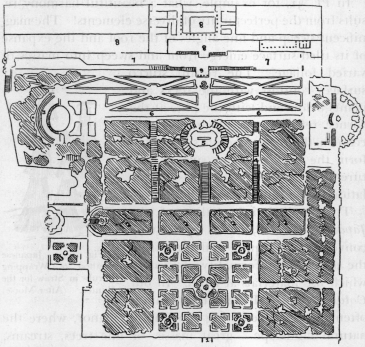

Fig. 70.   Plan of the Villa d'Este, and its Gardens. 1, Original entrance at
the foot of the hill; 2, ponds; 3, cascades; 4, ascending stone stairways
bordered by streams of water; 5, fountains and circular stone stairway;
6, Terrace of the Hundred Fountains (PL. 33); 7, terrace of the villa; 8, villa;
9, projecting terrace from which one obtains a fine view down through the
gardens along the main axis (PL. 32).

symmetry here in comparison with the asymmetry of the
Japanese! A double stone stairway curves from the upper
terrace down through the trees to meet this path, the fine
sweep of its stone balustrades bringing curves into a design

that is rectangular. Cutting across this central axis at right angles are paths which open up vistas to a fountain, or to an open terrace overhanging the valley, with a view out over the hills. Magnificent cypresses dominate and together with other trees, vines, and shrubs form dense shade, interspersed with open spaces for pools with fish and aquatic plants.

Yet, with all this refreshing shade, what would these gardens be without the water! Water used architecturally and at the same time supplementing the shade with its refreshing coolness. Spend a hot afternoon in these gardens. You cannot hurry in the cool soothing shadows. Leisurely you climb the lichen-covered stone steps and loiter along paths bordered by tiny jets of water and bubbling cascades (PL. 33). Their light music is the only sound except the song of the cicada. Look to the right and a broad silver spray terminates the vista through the overarching trees. Look back toward the villa from halfway down the central path and see the fountain, like a tall cypress of silver swaying gently in the breeze. How it unites the stone villa and its garden! Light, movement, sparkle, music, in the midst of the darkness of the shade, the solidity of the stone, the solemn silence of the cypresses. Now it rises in a long avenue of jets transformed by the breeze into misty spray. Here it gushes in miniature cascades or bubbles merrily in tiny fountains; there it falls in a thin sheet over a vine-covered arcade or in a triple cascade to be reflected in a quiet pool near by. The water at *Tivoli* is like the glass at *Chartres*.

Still another type of garden we can find in the Mediterranean lands or in America where Mediterranean architecture has found a logical place, as in *Florida* or southern *California*. In the *Craigie House* (PL. 27), at *Tivoli*

(PL. 34) , and in *Japan* (PL. 33) , the gardens form a setting for the house which looks out to them.   In the Mediterranean, or more specifically in the Spanish type of house, the building appears to have gathered the gardens within its embracing wings (PL. 34 and Fig. 71) .   In plan this type of house is loose and rambling instead of compact like the *Craigie House* (Fig. 67) .   The one indicates a warm climate, and suggests a cool, airy, shaded interior; the other indicates a cold climate by the grouping of the rooms closely to keep out the cold and to facilitate the circulation of artificially heated air.   Each type is logical and appropriate to its environment. That is why a Spanish bungalow on the Maine coast is not only impracticable but distressing.

Fig. 71.   Plan of a Typical Southern House with a Patio.   Notice how the house is spread out loosely to secure air in contrast to the compact house of the North (Fig. 67).

But in southern *California* how delightful is a house of tile and stucco that defies the heat and at the same time provides air and cool shade!   The windows of the *Heberton House* (PL. 34) look out to the greenery. Quiet unbroken lines and surfaces are enhanced by the broken dark masses of shadow-making foliage: lacy vine, shaggy eucalyptus, feathery pepper tree, and solid hedges. What a careful gradation of foliage as it varies from a solid base to the loose, swaying, ragged masses above!   Urns and walks again bring the note of stone or stucco into the greenery, and the reflecting pools mingle them.

As in the Japanese garden, unity and harmony have resulted from the use of the same means.   Shape, material,

PLATE 31

Garden of a Monastery. Kyoto. A sensitive unity of building and garden. Each completes the other through the interweaving and contrasting of lines, surfaces, and textures. (J. Harada, *Gardens of Japan*. London. The Studio)

PLATE 32

Gardens of the Villa d'Este. Tivoli. The central path from the gate up to the villa in the foreground is the axis which controls a symmetrically balanced design by which the villa and the garden are harmoniously united. Note the magnificent cypress trees.

texture, color — each plays a definite rôle of harmony and contrast in creating a pleasingly proportioned and balanced whole. In this whole it is the garden that links the house with its surroundings, and brings the surroundings into the house to enable it to perform its function more adequately and to delight the eye more graciously.

READING

CRAM, R. A., Impressions of Japanese Architecture, Boston, Marshall Jones, 1930.

HARADA, J., Gardens of Japan, London, Studio, 1928.

HUBBARD, H. V., and KIMBALL, T., An Introduction to the Study of Landscape Design, N. Y., Macmillan, 1929.

TRIGGS, H. I., Garden Craft in Europe, London, Batsford, 1913.

SUGGESTIONS

1. Gardens offer a large field for creative effort, whether the garden be a small city back yard or a large place in the country. After a study of the location and climate, make a plan of the entire site establishing a unity between the buildings and the garden. Select imaginative sites and design gardens in (a) the formal Italian style, (b) the informal New England, (c) the Japanese conventional, (d) the Spanish patio.

2. Find illustrations of "before and after" in back yards, empty lots, or streets.

Part Four

THE ART OF CITY PLANNING

" No city can have dignity, beauty, and distinction, or be a great city in the best sense of the word, unless its every element is an appropriate part of a greater whole." [1]

Has curiosity ever led you to look up the definition of a city? Although the usual meaning given is " a town or other inhabited place," " a large and important town," a little investigation into the origin of the word reveals a primary meaning of citizenship, the body of citizens, the community, with emphasis upon the human element. A city, a town, or a village means much more than a group of buildings. For buildings are not an end in themselves but a means to an end, the life of the people. A city is rather a group of people engaged in community living, community work and play. People may or may not make an art of it. If they do, one factor in their success is the intelligent planning of their physical city, that is, so de-signing it that the different elements form a balanced and harmonious whole, providing for its citizens the greatest possibilities for the highest type of living. To this idea everything is subordinated and, vice versa, every detail contributes toward this objective.

Most cities have just grown and have awakened too late to a realization of the need of design. An example of this is Manhattan Island in New York, where the long water-front has been lost for recreational purposes for the people, and where the cost of widening streets far too narrow for traffic is prohibitive. Many a city, large and small, reveals a beautiful river bank or seashore or some other spot of natural beauty despoiled and lost because a clear

[1] Milton Medary in *The American Architect*, May 20, 1929, p. 638.

design did not adequately provide for both the work and the play side of life. An example of how such a mistake can be rectified is seen in Chicago, which awakened to the fact that its lake front, an asset of natural beauty that should add to the life of the citizens, was almost lost to industry. The Chicago Plan Commission, however, by depressing, electrifying, and bridging over the railroads that skirt it, and by pushing the shore line out into the lake through reclamation and the making of new land, is creating one of the finest water fronts in the world for the benefit of the citizens.

A city is usually where it is, not from someone's whim, but for some definite reason. It may be the center of an agricultural or a mining region; near raw materials for manufacturing; a strategic point for transportation; a natural seaport; a recreational center. Therefore most cities have a preponderance of some interest; the steel industry in Pittsburgh; education in Oxford; government in Washington; shipping in New York. Its very existence is dependent upon the robust life of that interest. That is a focal point of the design, just as the dome is the focal point of *Saint Peter's* and of the *Taj*. But just as the dome, important as it is, takes its place in a unified design, so that vital interest in a city, important though it may be, is but one element in a well-designed community.

Such a design is complex and calls for vision. Consider yourself, in imagination, a builder of cities. Though in real life it never happens this way, a community summons you to lay out for it a city on a given site, a map of whose topography is laid before you. For what factors in the life of a city will your design have regard? At least five or six major factors will determine the important elements: (1) The industrial factor, industry located with regard to

transportation and raw materials, and with regard to healthy working conditions. (2) The home factor, where the workers may live with the greatest comfort, health, and facilities for recreation. What are the best locations for healthful living? What natural resources in the site should be preserved for the benefit of all? What small areas kept open for playgrounds? What river banks for drives? What wooded areas in the environs for preserves? (3) Then there is the civic factor. A city must govern itself and provide buildings not only suitable for the functioning of the government and conveniently located, but in appearance symbolic of community dignity and pride. (4) Education, (5) religion, (6) amusement — to bring these within the reach of all, liberal provision must be made.

No one of these elements, however, can operate in isolation. A city is well designed only when transportation functions with reasonable ease and rapidity from one part to another, to the environs, to other localities. Streets have well been called arteries, and, as in the body, are large or small according to their function. In planning your city, it makes a great deal of difference whether the street is to be a great thoroughfare for traffic, or a secluded tree-shaded avenue that suggests well-being in the home. Are your traffic arteries broad enough and straight enough for the amount of traffic poured into them? Are your railroad terminals so located that they serve all the interests of the city? Do your avenues in the residential parts give access to the controlling arteries and at the same time provide trees, grass, vistas, that bring both seclusion to homes and beauty for all? Have you provided for links between your parks, free from business traffic — especially important in these days of the automobile?

When all these factors are provided for, another element

PLATE 33

A Terrace at Tivoli (Pl. 32). Water is used here as an architectural element. Contrasting in texture, color, and movement with the stone and trees, it enhances their darkness and solemnity.

PLATE 34

Residence of Mr. Craig Heberton. Montecito, California. Here the garden brings cool shadows within the house and the combined beauty of the house and garden, with their contrasting light and dark, color, texture, is greater than that of each alone. (G. W. Smith)

arises — growth. City building is too complex and too costly to take into consideration one or two generations only. Far-seeing vision must reckon with the probable directions of growth. Even the wisest, however, cannot always foresee. Who could have prophesied fifty, even twenty-five, years ago the great problem now confronting all communities — traffic congestion due to the enormous development of the motor car?

To secure this proper apportionment of the different parts of the city to its various functions is the purpose of zoning regulations. This means that the city as a corporate body and not individual citizens shall decide what is the best use to which the various parts of the city shall be put for the benefit of the community as a whole. That is, the design as a whole is considered first, rather than the detail. These regulations not only decide which localities shall be zoned for industry, for homes, for apartments, for recreation, but also determine such problems as how high a building can rise without endangering health by obstructing air and light, and how near its neighbor it can stand.

Thus in planning your city the nature of the site on the one hand, and the logical demands of the work and play of the citizens on the other, with provision for growth, will determine your design.

Let us take our capital city Washington as an example of harmony between function and design in city planning. The focal interest of Washington is the administration of the affairs of government in relation to its own citizens and to the other nations of the world. Therefore a design for such a city would call for the adequate functioning of the different parts of the Government, and for the people, in their work and play, who participate in this functioning;

and also would call for an appearance, in the city, worthy of the nation, symbolizing its dignity and sovereignty. At the outset, it was the opinion of the President and his associates that the Potomac and the seaport at its mouth would be the great trade and transportation artery to the rich lands west of the mountains, and that the capital city would thus have a direct connection with the economics of the country. But they reckoned without a knowledge of the railroad and the dependence of trade routes upon this agency. That Washington has developed is due to its primary interest alone.

It was in 1800 that our Government moved from Philadelphia to " the backwoods settlement " on the Potomac. The plan of the city was intrusted to Major L'Enfant, a French military engineer who had fought in the Revolutionary War. Under the supervision of President Washington and Thomas Jefferson and also, apparently, under the influence of his native Paris and Versailles, Major L'Enfant took stock of the natural resources of the site and presented a plan whose vision and soundness have been proved by the fact that a commission appointed one hundred years later for further beautification of the capital based all its suggestions upon his fundamental plan.

What was Major L'Enfant's plan? With future growth in mind, as well as present need, he looked at the possibilities of the site. Here was a natural amphitheater surrounded by wooded hills and traversed by a broad river. The highest point in the amphitheater he selected for the *Capitol*, the focal point of his design, and he laid out avenues radiating from it in all directions in order to give free access to and from this center and also to enable the *Capitol* to terminate and dominate the vista of each avenue

(Fig. 72) . Another important center he established, the *White House,* on one of the radiating avenues not far from the *Capitol,* and from this too he sent out his avenues. So

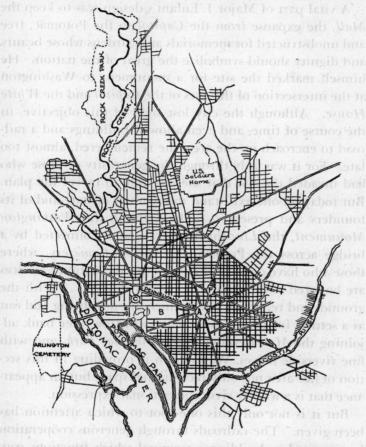

Fig. 72.   Plan of the City of Washington.   *A,* Capitol;   *C,* White House;   *F,* Union Station;   *B – D,* Mall;   *E,* Washington Monument;   *D,* Lincoln Memorial.

that the key to the plan of Washington consists of twin hubs, as it were, connected by a common spoke, *Pennsyl-*

vania Avenue. Within these spokes the streets are laid out regularly, making interesting intersections, known as *circles,* with the radial avenues.

A vital part of Major L'Enfant's design was to keep the *Mall,* the expanse from the *Capitol* to the Potomac, free and unobstructed for memorials and gardens whose beauty and dignity should symbolize the great of the nation. He himself marked the site for a monument to Washington at the intersection of the axes of the *Capitol* and the *White House.* Although the city lost sight of this objective, in the course of time, and even allowed buildings and a railroad to encroach on the area, she remembered, almost too late. For it was only through the generosity of those who had invaded the site that she was able to revive the plan. But today on one axis stand the symbols of state and of its founders and preservers — the *Capitol,* the *Washington Monument,* the *Lincoln Memorial,* and, connected by a bridge across the Potomac, *Arlington Cemetery,* where those who have devoted themselves to the nation's services are honored with burial (PL. 35 and Fig. 72). With the grounds and reflecting pools which are now being laid out as a setting for these monuments, with the river bank adjoining the *Mall* developed into *Potomac Park,* and with fine riverside drives, Washington is providing in this section of her area not only recreational space but an appearance that is a worthy civic and national expression.

But it is not only this one spot to which attention has been given. The railroads through generous coöperation have united in building a terminal which functions conveniently for all and at the same time, because of its site on one of the radiating avenues leading to the *Capitol,* takes its place in the city design harmoniously. The streets, avenues, and parks have been strongly emphasized; more

PLATE 35

The Washington Monument seen from the Lincoln Memorial. Stately dignity resulting from intelligent city planning. (Photo. by Horydczak)

PLATE 36

Photograph of the Hands of the Sculptor, Eric Gill. (Thorpe, *Eric Gill*. N. Y., Cape and Smith)

than half the area of Washington is given to these open spaces. The streets, unusually broad, are beautifully planted with elm, chestnut, linden, maple, oak, which in arching over the sidewalks and streets create deep vistas of refreshing sun-flecked shade. Not only have the circles at the street intersections been made into small spots of beauty by generous plantings of trees, shrubs, and flowers, but the sites of natural beauty about the city, such as *Rock Creek Park*, have been zealously guarded as one of the city's great possessions.

Thus Washington today is the result of vision, of fair-minded regard for all interests, and of insistence upon the coherence of all parts into the " greater whole."

READING

BENNETT, E. H., " City Planning," in The Significance of the Fine Arts, Boston, Marshall Jones, 1923.

LANCASTER, H. V., The Art of Town Planning, London, Chapman and Hall, 1925.

LETHABY, W. R., Form in Civilization, London, Oxford Press, 1922.

NOLEN, E. H., New Towns for Old, Boston, Marshall Jones, 1927.

SUGGESTIONS

1. As most of the larger cities of the United States have undertaken projects of town planning and have published reports which are accessible in the public libraries, make a study of your own city or another with which you are familiar; find just what the problems are and how they are being met.

2. Find examples of constructive city planning in European cities, both present and past. Berlin, Paris, Versailles, Rome, London, Vienna are a few among many examples.

3. Find examples of famous streets, harbors, public parks, and note the reasons why they are famous.

4. Find local examples of buildings too monotonously

placed; of those where some variety adds to the appearance; of successful planting in parkways; of good or impeded vistas.

5. Out of materials of your immediate or an imaginative environment: (a) make a plan for civic improvement: zone the city; lay out streets to handle traffic; a park and boulevard system; the civic center; the utilization of natural resources for the benefit of the community; (b) list the best examples of buildings, landscape architecture, monuments, bridges, sculpture, paintings, stained glass windows.

Part Five

THE ART OF SCULPTURE

"THE sculptor's job is making out of stone things seen in the mind." [1]

A block of stone, a consuming idea, a specific site — these form the basis of the art of sculpture in its truest sense, as the origin of the word implies — *to carve*. It sounds strangely like what we have been saying of building — a mass or volume, a definite purpose, a specific site.

We are inclined, in these days of specialization, to pigeonhole the arts. Architecture is one thing, painting another, dancing another; weaving, sculpture, music, writing — each in its own compartment. To be sure, each is a craft, subject to the laws of its own technique. But are there no common principles? No interrelations? Let us put a building and a statue side by side and, disregarding the discrepancy of size, look at them comparatively.

With a little observation and thought we begin to discern a kinship. This is due, in the first place, to the fact that a fundamental problem of both is the organization of mass. In making this comparison we are thinking only of sculpture *in the round*, that is, free-standing statues which we can walk around, in distinction to *relief*, which is attached to a background and thus only partly free (PLS. 50–52). First, then, the building and the statue actually exist in three dimensions; they have height, width, depth. Each is a volume or a group of volumes. Second, to design a building or a statue means to make the volume pleasing and harmonious by means of line, light and dark, texture, color; and to make this ordering of the parts harmonious with the purpose, or subject matter — "things

[1] Eric Gill, *Sculpture*, p. 21.

seen in the mind." Third, this design is to be seen from several points of view, not from one only as in a painting, an etching, or a textile, which is on a flat surface. So that while in some cases one point of view may be more favorable, in general the design must be pleasing from several angles.

Both the building and the statue, again, being volumes, are subject to the laws of stability, which results from a balance between two forces, downward pressure and upward thrust. Balance is one of the fundamental principles of life. To learn to walk is a matter of learning to balance the body; and in the process we discover only too well the results of breaking its laws. This is so impressed upon us that we demand the same of a building or a statue. As we can imagine a vertical line drawn through our bodies to represent the force that is pulling the body to the ground if the parts are not balanced, so in other volumes, whether buildings or statues, there is this imaginary line which requires that the masses be balanced in a like manner. Do you not sometimes have a feeling of equilibrium in your own body when you see a finely balanced building or statue and, vice versa, seem to feel yourself toppling over when you see one out of balance? Thus the builder and the sculptor are dealing with the same fundamental problem — organizing a mass into a balanced harmonious unit that is pleasing to the eye.

A second reason for the kinship between architecture and sculpture lies in the fact that so much sculpture was originally an integral part of a building; of the same material, stone; as architectural as the piers, columns, walls, and roofs, and not merely a decoration applied as an afterthought. Remove it and the building loses a vital part of its form and of its meaning; in the *Parthenon,* for example,

in *Chartres,* and in the *Nebraska State Capitol.*   Much free-standing sculpture in museums and private collections today was intended for a specific site and lighting.   To understand these statues with any intelligence, then, we must restore them to their original settings.   It is of vital importance whether the artist intended his statue to stand out of doors, at a distance, in a diffused light, or indoors, near by, in a dim or concentrated light.

Yet notwithstanding these marked similarities, strong dissimilarities appear.   A building is *abstract* [2] in form, based upon geometric shapes.   It does not represent anything.   The statue, on the other hand, is representative; in the vast majority of cases, of the human or animal figure. Again, the building is hollow.   Its interior is as important as its exterior and is molded by it.   Its stability means a nice adjustment between mechanical forces controlling walls and roof so that the interior can be open and safe. In other words, a building looks both inward and outward; a statue, on the other hand, outward only.   Yet the sculptor realizes that within the figure of the man or the horse which he is seeking to represent, there is an inner life — not to be found in the building — that is the vital force which determines the movements of the figure; and that the significance of the finished work is a balance between the outward form and the inner life.

What, then, is the purpose of the sculptor?   Is it not to make the mass with which he is dealing not only an interesting design, but a design that is significant of this inner life; with regard, at the same time, for the place which the statue is to occupy?

What is the mass, you ask, that is to be made interesting?

---

[2] A drawing away from realistic and representational form toward simplified and nonrepresentational.   Geometric patterns and solids are abstract.

It is the material with which he is working — stone, wood, ivory, clay, bronze, a great variety of materials, each to be worked according to its own peculiar qualities. Sculpture in its truest sense, we have said, means *to carve*. In other words stone is the material of much of the world's best sculpture. All stone is hard but some much more so than others; limestone and sandstone are comparatively soft; porphyry and diorite very hard; marble intermediate. Some stone is dark, some light; some dull, some glistening. Some has a coarse texture, some is fine and smooth. Some stones chip evenly; others split along a cleavage.

Whatever the stone, to carve is hard, difficult work, involving danger from a slip that would spoil the entire block. Does this character of the material in any way affect the work? Or the artist's conception? With wooden hammer and chisels (PL. 36) he stands before his roughly hewn block of stone. A convincing idea, "things seen in the mind," calls for expression. The block of stone must become the idea in visible form. So there is ever an interaction between the idea and the stone. As he works at the unyielding material he sees and carves large masses. Stone requires that in its hardness. Details slip away. The statue becomes large and monumental, small though it may be in size.

This influence of the material upon the artist is seen in wood-carving, though of a different kind, because wood is less stern than stone, is softer and more easily worked. Yet the fiber or grain of which it is composed requires the cutting be done, as far as possible, "with the grain" in order to avoid splitting. This tendency to crack, and the disastrous reaction of wood to atmospheric conditions, except in a very dry climate, make it a far less permanent material than stone or bronze.

Another great class of material is metal, chiefly bronze, though gold, silver, brass, and alloys are used. Bronze is dark, even when gilded, and has a reflective power, causing strong high lights and deep shadows within which detail is lost (PLS. 47–49). Bronze-working is not carving but consists of building up a core about the size and shape of the contemplated figure, covering this with a layer of soft material like clay or wax, in which the modeling is done, and then casting it in the metal.[3] Engraving brings out the detail in a sharp, crisp manner that is necessary if it is to show in the dark color of the metal. Bronze has a dusky splendor, a sharpness and precision not found in marble, which is due not so much to the artist's intention as to the rigidity, color, and reflective character of the material.

Finally there is clay, the medium for modeling. " Modeling and carving are different human actions, originating respectively in the boy making a mud pie and the boy whittling a stick " [4] (PL. 37). In the latter the artist takes away from a given volume, subtracts until the result is reached, and the planes of the original block determine the limits of his design. In the former, he builds out from a slender framework called an *armature* (Fig. 73) with chunks of clay to form a volume, adds until the result is reached, unlimited by any bounding planes. In another respect modeling is the opposite of carving, for the material is soft, shapes easily, and affords possibilities of building up and tearing down. Thus in clay there is more freedom, more opportunity for quick momentary expression, but less for the grandly monumental. To become permanent

[3] For an explanation of bronze-casting see H. Gardner, *Art Through the Ages*, N. Y., Harcourt, 1926, p. 115, note 6. For a dramatic account of the casting of a statue, see Benvenuto Cellini, *Memoirs*, Everyman's Library, pp. 402 ff.
[4] J. Thorp, *Eric Gill*, London, Cape, 1929, p. 6.

the clay must be fired, or cast in plaster or metal. The truest clay forms are those in which the feeling of the soft clay remains, hardened by fire into permanency (PL. 37A).

Each medium,[5] thus, has its own peculiar character, limitations, advantages and disadvantages. And the quality of the final work depends upon the judgment of the artist in selecting the medium that will harmonize best with the idea that he wishes to express.

Fig. 73. Armature. Made of piping, wire, and wood. (After A., Toft, *Modelling and Sculpture*, Phila., Lippincott, 1915)

Because the character of the sculptor's medium, taken as a whole, suggests strength, endurance, and monumentality, and because sculpture, like all the arts, is an art whose inherent quality does not conflict with the medium but harmonizes with it, suitable subject matter at the disposal of the sculptor is quite limited. Look at the sculpture that the world has produced, east and west, from the twentieth century to earliest times, and you discern an astonishing limitation in subject matter — overwhelmingly the human and the animal figure. Has this happened from mere chance or coincidence?

To answer this question, let us return to the purpose of the sculptor: "making out of stone things seen in the mind." He does not abandon the material. He makes it live. This is what Michelangelo meant when he said, " Life moves within the stone." The statue does not give you a copy of the appearance of the person represented, but a feeling of his reality, his life, in stone. It is this bal-

[5] *Medium* is a general term for the material with which the artist creates form. For the writer it is words; for the builder, stone, wood, steel, brick, concrete; for the painter, pigment; for the weaver, threads; for the potter, clay; for the musician, tones.

PLATE 37

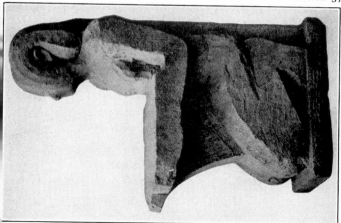

A. Chinese Figurine. (Metropolitan Museum)

B. Unfinished Egyptian Statue. (Cairo Museum)

In A one feels the soft pliable clay built up by the fingers; in B the hard, resisting stone carved out by the chisel. B is conceived as a four-sided form in which the block of stone and the figure seem inseparable. A, though compact in mass and simple in contour, has no ideal space (like the block of stone) to define its limits.

PLATE 38

Porch of the Maidens. Erechtheum, Athens. The figures are compact and column-like so as to function architecturally in supporting the roof. How certain surfaces catch the light and present to the eye a charming rhythm of light and dark, and how harmoniously figure, building, and landscape unite. (Clarence Kennedy)

ance between life and stone that constitutes the art of sculpture — to transmute the block of stone into a concrete expression and still retain the feeling of the stone.

And still more, the sculptor not only makes the stone live but makes it present to the eye a pleasing mass, a mass made stable, balanced, rhythmic, and harmonious by line, and by light and dark. Just as in a building. The building may perform its function adequately. Yet only when its mass is organized into something that pleases the eye with its stability, balance, proportions, and harmony does it become a work of art.

Why, then, the use of the human or the animal figure? Though there have often existed secondary reasons for its use, such as the religious significance of Egyptian portraits, the personification of nature among the Greeks, commemoration of great men among all peoples, still behind these reasons lie the artistic possibilities of the human figure. Why did Michelangelo say that the most beautiful thing in the world is the human figure? Because it is made up of closely related masses — head, trunk, and limbs — which can be composed into an indefinite number of designs. It can stand stiff and stern with a symmetrical balance, can turn into graceful curves, or can violently contort its parts and interweave them into a complex pattern, maintaining its balance either symmetrically or asymmetrically. This is the essence of the dance when the dancer captures for a moment or makes progressive what the sculptor makes permanent.

Thus the art of the sculptor involves three things. First, to understand the material, its limitations and its possibilities, a material which, with the exception of clay, is hard, enduring, and monumental; second, the use of the figure to convert this raw material into an interesting de-

sign with a significant meaning; and third, to relate the design to the site it is to occupy.

All this, however, is theory. What do the statues themselves say? Shall we go directly to them and see with our eyes what the sculptor intends us to see?

READING

FLACCUS, L. W., The Spirit and Substance of Art, N. Y. Crofts, 1931.

GUILLAUME, P., and MUNRO, T., Primitive Negro Sculpture, N. Y., Harcourt, 1926.

RINDGE, A., Sculpture, N. Y., Payson and Clark, 1929.

SUGGESTIONS

1. Experiment as far as possible in handling materials — stone, wood, metal, clay — for a realization of hardness, texture, plasticity.

2. Visit a stonecutter's yard, if possible, and see the use of the hammer and chisel.

3. As actual carving in stone presents insurmountable obstacles, use soap or clay bricks, in order to realize, with the help of the imagination, what carving really means. The pamphlet published by the National Small Sculpture Committee in connection with the annual Proctor and Gamble competition offers many suggestions.

4. Select a simple subject. Model it in clay and carve it in soap. Compare the influence of the material and of the process upon your work while it is going on. Compare the finished pieces.

5. Study posing the figure to see how many interesting designs you can work out with it. Much on this topic can be done in dancing and gymnasium classes. Select poses suitable for stone; for bronze.

THE COLUMBUS MEMORIAL

FROM the harbor of Palos in southwestern Spain, legend says, three ships sailed forth in 1492 on a mighty adven-

ture. It required courage and faith as well as the joy of daring to embark on that westward voyage.

Today, overlooking the same harbor, rises a monument to commemorate that setting forth (PL. 39).[6] Grandly impressive, it towers above the land and the sea. Its stern simplicity compels the observer to follow the long unbroken lines and the large uninterrupted areas of light and dark. There is no irrelevant detail to distract. What *Columbus* looked like does not matter. What does matter is his impelling courage and the will to adventure. The grandeur, the directness, and the dignity of this conception harmonize with the grandeur, the directness, and dignity of the design.

Though built up of masonry, the statue gives the impression of one colossal block of stone carved by giant chisel and hammer. The base is a simple geometric form, a truncated pyramid, out of which the figure and the cross grow as naturally as a plant thrusting itself up from the earth. There is no sharp dividing line between the figure and the base, but a skillful interplay of forms: the unbroken face of the base and cross, the narrow plinth on which the feet rest, and the embracing cloak. The base rests upon a platform with a triple step, and is broken near the bottom by a repetition of this triple-step motif. At its corner is an entrance to the room in its base, breaking the contour at that point and giving an angular profile like that of a setback skyscraper. How many people, do you think, would have thought of placing the entrance at the corner instead of in the center, so as to give variety to a symmetrical balance? Near the top of the base, where the

[6] *The Columbus Statue* overlooks the harbor of Palos. Base, 30 ft. square; figure, 64 ft. high. Gertrude Vanderbilt Whitney, a contemporary American sculptor. 1929 A.D.

sternness of the unbroken masonry needs interruption, are four accents, four reliefs symbolizing the continents. The cloak envelops the figure and brings its parts into one large unity and with its flowing edge provides the bold diagonal that gives power to the design. Cover this diagonal and see the result.

All the parts of the statue, being broadly generalized, form large simplified areas of light and dark in much the same way as we saw in a *Chapel* (Fig. 3) . There the bold simplicity of the two volumes creates, when seen from any angle, an expression of strength and aspiration. Or, make the comparison with the *Nebraska State Capitol* (PL. 24) . Here again simple geometric volumes unite, by their shapes, proportions, lines, and light and shadow, into a lucid, coherent, rhythmic whole. So too in the *Columbus*. Its big simplified masses are like the impelling masses of the *Chapel* and of the *Capitol*.

To be sure the statue represents some one — *Columbus*. But not the individual *Columbus* except as the individual *Columbus* is an epitome of courage, faith, and daring. So that the statue symbolizes the faith and courage of any adventurer, as the *Chapel* and the *Capitol* symbolize the strength and aspiration of any people. In each case a convincing idea has found suitable form.

SUGGESTIONS

1. Carve in soap the chief masses and planes of this and the succeeding stone statues that we study. Be sure to show the important masses and planes only. Omit all detail. To do this satisfactorily it is necessary to have illustrations from several angles. (See Fig. 75 for a suggestion.)

2. Find statues which commemorate historical events. Study them as to (a) what the artist felt and thought about the subject; (b) design: mass, contour, light and dark; (c) re-

PLATE 39

Columbus Memorial. Gertrude Vanderbilt Whitney. As in certain buildings (Pls. 2, 3, 24, for instance), grandly simple masses convey a grandly simple impression. (Mrs. Whitney)

PLATE 40

Khafre, an Egyptian Pharaoh. A simple organization, with planes generally parallel to the sides of the block of stone, which creates an impression of repose and majestic dignity. (Metropolitan Museum)

lation of the design to the artist's conception; (d) relation
of the design to its setting.

KHAFRE, AN EGYPTIAN PHARAOH

TURN from *Columbus* to *Khafre* (PLS. 40 and 42).[7] How
much alike they are! There is the same simplicity, dignity,
enduring monumentality. To be sure the *Khafre* is small
in comparison, though it is of life size,
and is cut from one block of stone.
Seated quietly, he turns neither to the
right nor to the left. Figure and throne
form a very compact unit with a simple
contour to which everything is subor-

dinated, and their
surfaces closely fol-
low the surfaces, or
planes, of the orig-
inal block of stone
(PL. 37B and Figs. 74
and 75). You are
constantly reminded

Fig. 74.   Front
View of Khafre
(PL. 40).

Fig. 75. Organi-
zation of Planes in
Khafre (PL. 40).

of this block by the general squareness
of the design. From a frontal point of
view the only variant to a perfectly
symmetrical balance is the different
position of the hands, the right holding
a handkerchief, the left resting flatly on
the knee. The arms are so placed that
their cylindrical shapes are brought into
harmonious alignment with those of the legs. The head
rests squarely on the broad shoulders and is connected

---

[7] *Khafre* also called *Cephren* or *Cheops*. Sculptor unknown. Of diorite, about
life size. About 2850 B.C. Cairo Museum.

with the trunk by the folds of the headdress and by the beard.

The volumes of which the entire statue is composed — the head with its enclosing headdress and hawk, the trunk, the arms, the legs, the throne — all are clearly revealed by largely unbroken masses of light and dark, because the planes that bound these volumes are highly simplified. Take one detail, for example, the upper part of the figure seen in profile. The spherical volumes of the head, the shoulders, the bird, and the rectangular volume of the throne, are fitted together with the precision of the architectural members of a building. The volumes of the head and shoulders are united to the throne by the body of the hawk that stands upon the back and enfolds the head with outspread wings. The curved contour of the shoulder repeats that of the head, of the bird's head, and of the under edge of the wing; and the contrasting straight lines and angles of the headdress and the upper line of the wing add virility. The clear, direct coördination of these parts recalls the same kind of harmonious unity that we saw in building, for example in *Santa Maria in Cosmedin* (PL. 16A). *Khafre* is as architectural as the church; or, in other words, the church is as sculptural as *Khafre*.

Another element that assists the eye to travel through the design is the differentiation in texture between the smooth surfaces of the flesh, the headdress, and the throne, and the broken areas of the hawk's plumage, the flaps of the headdress, the kilt, and the decoration of the throne.

Here then is a statue that conveys to us by the organization only or by its mass a feeling of dignity and majesty. What is its subject? Why did the sculptor carve it? Only to compose his stone into an interesting design? We have

already called our statue by the name of an Egyptian king. That implies a portrait.

To understand the reason for such a portrait, let us recall something of the spirit of Egypt as we met it in the *Temple*. Contrasts of geography are reflected in contrasts of building. A rich narrow valley is squeezed in the grasp of relentless deserts; rich decoration is held subordinate to overwhelming mass. Happiness, gayety, and wistful awe of the mysteries of life and death characterize the Egyptian. With a strong conviction of a life beyond death for which the body must be preserved, he laid great stress on tomb building and even provided a likeness of the body to take its place in case of its destruction. Hence the importance of the *Great Pyramids,* which are royal tombs (Fig. 2). The statue of *Khafre* was one of a row of statues in the vestibule of one of these pyramids (PL. 42).[8] The room is severely simple, and its impressiveness results partly from its proportions and partly from the great piers and roofing stones of beautifully cut red granite. Its only decoration is the row of portrait statues, as quiet, as austerely simple, as the room itself.

Here then was the original setting and the purpose of our statue: to stand in the vestibule as a decorative element and at the same time to present a likeness of the king. Does it look like *Khafre?* No one can say. Probably in a general way it does. He wears the usual dress of his time: a headdress of linen brought smoothly over the forehead, where was affixed a serpent (now broken off), the mark of royalty; an artificial ceremonial beard (also broken off), held by straps up over the head; and a plaited kilt. The hawk, enveloping the head, is the symbol of the sun god,

---

[8] The *Pyramid of Khafre* (Cephren or Cheops) is the second of the three *Great Pyramids*. At Gizeh, near Cairo. About 2850 B.C.

for in flight it flies toward the sun. Now to the Egyptian the pharaoh is half divine, the son of the sun, and hence the presence of the hawk is indicative of his semidivine station.

The conception of the unknown artist who carved the *Khafre* had regard partly for the appearance of *Khafre,* but largely for that for which he stood: a majesty and kingly feeling not granted other mortals. Just as in the *Columbus Memorial* it was the idea rather than the man that mattered most. The quiet pose, the simplified expression of form, the clear simple relationships of the parts of the mass to each other and to the block of stone — all these factors contribute to an expression of calm and lofty dignity. It is this harmony between the form and the idea that gives the statue its quality.

It is carved from one of the hardest of stones, diorite. To attack a stone like this with hammer and bronze chisel meant patient, persistent effort which would force upon the sculptor a drastic kind of simplification and a terse expression of form. Would not a feeling of monumentality and endurance inevitably result?

THE TOMB OF A PRINCE

WITH the simple organization and quiet gravity of *Columbus* and *Khafre* in mind, journey to Florence (Fig. 53) and make your way at once to the *New Sacristy* of the *Church of San Lorenzo* and without noticing the rest of the room, take your stand directly in front of *Day* (PL. 41).[9] What a difference! The half-reclining giant peers

---

[9] *Day*, a figure from the *Tomb of Giuliano de' Medici* (Pl. 43), son of Lorenzo the Magnificent. Michelangelo not only carved the figures, but designed the entire room (1524–33 A.D.), which was never completed. The portrait of *Giuliano*, in the niche, is highly generalized.

out at you directly over his great shoulder. Thence your
eye is carried backward and forward, in and out, by the
spiraling limbs. It is the opposite pole from *Khafre*.
There, was quietude and poise; here, restlessness and
tumult. Both are obedient to the laws of stone-carving;
yet the results are diametrically opposed.

In *Khafre* there is no crossing of the parts of the body.
The planes are mostly parallel to the planes of the original
block of stone (Fig. 75) ; are vertical, horizontal, at right
angles. In *Day* these same volumes of the same human

figure cross and swing
around each other, turn
and bend; they seem to
have gathered into them-
selves the maximum ca-
pacity of the human fig-
ure for movement. Yet
the movements are not
haphazard or disorderly.
With both consonance
and dissonance they move
rhythmically about the

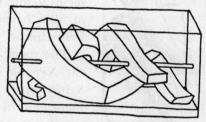

Fig. 76. Organization of the Planes in
Day (PL. 41). The figure consists of
three primary masses which spiral
around the axis within the space determined by the block of stone. Compare PL. 44.

imaginary axis of the figure (Fig. 76) . The great sweeping plane of the back and flanks forms a base of strength
and solidity, with a largely unbroken contour which balances the jagged contour above. Compare in the profile
view of *Khafre* the repetition of similar contours rather
than the opposition of dissimilar.[10] Yet the restless *Day,*
even as the quiet *Khafre,* occupies a space determined by
the original block of stone, a rectangular mass which one
easily feels as he looks at the figure from several points of
view (Fig. 77) .

[10] Compare also in this connection Pls. 37 B and 44.

The head of *Day* is turned sharply to the right, so that it faces the spectator squarely over the shoulder. The right arm, turning in the opposite direction, encircles the body. The right leg, paralleling the right arm, moves to the left, while the left, swinging forward, cuts sharply across the upper right and then flows into harmonious unity with the lower part, a harmony that is emphasized by the lines of the drapery. In fact all the restlessness of the movement

that flings itself about the shoulders and rears itself in the sharply bent knee seems to find final rest in the quiescence of this harmonious grouping of the lower limbs.

The room in which the tomb stands, the *New Sacristy*, shows similarities to *Saint Peter's* (PL. 23): upward movement held in restraint. The dominant motifs are the rectangle and the curve, both linear and spatial. Shallow projections and recessions catch the light and hold shadow and half-shadow, creating a movement that is backward and forward as well as on the surface. Study for a moment the corner of the room.

Fig. 77. Side View of Day (PL. 41). Note the compactness of the figure and its subordination to the block of stone.

The pilasters and cornice form a sharply defined rectangle divided into a doorway and a niche. The parts move backward and forward; some are deep, some shallow. The series of rectangles plays up into the curve; the curved brackets carry the curve down in the rectangle of the door and break the angularity at that point; the garlands and discs repeat the curve inversely — every detail so relates to every other that the corner becomes a harmonious design in three dimensions. It is really abstract sculpture.

The tomb not only fits into this design through its use of the same motifs, but also becomes a focal point in the room because of the enrichment of details and of the addition of figure sculpture.

The architectural framework of the tomb is rather quiet, with well-balanced verticals and horizontals and a slight use of the curve. In the upper part the strong shadow, the broken cornice, and stronger ornament balance the more powerful masses below. The sculpture forms a triangle, inclosing similar triangles, happily combined with the architectural setting, for the diagonal lines give virility and contrast (Fig. 78). But the design is not on a two-dimensional surface, as the drawing might indicate. Like the corner at which we have been looking, the forms are three-dimensional masses that move backward and forward — within narrow limits, to be sure — and throw strong shadows that play so important a

Fig. 78. Linear Pattern of the Tomb of Giuliano de' Medici (PL. 43).

part in the design; as, for example, the horizontals made by the cornices, the masses of dark in the upper part of the niches and beneath the sarcophagus which contribute to the strength of the base.

Just what significance Michelangelo attached to these figures is not clear. To him, as we have already said, the human figure contains an infinite number of beautiful designs. These, however, are valuable not only as abstract designs but also for the expression of that inner life which makes the movements of the figure significant. Certain positions and movements express quietude, poise, serenity;

others, restlessness, tragedy; some, profound thought or epic grandeur; others, facile gayety or lyric grace. It is the same principle that we have seen in *Columbus* and *Khafre,* that of fitting a form to an idea. With Michelangelo there is no quietude, no calm. His own restless soul reflected the restlessness and the conflicting forces of his day. " Lay blame on the times," he says in a letter, " which are not favorable to art." *Day* is a giant of conflict. Beyond this we cannot go. Why is it so? Because, though the block of stone still holds sway over the space that it occupies, the planes swing backward and forward through the mass, keeping the eye ever in motion. Is it not well that surrounding *Day* there are reposeful spaces?

THREE FIGURES FROM THE PARTHENON

IN *Khafre* and *Day* we have seen two general types of stone sculpture: one, with its planes closely following the planes of the block of stone, quiet, static; the other, with its planes spiraling about the axis of the block, restless, dynamic (Figs. 75 and 76). Turning to the *Three Figures* of PL. 45,[11] do we see any relationship with either of these two types? The figures are quiet and majestic, figures of stone — you do not forget that nor do they intend that you should — with all the feeling of the mass and texture of stone, yet with a vitality of their own; figures that give you not an illusion of the flesh and blood prototype, the model, but a suggestion of its potential grandeur, a feeling en-

[11] From the sculpture of the east pediment, the subject of which was the *Birth of Athena.* These figures have never been identified satisfactorily. Three Fates, Three Attic Horae, Clouds, Sea in the Lap of the Earth, have been suggested. Of Pentelic marble, colossal in size. Though they may be the work of Pheidias, one of the great Greek sculptors of the fifth century B.C., this cannot be proved. About 438–32 B.C. Taken to England in 1801. British Museum, London.

PLATE 41

Day, from the Tomb of Giuliano de'Medici. Michelangelo. A complex organization, with planes spiraling about the axis of the figure though still under the control of the block of stone, which creates an impression of restlessness.

PLATE 42

Vestibule to the Tomb (the Pyramid) of Khafre. The reposeful and majestic
Khafre fits perfectly into this simple room.

PLATE 43

The New Sacristy of San Lorenzo. The restless Day fits perfectly into this restless room.

PLATE 44

An Unfinished Statue. Michelangelo. Notice how the space occupied by the figure is determined by the four-sided block of stone. The body is so turned that one arm is parallel to the front plane (compare Pl. 37B) and the head, in the piece of stone still uncut, faces the side plane. Notice the chisel marks.

hanced by the quiet undulating rhythm that binds them together, a movement like that of a deep and quiet sea (Fig. 79).

One, at the left, is erect and alert, and is turning expectantly to the left; the second sits in a crouching position, bending over the reclining figure that rests upon it in complete relaxation. How the three flow together into a unity that seems so casual and yet so harmonious and inevitable! Serenity and harmony seem to be the words we keep repeating. Stone made beautifully serene and harmonious, suggesting a serene and harmonious life in the person represented; and, at the same time, fitting into its place in the corner of the pediment unostentatiously, as if it belonged there. To be sure this group is now in London, but in imagination let us see it in its original place on the temple.

Take the single figure at the left. It has neither the immobility of *Khafre* on the one hand, nor the restlessness of Michelangelo on the other. Though seated in a frontal position like *Khafre,* the figure shows a slight movement to the left to which every part of the body responds, one shoulder lowered, one leg thrust back, the head turned, the right arm raised, giving life and movement to the statue. In *Khafre,* we are practically unaware of this movement; in the Greek figure we are fully aware of it; in the *Day,* dramatically so. In the Greek, the easy movement throws the body into curves so that the eye is carried from one mass to another by an easy, flowing rhythm which produces a feeling of tranquillity.

But what about the block of marble? Whether you look at the figure from the front or from the side, you feel a predominance of planes that parallel the planes of the original block (Fig. 75), that is, a four-sided organization.

Yet there is a movement, a tilting of the planes without crisscrossing (compare Fig. 76). They are simplified and broadly modeled; that of the chest, for example, presents a surface but lightly broken. This gives a broad quiet expanse of light which enhances the monumental effect. In the rest of the figure the drapery plays an important part. Let your eye be guided by its folds and see how closely its lines follow the surfaces. How insistently you feel the backward movement of the plane made by the back thrust of the right leg, because of the few strong lines

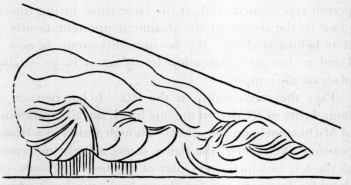

Fig. 79. Organizing Lines in the Figures from the Parthenon (PL. 45).

radiating from the left knee! These lines, you will notice, are really shadow obtained by undercutting the marble deeply. Follow them through the group and see how they form a quiet rhythmic rise and fall (Fig. 79) that is pleasurable in itself. It is an easy, continuous flow of line in which change of direction is made without abruptness and minor lines are kept subordinate. The fact that broadly treated planes dominate the lines of the garments and the lines in turn accent the planes is an important reason for their harmony; and harmony in the organizing of the

block of stone reflects a harmony of inner life in the figures represented in the stone.

What, you ask, do the figures represent? We do not know specifically, except that they are divine or semi-divine personages, who in the eye and mind of the Greek of the *Parthenon* age, like Agathocles, were serene, majestic, idealized humans. One purpose of these figures, then, was to give expression to this idea of a majestic humanity. In Greece man was the unit of life and among the citizens there was democracy. Even in the popular Greek religion

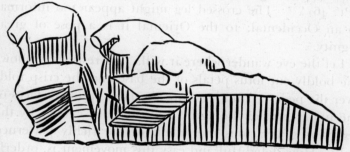

Fig. 80.   Organization of the Planes in the Figures from the Parthenon
(PL. 45).

of the *Parthenon* age " man was the measure of all things," so that the gods were visualized as like him. Thus the idea to be represented, a serene, balanced type of life, accords with the design of the block of stone, a design that is peculiarly majestic yet reposeful in the flow of its planes, lines, and lights and darks.

But there is one more element to consider in our understanding of these figures. And that is the original site. *Khafre* was a decorative element in an astonishingly simple room with overhead lighting, a situation into which it fitted with perfect harmony. These Greek figures belong to a decorative group that filled the pediment of the *Par-*

thenon, in a diffused, out-of-doors light, a group that we saw was necessary to give broken light and shade and curved lines to balance the severity of the rectilinear character of the building (Fig. 22). The sculptor in each case had the discerning eye to realize that there must be harmony between the statue and its function.

A JAPANESE SAINT

WHAT a brooding tranquillity in this figure seated on a high pedestal, meditatively resting his chin on his uplifted hand (PL. 46)! [12] The crossed leg might appear too informal to an Occidental; to the Oriental it is a pose of great dignity.

Let the eye wander where it will. It irresistibly follows the boldly cut lotus petals of the base and the crisp folds over the pedestal and legs into the large quiet surfaces of the upper part of the figure and thence is caught by the contrasting vivacious movement of the richly patterned halo. How delightful and easy this movement is, orderly yet forceful, giving the figure a feeling of tranquillity and power that seems to reflect an inner poise born of some great conquest!

What has the sculptor done to convey this impression even to a Westerner who understands but little of the meaning of the figure? From a base fringed with lotus petals rises a cone-shaped seat covered with a drapery and a cushion, on which the *Saint* is seated in a frontal position with no turn of the body to the right or to the left, like *Khafre* (PL. 40), but with considerable freedom of pose because of the crossed leg and the lifted hand, and also because of the bending of the figure as the head rests upon

[12] *Japanese Saint.* Of wood. In a monastery, Chuguji, near Nara. Suiko period, 552–645 A.D.

the hand. A strongly felt vertical axis falls from the point of the halo about which the figure is balanced. On the left the arm is in alignment with the leg. Together, whether seen from the front or the side, they present a unit, both of mass and of line. On the right is the opposing movement of the crossed leg and uplifted arm. Thus vivacious variety balances reposeful uniformity. The abrupt right angle made by the legs is softened by the curves and diagonals of the folds of the dress, which unite with the folds of the stuff thrown over the pedestal to bring the figure, cushion, and pedestal into one inseparable unity. Notice how, from the side view, the smaller curves are united by one sweeping fold from waist to ankle that repeats the sweeping line of the arm and leg.

You probably are thinking of the similar rôle that the drapery plays in the *Parthenon* figures (PL. 45). There the garments are more naturalistic, look more like cloth. In the Japanese figure they are more conventional, with greater insistence upon a decorative pattern. Each, we feel, is exactly right in its own place. To interchange them would be ruinous.

The crisp cutting of this drapery as well as the rather loose contour of the figure do not suggest stone but wood. The features too show the same incisive carving. The lines of the brows, lids, nostrils, and mouth cut directly across the vertical axis with precise regularity, giving the face an impression of quiet symmetry and harmony. This impression results, then, not from an attempt to imitate natural appearance, but from an arrangement of natural features into an oval-framed pattern. All its lines are curves set forth by shadow, which harmonize with the curve motive of the entire design. For, looking at the figure as a whole, it resolves itself into rounding surfaces

and curved lines, a flow of both surface and line yet with invigorating contrasts and stabilizing verticals.

Thus we have seen that the nature of the design harmonizes with the nature of the general impression that the statue gives us. What is its meaning? This we may learn from a Japanese Buddhist. According to Buddhist belief, a person pursues a long series of lives, each of which advances or retreats, according to its rightness, to or from the " attainment of wisdom," which is Buddhahood. Now the last step to that " enlightenment " is the stage of the Bodhisattva, who corresponds in a general way to the saint of Christianity. This particular Bodhisattva is called *Maitreya,* a name based on the word " to love." He loves all living things tenderly, birds, animals, and flowers as well as man, and is not only compassionate toward their weaknesses but actively working for their salvation, that is, for their attainment of Buddhahood. Through his long series of lives and his gradual conquests over himself he has won his own inner poise. Thus his character combines strength and tranquillity. In visualizing such a *Saint,* the Japanese artist felt that he was concerned not with a being that was like a human, as did the Greek, but with something mysterious, something less easily understood. Therefore his tendency was to depart from naturalistic appearance and to use symbols to express his ideas. The figure has broad shoulders and a narrow waistline; the different parts of the body are modeled with no detail but with gently rounding broad surfaces; and the face, as we have already said, is conventionalized. Symbolic meaning we see in the base decorated with petals of the lotus, as we saw in the *Taj Mahall,* in the knob of wisdom on the head, and in the elongated ear lobes which have renounced the costly jewels that weighed them down.

Thus when we see the *Maitreya* with our Western eyes we see a figure whose form conveys to us the delight of a fine design. When we understand something of its inner meaning we then realize that here is not only carving of wood into a rhythmic design of great beauty, but also a noble design befitting a noble idea.

READING

COOMARASWAMY, A., Buddha and the Gospel of Buddhism, N. Y., Putnam, 1916.

OKAKURA-KAKUZO, Ideals of the East, London, Murray, 1920.

TAKI, S., Japanese Fine Art, Tokyo, Fuzambo, 1931.

A BRONZE MAIDEN

IN contrast to the Oriental figure with its emphasis on conventions and symbols, we turn to a statue whose form lies closer to natural appearance (PL. 47).[13] Its compact mass is dominated by a supple rhythm and its planes and contours flow with grace and charm. We do not know the purpose or the original placing of the statue. It seems to represent a girl removing her garments as she prepares for the bath. The left arm rests on a low pillar; the right holds the drapery, about to drop it; around the head is wound a scarf. This simple everyday incident gave the artist the opportunity of revealing the beauties of the human body.

For at least two reasons the Greek emphasized the human figure in his art. First, because, as we have seen, he visualized his gods as men and women, and much of his sculpture consisted of temple statues. In the second place, athletics played a great part in Greek life. The Greeks were an

[13] *Bronze Maiden.* Height, 10 in. Greek, late fifth century B.C. Antiquarium, Munich. Parts of the statue are lost — the arms, a low pillar, and the drapery held in the hands.

out-of-doors people who made the development of fine
bodies an essential of education and of life. Every day in
the gymnasium the youths boxed, wrestled, danced, and
ran, naked, to the accompaniment of music while the
elders watched and discussed philosophy and politics.
Thus all the Greek people were trained to see the beauties
inherent in the figure, and the artists in particular always
had before them examples of how the body in its parts and
as a whole reacted to different conditions. Thus they
looked to nature as their teacher rather than to abstraction
and symbols. This, however, is very different from saying
that they copied nature.

The nude, then, to the Greek was a natural everyday
commonplace; and in it he saw the most beautiful thing in
nature, just as Michelangelo saw it, with infinite capacities
for the organization of its parts into significant arrange-
ments. So that whatever his subject matter — a god or an
athlete, an expression of austerity, majesty, or simple
charm — he could mold the body to an expression of it.

In the little *Bronze Maiden,* then, the figure is used because of its capacity to express lyric charm. If the figure
was a portrait or a commemorative statuette, probably
such was the personality portrayed. Just how did the
sculptor produce this result? The figure is swung on a
great S-curve so that the surfaces of the volumes catch the
light, giving, in our view, a rhythmic movement with four
strong accents. This results from the pose of the figure.
The weight is thrown on to the right side, leaving the left
leg free, slightly thrown back and with the heel raised. The
left arm rests firmly on the low shaft; the right freely holds
the garment. This pose brings about a balance between
the free and the weight-carrying parts and an easy balance
to the entire figure (Fig. 81). A statue so posed is like

PLATE 45

Three Figures from the Parthenon. They partake partly of the majestic repose of Khafre (Pl. 40) and partly of the movement of Day (Pl. 41). (British Museum)

PLATE 46

A Japanese Saint. The brooding repose of the figure is expressed through a conventionalized form (compare Pl. 72 for a similar attitude toward form in another medium). The crisp cutting, the less compact grouping of the parts and the irregular contours indicate wood carving. (Okakura-Kakuzo, ed., *Japanese Temples and their Treasures*. Department of Education, Japan)

PLATE 47

A Maiden in Bronze. Grace, charm, and great unity in the easy rhythmic flow of masses and of contours, as one great rhythmic sweep incorporates all minor rhythms. The dark color and the high lights indicate bronze. (Clarence Kennedy)

PLATE 48

A Victorious Charioteer. An expression of balance and self control. The compact mass with quiet contours varied by the outstretched arms, the dark color of the bronze and the crisp detail carry well in the out-of-doors.

a sentence with chiasmic structure. In both there is a cross arrangement of the parts:

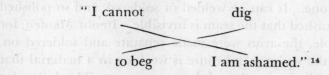

"I cannot   dig

to beg   I am ashamed." [14]

But easy curves intensify their charm if combined with straight lines. These are here afforded by the decided feeling for the vertical axis about which the parts are balanced, by the verticality of the right leg and of the low pillar on which the left arm rests, and by the vertical folds of drapery. Further contrasts we find in the surfaces. The folds of the headdress, the silver inlay of the eyes, the finely engraved mass of hair over the forehead and stray locks near the ears, the folds of the drapery — all these animated surfaces emphasize and enhance the smooth-flowing surfaces of the body itself.

Fig. 81. Chiasmus in Sculpture. The right leg and the left arm carry the weight; the left leg and the right arm are free.

There are several ways in which this statue differs from the others that we have studied — in its sharper contours, darker color, much stronger accentuation of light at certain points, and sharper differentiation between the light and the dark; also, when the lost drapery is added, in a greater freedom of pose, as if

[14] H. W. Fowler, *Modern English Usage*. *Chiasmus* is from a Greek word meaning to make the letter chi, which is like our X. In writing it means that the order of words or phrases in the second part of the sentence is the opposite of that in the first part.

not limited by an original block of stone. All these qualities are due to the bronze technique. Bronze is not brittle,
like stone. It can be welded or soldered, and so polished
and finished that the seam is invisible. In our *Maiden,* for
example, the arms were made separate and soldered on.
Thus the sculptor in bronze is working in a material that
is not as limited as that of the stone-carver. The dark color
of the metal against the light sharpens the silhouette.
Metal has a strong reflective quality, causing concentrated
high lights, and the artist must so design his figure that
these lights will accent and harmonize, rather than obstruct
and confuse. So in our *Maiden,* the four masses of light
mark the controlling rhythm. How we would like to run
our hands over this bronze and feel the rhythmic undulations of its surfaces and thus let our hands feel what our
eyes see!

TWO COMMEMORATIVE STATUES
A Victorious Charioteer
An Indian Warrior

THIS youth is a *Charioteer* (PL. 48),[15] and more than that,
a victorious *Charioteer.* Yet he stands so restrained, so
dignified, so impersonal. Our eyes observe it all, easily
and clearly — the clean-cut contours of the compact mass;
the fine curves of the head; the firmly erect yet easy pose;
the contrasting outstretched arm; the crisp lights and
darks; the strong straight folds at the base swinging into
curves above the girdle, then wavering lightly as they rise
over the shoulders. The simplicity of the statue seems so
direct, the quiet strength so inevitable.

[15] *Charioteer.* Greek. The figure is one of a chariot group, and was discov-
ered (1896) at Delphi, in two pieces by a retaining wall covered with rubbish.
Only fragments of the other figures have been found. Height, 6 ft. 480–50 B.C.
Delphi Museum.

Upon the base runs the inscription, "Polyzalos dedicated me. Prosper him, O glorious Apollo." For the
statue was dedicated to Apollo and stood near his temple
at *Delphi*. At this shrine, in a wildly majestic gorge on
the side of Mt. Parnassus, the Greek sought advice of the
god of wisdom and held games and contests in his honor.
Rich gifts filled the sanctuary and statues without number
dotted the site. Fittingly the
place became known as *Bronze-
crowned Delphi*.

The *Charioteer* was one figure
of a group consisting of a four-
horse chariot, in which the victor
Gelon, tyrant of Syracuse, stood
with his *Charioteer;* possibly a
Victory held a crown over the
victor's head. The group, standing on a high terrace, could be
seen for a long distance against
the rugged cliffs and deep-blue

Fig. 82.   Coin of Syracuse
Showing a Victorious Charioteer.   Below the figure is a
set of armor, the prize in the
race.

sky or the low-lying clouds and rain.   Now the most popular sport of the Syracusans was chariot-racing; so popular,
in fact, that a victorious charioteer was used to decorate
their coins (Fig. 82) .   Hence it seems probable that Polyzalos, brother of Gelon, dedicated this group to commemorate one of his brother's victories in the race.   The moment represented is not the race itself, as on the coin, but
when the chariot had stopped or was driving slowly around
the arena after the race to receive the acclaims of the
crowd.

Because of the site in the open, in a diffused light, it was
essential that the statue carry clearly, that is, that it present
a mass which the eye could grasp easily, compact enough to

make a strong silhouette, yet loose enough to let the light, air, rain, or blue sky play into it to bring it into harmony with its environment. Detail, because of the dark color of the bronze and the distance, must be strongly accented. These are just the characteristics of our *Charioteer:* a compact, almost cylindrical form, highly simplified contours, with an effective variety in the outstretched arms, and detail sharp and strong.

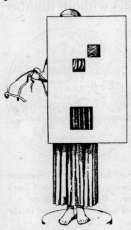

Fig. 83. A Finder to Isolate Details for Comparison.

Let us look a little more closely. The figure stands erect with weight balanced firmly on both feet. The deeply cut folds of his dress, holding deep shadow and catching the light along the ridges, emphasize the erectness of the figure. There is a slight turn of the torso and head, giving movement and vitality to the figure. The dress above the girdle is again deeply cut, with sharp edges and a curvature suggestive of the turn of the body. Over the shoulder and arm the cloth falls into many small irregular folds not as deeply cut, giving more rapid and more delicate play of light and shade. To see this variety in the folds comparatively, isolate each with a finder (Fig. 83). In the head also the sharp cutting of planes brings the features out clearly and emphasizes curves — in the brow and the nose, the lids, and the mouth — which repeat the curves of the brow, the fillet, and the contour of the head.

Is this a portrait, you ask? There is not enough individuality about it to suggest more than a generalization. But that was exactly what the Greek desired. He was in-

terested not so much in the individual as in the species.
So here it is the species of the chariot-driver, calm, poised,
with great capacity for alertness when called upon to be
alert, all the body and mind under complete control. That
is the characterization which the sculptor wanted to por-
tray. And how has he done it? Taking suggestions from
natural appearance, he has so organized the mass of the
figure that its proportions, its quiet unbroken contours, its
line, and its light and dark all harmoniously work together
to express the quality of restraint and quiet balance that
is his subject. Again it is form and idea, neither the one
nor the other predominant but the two inextricably fused.

Now let us turn for comparison to another group, in a
twentieth-century American city (PL. 49).[16] Although the
artist's conception of his subject is dramatic and his expression one of tense energy rather than of restraint, never-
theless the controlling principles have been the same. The
statue stands in a large open space; on one side, the expanse
of Lake Michigan stretching to the horizon; on the other,
a solid line of huge buildings with a busy thoroughfare
skirting its base. Standing now beneath clear blue skies,
now almost enveloped in mist, snow, or smoke, whether
seen against the open sky toward the lake or against the
wall of windows and the moving fringe of traffic, the group
presents a clear silhouette.

While the subject matter — a man and a horse, therefore
two bodies, two heads, two arms, six legs, a tail — makes
impossible as simple a mass contour as with the single
figure, yet how clear and unified is the entire space sug-

[16] *An Indian Warrior.* Ivan Meštrović, a contemporary sculptor of Yugoslavia.
The statue is one of a pair of mounted Indians made in Meštrović's studio in
Zagreb and cast there in a primitive way by the *cire-perdue* method (see p. 145
note 3). They were shipped in pieces and reassembled, 1929, in Grant Park,
Chicago, where they now stand.

gested! A rectangular volume controls the mass as sternly, though not as obviously, as the block of stone controls *Day* (PL. 41). At the same time the unity of the masses, from many points of view, is varied and coherent. From the side (PL. 49) the rider holds himself closely and firmly to the horse and draws the bow with the full strength of his sinewy arms. The omission of the bow is effective — the pose is perfectly intelligible without it and much more stimulating to the imagination — because it saves the group from distracting lines which would mar the unity of the design.

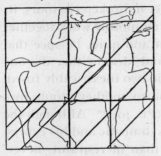

Fig. 84. Vertical, Horizontal, and Diagonal Lines of Organization in the Indian Warrior (PL. 49). Through these lines sweep great curves.

Note this unity in the silhouette (Fig. 84). The two figures interlock compactly because the square mass of the horse's head and mane fit into the angle formed by the erect body and the outstretched arm of the *Indian*. The silhouette fills a square whose vertical and horizontal lines are constantly repeated. What stability is given the group by the strong vertical that starts at the horse's ear, follows a muscle in the neck, and is taken up by the firmly placed left foreleg! Then across the pattern of squares play the strong diagonals of the *Indian's* taut arms and legs, continued and repeated by those of the horse, and by the strong curves of the horse's flank and tail. To bring variety into the design, the contrast is stressed between the smooth and the animated surfaces. The broad areas of the body of the horse contrast with the broken areas of the mane, tail, and feathered headdress. The muscles too create a vivacious

pattern. For this reason they seem exaggerated when seen at close range. But as with all detail in bronze, strong emphasis is necessary if it is to carry at a distance. Thus your eye is guided by these accented areas until you feel a rhythm that carries you throughout the group and holds you firmly there because of the strong contours of the dark mass.

Yet again we remember that the design is not a flat pattern but a group of volumes. The effective grouping is largely due to the fact that while the horse is in a direct frontal position, four-sided like *Khafre* (PL. 40), the rider, because he is pulling back upon the bowstring, presents his arms and torso in profile from the frontal view of the statue and in front view from the profile, thus creating a twisting movement similar to that of *Day*. This combination of two sculptural types creates the final impression. The dramatic intensity of the *Indian* is balanced by the greater poise of the horse. Yet the two are so unified that the total effect is one of controlled intensity of life and action. And this is the meaning and purpose of the statue — to commemorate the heroic days of the Middle West, when life was dramatic and tense but not uncontrolled.

READING

CASSON, S., Some Modern Sculptors, London, Oxford Press, 1920.
POULSEN, F., Delphi, London, Gyldendal, 1928.

Part Six

THE ART OF SCULPTURE IN RELIEF

SCULPTURE in relief lies between the three-dimensional and the two-dimensional arts and partakes of the characteristics of both. Like sculpture in the round, it has at least some mass, almost as much as the latter in high relief (PL. 50B), and a practically negligible amount in low relief (PLS. 51–52) where, like a painting, it only suggests depth. But whether high or low, it is always attached to a background and like a painting is seen from one point of view only.

The *Parthenon* again will illustrate. PL. 50B shows a metope (see PL. 7 and Fig. 22) in which a struggling *Centaur* and *Lapith* [1] furnish vigorous movement within a square area. Yet the figures are so fitted into the square that the contours repeat, with variations, its four sides; and notwithstanding their vigorous action, they move from side to side only (not forward and backward) and present to the eye large areas of almost unbroken surface, which emphasizes the frontal plane and the plane of the background. These two planes, like two parallel sheets of glass, determine the space occupied by figures. Nothing projects in front of or behind them. So clearly and definitely does the eye move from the front to the back that the mind easily grasps the suggestion of the space occupied by the figures and their orderly relationships within the space. Compare PL. 50A. [2] The crowded figures, moving in all directions, suggest no definite space and no harmonious unity; and the eyes soon weary of looking at them.

In low relief the controlling front and back planes are

---

[1] From the south side of the *Parthenon*. British Museum, London.
[2] *Roman Relief* of the late third century A.D. Terme Museum, Rome.

PLATE 49

An Indian Warrior. Ivan Meštrović. Intense energy controlled by a simple organization: two compactly grouped figures of dark bronze with a vivacious broken silhouette held sternly within a square. (Art Institute of Chicago)

PLATE 50

A. A Late Roman Relief. The figures are crowded confusedly into the space without organization (compare Pls. 50B and 51).

B. A Struggling Centaur and Lapith. Vigorous movement held sternly within a square and between two parallel planes (compare Pl. 49 and Fig. 84). The two figures are so posed in relation to each other and to the square space that they present large areas of unbroken surface parallel to the plane of the background and with the help of the shadow which the projections cast create an interesting pattern within the square. The ground was painted, probably red, thus emphasizing this pattern. (British Museum)

PLATE 51

Detail of the Parthenon Frieze. In distinction from Pl. 50A, in which the confusion, due to lack of any organization, becomes wearisome, this relief is clear, definite, and pleasurable because it is controlled by stern principles of organization. (British Museum)

PLATE 52

Grave Relief. Eric Gill. There is the same clarity here as in Pl. 51 due to the same practices in carving a relief from a slab of stone: two parallel planes of stone control the space, and movement is from side to side, not from front to back or vice versa (compare Pl. 50A).

very close together. In PL. 51 [3] see how convincingly you
feel the horses one behind the other. The eye moves from
a definite front plane by definite steps to a definite back
plane and you have no difficulty in understanding the
space, though your fingers, touching the stone, can find a
depth of but an inch or so. Notice again that the figures
are in profile and that the movement is from side to side.
How clearly and how pleasantly there are presented to the
eye several mounted youths of stone moving across the line
of vision! And how beautifully harmonized are the abstract idea of movement
and the concrete expres-
sion of a cavalcade! Seen
between the contrast-
ingly static columns (Fig.
85), now it becomes
rhythm only. You forget
the youths. Then, be-

Fig. 85. Parthenon Frieze Seen between the Columns.

cause you are a Greek, imaginatively, you remember them
again. For this is the great *Panathenaic Procession,* the
cavalcade in which Agathocles took part that August morning. So the idea of rhythm and the idea of the procession
and all that it means to a Greek are fused.

Look at the frieze a little more closely. The riders,
three and four deep, gallop along easily and naturally.
There appears to be ample space for them. Though there
is great variety in the movements of both the horses and
the men, they just fill the space from top to bottom,
whether they are standing or mounted, giving a level line
of heads at the top that produces a definitely felt rhythm.
Such an arrangement, of course, is not based upon natural

[3] A fragment from the *Parthenon Frieze* which ran around the top of the
temple wall inside the colonnade. Of Pentelic marble, 40 in. high. British
Museum, London.

proportions.   Perhaps the cavalcade is not as naturalistic
as we first thought.

Let us look further.   As everything is kept in profile,
except for an occasional turning of a youth toward a front
view, the broad expanse of the horses' bodies provides
large quiet areas in contrast to the breaking up of the space
below by the legs.   The horses' bellies form another horizontal to parallel that of the heads; and the hoofs that
touch the ground, another.   Verticals are felt frequently,

falling from head to
hand to hoof, while
through the resulting
angular pattern sweep
great curves (Fig. 86) .

You may say that
nature, not the artist,
provided this pattern.
To be sure nature pro-
vided the elements —
heads, bodies, arms, legs
— but it was the artist

Fig. 86.   Line Organization of a Section
of the Parthenon Frieze (PL. 51).

who organized them into something that our eyes delight
to see just as our ears delight to hear the tones that some
musician has organized into harmony.   Compare this with
any photograph of moving mounted horsemen taken in
profile.   Do you find that the figures organize into a pattern of repeated horizontals, verticals, and curves?   Herein
lies the difference between nature and art.

We see the same clarity of expression, due to the same
handling of stone, in a relief by Eric Gill (PL. 52) ,[4] the
artist who said that " the sculptor's job is making out of
stone things seen in the mind."   Here again we find the

---

[4] *Gravestone.*   Of Portland stone, 4 ft. high.   1928 A.D.

feeling of two definite planes, the front and the back, with movement from the central figure to the side and from the side to the center but never from front to back. See how skillfully these two directions of movement unite in the central figure. The head, the outstretched arms, and some of the lines of the drapery carry to the right, while most of the drapery lines and the sharply bent knee carry to the left. How clearly does a thin slab of stone, without losing its identity, convey to us what the artist sees, feels, and thinks!

READING

Brown, G. B., The Fine Arts, London, Murray, 1916.
A Short Guide to the Sculptures of the Parthenon, London, British Museum, 1925.

SUGGESTIONS

1. Make a detailed study of the sculpture of the *Parthenon* as architectural design, showing why the sculpture in the round in the pediments, the high relief on the metopes, and the low relief of the frieze are each architecturally right in its own place.

2. Find photographs of processions of mounted horsemen to compare with Pl. 54 A.

3. Adapt the suggestion given under sculpture in the round (p. 150) to sculpture in relief.

4. As the examples in this chapter are confined to stone relief, it would be well to compare with them examples in bronze and to note the same differences that we found between stone and bronze sculpture in the round. The doors of the *Baptistery* in Florence (Pl. 21) offer a good point of departure. Find also examples in wood.

Part Seven

THE ART OF PAINTING

Should any one ask you which of the arts you enjoyed the most, would you answer music and painting? The majority of people probably would; music, they say, because of its rhythm and painting because of its color. Yet many paintings of the highest quality, such as the *Chinese* (PLS. 59 and 72), have been painted in monochrome, that is, with one color only: black, white, and the intermediate grays. Color, in fact, is but one element or means of expression in the hands of the painter.

Other means are line, and light and dark. He has no mass to organize, as the builder and the sculptor have; only a flat surface — wall, canvas, wood, silk, paper — that has two dimensions, height and width. But a painter can create an illusion of depth which often seems very real. In PL. 71, for example, you walk a long way before you reach the farthest house and the poplar tree.

With these means, then — line, light and dark, and color — he creates forms and space, and organizes them into a coherent design, all on a flat surface. Is not painting then more limited than the other arts? On the contrary, it is much more flexible, with capacity for greater range of subject matter and of expression. A painter can successfully represent or suggest movement that goes on indefinitely, like wind in the bamboo (PL. 59) and flowing water (PLS. 72 and 73); a builder or sculptor can only represent, successfully, arrested movement. For the painter this is both an advantage and a disadvantage. For while it gives him a much wider range of expression and appeal, at the same time there is danger of its degrading into mere copying of nature.

To continue our comparison of painting with architecture and sculpture, does painting impose upon the artist
a definite site and a definite function? It would seem as
if these limitations hardly existed when we wander past
miles of museum walls covered with paintings. But here
also we must recall the fact that many pictures, like statues,
have been torn from their original homes and are now in
an artificial setting. Their stories have been both romantic and tragic, stories not only of the older pictures but of
such recent work as that of Cézanne or Van Gogh. Great
altarpieces have been taken apart and tossed aside when
a whim of style banished them, one part finding its way
to one collection in one city and another into a museum
in another city. Most have been repainted or revarnished.
They have suffered from dampness, lain forgotten in cellars
and attics collecting dust and grime; they have been
scoured with destructive cleansers, made over to serve a
new master, inscribed with well-known signatures to trap
a collector. Series of frescoes have been whitewashed —
fortunately, for whitewash is an excellent preservative —
but when later discovered beneath it, have been ruined by
the " restoration " of a tenth-rate painter. Many a painting has passed from hand to hand until with a sudden turn
in popularity it finds a resting-place in a wrong environment, in company with other works of art suffering from
the same fate. But when we have traced the life story back
to its beginning, again we often find that a definite function and especially a definite location limited the artist and
that the picture is successful not in spite of that limitation,
but because of the harmony between the limitation and
what the artist wished to express.

Once more to make a comparison, painting like all the
arts is a craft and subject to the principles of the craft. It

is one of the oldest in the world. The earliest cave paintings were made before man learned to build for himself.
Yet from the time of these to this very day, in all the continents of the globe, the painter has created form with
the same means — lines, light and dark, and color on a flat
surface; sometimes with one only, as with line; or with
varying combinations.

Line. It sounds like a commonplace. Yet how many
kinds of line there are and how many things you can do
with it! Of itself it may be delicate or virile, firm or
wavering, broken or unbroken, flowing or angular. This
may be the result partly of the instrument. A very delicate
and sensitive line can be made with the *silver point,* a
silver pencil that must be used on specially prepared paper;
or by a fine brush; or by pen and ink. Then there is
heavier ink, there are pencils of all grades of hardness and
softness, brushes of all widths and pliability, the bold red
and black chalk, and the brush of the Oriental, which has
a possible range from the most delicate hair line to that
of the greatest strength. Again, line, whatever its quality,
may be straight, curved, or zigzag; horizontal, vertical,
cutting across on a diagonal. Each has a significance.
The vertical suggests uplift, majesty; the horizontal, repose,
quietude; the diagonal, movement, so that it is very dynamic; the curve also suggests movement, but a movement
of suavity or grace. Whatever its direction, the line may
be interrupted in its movement, visible here, lost there,
picked up farther on; or it may be strongly felt but quite
invisible. It may combine with other lines in an infinite
number of ways.

Light and dark differentiate the parts of the design more
clearly than can line alone. Compare the drawing of *Botticelli* (PL. 58) with the *Persian Miniature* (PL. 64) as an

illustration. In the latter the figures stand out more emphatically because each is an area of color. Some colors are much darker than others. For example, yellow is light; blue, intermediate; and red, dark. Or the tints and shades of one hue alone produce an effect of light and dark, as we see in many textiles and wall papers. When there is natural illumination of the objects in the picture, from the sun or from any artificial source of light, then we have light and shadow that give an effect of roundness and depth (PL. 67).

Color is one of the most effective and varied means of expression. Its power is partly physiological. We are all familiar with the feeling of cheerfulness aroused by yellow; that of quietude, by blue; and that of excitement, by red. Because of this physical response, as well as from association of color with nature — such as the white and yellow of light and of the sun, the blue of the sky, the green of foliage, the reds and yellows of fire — colors have taken on meaning. Yellow, for example, symbolizes the sun god; blue, heavenly love, truth, and fidelity; red, ardent love, fervor, and passion. The power of color is also partly due to its inherent characteristics. Some colors are warm, like red and yellow; some are cool, like the blue and the blue-green. Some appear to advance, like red; some retreat, like blue (see page 90). So it is the problem of the painter to study each color both in itself and in its relation to the other colors, and then to decide which harmonies, which contrasts, which discords, will convey most exactly the feeling that he wishes to express.

We have been talking of the elements with which the painter works — line, light and dark, and color on a flat surface. But back of this we may go and ask where he gets his colors and how he fixes them permanently on the flat

surface. It is only recently that the painter has been able to purchase color put up in tubes and pans ready for use. Heretofore he bought the raw pigment — the Italian painters at the apothecary's shop — and ground and mixed it for himself. Pigments come from earth, from vegetable and mineral products, or are made artificially. The earth supplies some reds, yellow, browns, in soil stained by iron, from which the color is obtained by grinding and washing. Copper is one source for greens and blues. Lapis lazuli produces, by a long, tedious process, a much-treasured ultramarine blue. Scarlet or vermilion is secured from cinnabar, an ore, or made artificially. Blacks are based upon carbon, obtained by burning twigs, bone, fats, and other substances. Thus many forms of nature as well as man's ingenuity are called upon to provide the raw materials of color.

Having obtained his pigments in dry powdered form, how is the painter able to render them sufficiently fluid to be handled with his brushes and at the same time to adhere to the surface permanently? That is our second question. There are several ways, quite different both in method and in effect. Those that we shall discuss are *fresco, tempera, oil,* and *water color.*

Fresco is very old and almost universal. Its name most appropriately suggests the process: *a fresco,* the original Italian form, meaning " on the fresh " (plaster) , that is, painting on moist plaster with color mixed with water. The color does not sink deep into the plaster but remains close to the surface, of which it becomes a part by chemical action, permanent and inseparable, surviving with the wall, and destroyed with the wall.

Let us watch Michelangelo paint a figure in fresco on

PLATE 53

Madonna and Child. Detail from an unfinished Adoration of the Magi.
Leonardo da Vinci. The figure of the Madonna is sketched on the white
ground; that of the Child is modelled in light and shade and is ready for the
local color. Yet notice that all the grace and charm of the Madonna that
Leonardo wished to express is already complete in the preliminary work.
To him it may well have been complete.

PLATE 54

Head of the Delphic Sibyl. Michelangelo. Great simplification of form;
free bold brushwork. Fresco.

PLATE 55

Head of a Lady. Florentine, artist uncertain. Fine brushstrokes, sharp contours, generally flat and decorative. Tempera.

PLATE 56

B. Sunflowers, Detail. Vincent van Gogh. Short vigorous brushstrokes of thick pigment give a vibrating texture to the surface. Direct oil.

A. Cyclamen, Detail. Charles Demuth. The white paper left untouched by the paint forms the petals of the flowers about which are built up, in water color, the leaves and stems. (Art Institute of Chicago)

the ceiling of the *Sistine Chapel*.[1] It is very early in the morning. The chapel with its lofty scaffolding resounds with rapid steps and cheery voices, for yesterday word came that today the master would begin the *Delphic Sibyl* (PL. 54), starting with the head; and by the time he appears everything must be ready for him to take up his brushes. From his drawings the apprentices know the exact location of this head and already have laid the final coat of fine plaster about an inch thick so that it will dry just enough to stand the master's test — a slight impress of his finger. Some of the younger boys are mixing the colors; others are climbing the scaffolding with brushes and pots of freshly mixed paint. The oldest has the master's drawing of the head, the main lines of which he is tracing on the moist wall. All is ready as the master appears at the door. Climbing the scaffolding, he looks about him with a critical eye, tests the plaster, tries a bit of color. Comparing the tracing with the drawing, he makes a few changes. For painting on wet plaster is done so swiftly and so surely that it must be carefully thought out in advance and a preliminary drawing made in detail. Then, dipping his brushes into the pots, with broad bold strokes he models the features, the folds of the headdress, the hair. He must be sure of himself, for once the color has been laid on it can be neither removed nor changed; and he goes over any part of the work twice only if the plaster is still wet. Hour after hour he works, sometimes sprinkling the surface if it appears to be drying too quickly. He has but a limited number of hues, for not all colors can withstand the effects of the lime. Finally the day's work is done. The head is finished, a good day's work,

[1] *Delphic Sibyl*. Vatican City. 1508–12 A.D.

for the figure is to be of colossal size. Along the joining of the neck and the dress he leaves a mark where an inconspicuous joining of plaster can be made for the next day's work.

When he sees the work dry, the next day, he may wish to make a few changes. He may add a detail or darken a shadow *a secco,* that is, " on the dry " (plaster) with paint mixed with gum or egg. But he knows that it will look hard, lack the freedom of the true fresco, and also be likely to peel off. Hence rarely did such a craftsman as Michelangelo resort to retouching. His work must stand as he did it first. Hence the difficulty of the technique. Yet how he gloried in it! For it was the mark of the real master to work successfully in fresco. Its requirement of rapid work results in a large boldness, directness, and spontaneity; and its restrictions of color, in a softened and rather even tonality, so that in the hands of a genuine artist it is one of the most successful wall decorations, especially since it can be carried out on a large scale. Since it is of the same material and texture as the wall, one might say it really is the wall, made pleasing by having its surface broken into harmonious and contrasting masses.

Tempera (PLS. 55 [2] and 65) means painting on a wooden panel with color mixed with some material to make it adhere firmly, such as gum, honey, or egg, diluted with water. To a panel of seasoned wood is glued linen over which are applied coat after coat of *gesso* (plaster of Paris mixed with glue or size). Each coat is smoothed and polished until the final surface has a finish like ivory. The design may be drawn first on paper and then transferred, as in fresco, or directly upon the gesso. If the background

---

[2] *Florentine School*, about 1460 A.D. Poldi Pezzoli Museum, Milan. Color reproduction, Medici Society of America, Boston.

or any details are to be gold, this is put in first and burnished. Then begins the underpainting, that is, the lights and darks are painted in a green or brown (PL. 53) .[3] Over this are laid many coats of local color — the blue of the sky, the greens of the trees, the reds, blues, yellows, and greens of garments, the flesh-colors. The paint is applied in fine, close brush strokes, and dries so quickly that it is impossible to fuse the strokes or to alter them. Deep tones and dark shadows are difficult to secure because they must be built up by many coats and by *hatching* — that is, by close parallel strokes. Finally it is varnished, except on the gold parts, and put in the sun to dry. It is obvious that tempera cannot be used on large-scale paintings, as can fresco. Yet it is very decorative, for the small clean-cut brush strokes create precise, rather sharp contours. The forms are slightly modeled, with no deep shadows and no violent contrasts, creating a rather flat pattern and a smooth enamel-like surface. The color is more limpid than intense. The light, penetrating the translucent coats, is reflected by the gesso and underpainting, creating the impression of depth and luminosity that harmonizes so well with the gold. Tempera is a precise, painstaking method, with great capacity for the expression of restrained feeling.

The disadvantages of tempera — the tedium of execution, too quick drying, difficulty in blending colors and in fusing light and dark — led painters to experiment with some more flexible vehicle in which to mix the pigment, something that would dry hard, but not too quickly, would blend and fuse, and would protect the painting from harmful effects of moisture. Out of this experimentation has

[3] Leonardo da Vinci was commissioned to paint this altarpiece in 1480 A.D. but never carried it beyond the underpainting. Entire panel, about 6 ft. square. Uffizi, Florence.

grown the *oil* technique. Though there are many kinds of oil painting, they may be roughly classified as *indirect* and *direct*. The *indirect* is closer to the tempera, for its initial stages are the same. The design is worked out in detail and the figures are modeled in light and dark in an underpainting of brown, red, or green, usually opaque, which forms a solid ground. Over this are superposed many thin layers of local color made by mixing the pigment with oil until it is quite fluid. Some of these layers are transparent or translucent (*glazes*) ; and the light, penetrating them and reflected by the solid ground, produces an effect of inner radiance. Others are opaque. Thus the surface carries contrasting effects. With each coat the picture is thoroughly dried and bleached in the sunshine so as to extract all superfluous oil, which in time would yellow the painting.[4]

In *direct* painting the surface alone carries the effect, for the pigment is mostly opaque. There is little or no underpainting and the composition is sketched in lightly. The color is not added after the light and dark, as in the indirect method, but along with it. The brush stroke is important, for much of the effect depends upon surface beauty. The paint may be very thin, showing the texture of the canvas, or thick enough to cover it solidly, or so thick and rough that it catches the light and casts shadow as in a low relief. In the *Sunflowers* by Van Gogh, for example (PL. 56A) ,[5] the pigment is so thick that it creates a vibrating surface which combined with the intensity of the yellow produces a powerfully emotional effect. In

[4] Early works of Titian illustrate this method; fifteenth century Flemish paintings are among the best examples. See H. Gardner, *Art Through the Ages*, N. Y., Harcourt, 1926, Chap. XX.

[5] Vincent Van Gogh, a Hollander, 1853–90 A.D., lived chiefly in France. Small color reproduction, Artext Prints, Westport, Conn.; large, The Arts Publishing Corporation, 232 East 54th St., N. Y.

PLATE 57

Monkey Pursued by a Hare and a Frog. Toba Sojo. A maximum of life and spontaneity expressed with the slightest means, line alone.

PLATE 58

Dante and Vergil in Purgatory. Botticelli. An illustration for a Dante which indicates, by line alone, the very essence of what is represented — flames, people, cliffs — and at the same time presents a form that harmonizes with the written text and is beautifully decorative.

addition, the heavy pigment suggests the coarse texture of the plant, so that the reality of the *Sunflowers* is felt more keenly because of this surface quality. How Van Gogh, merely by the way he uses his pigment, glorifies the flowers of the sun!

Thus the oil technique offers the painter a wide range of possibilities and, especially in the indirect method, a freedom in handling that is suitable for a quick impression. The process has inherent in its very nature a capacity for force, impetuosity, or vagueness in contrast to the clear-cut, restrained, and painstaking tempera.

In *water color* painting the pigment is mixed with water, as in fresco, and applied to paper. The paint may be transparent, allowing the white ground of the paper to show through, or the paper may be left uncovered in patches to furnish the light (PL. 56A).[6] The paper may be tinted, thus giving a dominant hue to the picture, or it may be very rough, causing some of the liquid pigment to sink into the hollows and leave the projections white, thus securing a vibrating, almost sparkling surface when the artist needs such an effect. One wash, like a shadow, may be carried over another, though very little repainting is possible. For water color, like fresco, depends for its effect upon its freshness and spontaneity. A faint pencil sketch is usually made as a guide to the brush. The color is then washed over the paper, suggesting what is represented but giving little detail. Perhaps in no other medium can the painter gain such an effect of exquisitely delicate tones, and of ephemeral types of expression. The pigment may also be opaque, or *body color,* as it is sometimes called. The colors are mixed with opaque white, which furnishes the

[6] Charles Demuth, a contemporary American painter. Birch-Bartlett Collection, Art Institute of Chicago.

light instead of the white paper. Sometimes the transparent and the opaque colors are used side by side to obtain a vibrating surface, just as transparent and opaque layers are used in oil painting; as translucent and half-opaque streakings are used in Gothic glass; varying tones of a single hue in the ground of Persian carpets; the playing of a theme by several differently pitched instruments in a symphony.

Each of these methods of placing the lines, lights and darks, and colors on the flat surface — fresco, tempera, indirect and direct oil, water color — is a craft in itself, with its own advantages and limitations. By each method paintings of the highest quality have been produced. But quality, which is the mark of a great painting and without which no painting is great, is not dependent upon craftsmanship alone. For hand in hand with craftsmanship go sensitive vision, emotion, imagination, and intelligence.

READING ON THE TECHNIQUE OF PAINTING

BLAKE, V., Art and Craft of Drawing, London, Oxford University Press, 1927.

HOLMES, C. J., Notes on the Science of Picture-Making, London, Chatto, 1920.

LAURIE, A. P., Materials of the Painter's Craft, London, Foulis, 1910.

SPEED, H., Science and Practice of Oil Painting, London, Chapman and Hall, 1924.

SUGGESTIONS

1. Line. Find drawings or paintings to illustrate different kinds of line: delicate or strong, broken or unbroken, firm or wavering. Note in each case the instrument used. Experiment in making different kinds of line with pencil, pen, brush, charcoal, crayon.

2. Line direction and combination. Find examples of drawings or paintings to illustrate a predominance of vertical,

horizontal, straight, curved, or diagonal line; and varying combinations of these. R. Pearson, *How to Look at Modern Pictures,* N. Y., Dial Press, 1925, will prove helpful here.

3. Light and dark and light and shade. Make drawings or paintings to illustrate the difference. Textiles may be used for the former. See C. Pearce, *Composition,* N. Y., Scribner, 1927; J. Littlejohns, *How to Enjoy Pictures,* London, Black, 1927.

4. Color. For many suggestions on understanding color, see W. Sargent, *The Use and Enjoyment of Color,* N. Y., Scribner, 1923; and A. H. Munsell, *A Color Notation,* Boston, Munsell Color Co., 1919.

5. Find examples of fresco, tempera, oil, and water color. Find originals if possible or the best prints obtainable to illustrate differences in effect. Experiment in the actual use of these techniques. Select simple, perhaps abstract, compositions and carry them out in as many ways as possible. Fresco and tempera offer the greatest obstacles but these are not entirely insurmountable.

SOME MASTERS OF LINE

A Hare Pursuing a Monkey
An Illustration of Dante   Bamboo in the Wind

To use line alone! What can one accomplish with this slender means? Look at PL. 57. What an epitome of ferocity in the *Hare!* Aroused to righteous indignation, he pursues a whimpering *Monkey* with a zeal that is equaled by that of the frog who croaks in anger at some injury to his dignity.[7] The picture is a spontaneous expression of a living reality (not an imitation of what is represented to the eye) by means of line alone. This line is now strong and assertive, now so delicate that the brush seems to have touched the paper but lightly. Though

[7] The meaning, though uncertain, appears to be a satire on certain practices of the Buddhist priests and pilgrims. It was painted by Toba Sojo, who, as the name implies, was a Buddhist bishop of Toba, a city south of Kyoto, Japan. He lived 1053–1140 A.D.

broken, it creates a form, as in the *Hare,* as powerful as it is terse and stimulating to the imagination in aiding the eye. In the landscape too, a wavy line suggests a hilly country, and a few delicately graded strokes suggest a bunch of grass. By means of line alone everything takes its place in relation to everything else and the mind is so free from distraction by details and by an illusion of nature that it is ready to grasp the significance of the forms.

A similar accomplishment we see in a drawing by *Botticelli* (PL. 58) [8] to illustrate a passage in *Dante's Divine Comedy* (Purgatory xxv–vi). *Dante* and his two friends are skirting a narrow ledge bordering the flames; Dante stops in the center to converse; at the left the friends move away. A few delicate lines suggest precipitous cliffs above and below; between, flames leap, writhe, and lightly vanish into the air as the line sweeps upward, now heavy, now light, now lost, again caught and tossed upward. The impression of these lines — a swirling, rhythmic movement — is the essence of fire. To create a form which suggests the essence both of the flames and of the confining cliffs, was the purpose of Botticelli — not to give an illusion of their appearance.

Depth too is suggested rather than presented to the eye. The fact that the figures are drawn in front of or in the flames hints at their places in space, while the lightness of the lines in the upper cliffs, in comparison with the strength of the lines in the flames, gives a definite feeling of distance. This suggestion instead of illusion of depth keeps the surface comparatively flat and thus contributes to a decora-

[8] Sandro Botticelli, an Italian painter, 1444–1510 A D. The set of drawings from which Pl. 61B is taken were made in silver point and pen and ink, about 1492–97, for a finely written copy of Dante which was never completed.

tive effect. The uniform ground is broken by line alone
(compare PLS. 60–62) into three horizontal bands. The
strong central band of darting flame is given ample space;
both above and below the lightly broken areas of cliffs
and the delicate quality of their contours set off the contrasting strength and movement of the fire. At the sides
the curving lines terminate naturally and unobtrusively
parallel to the outer edge. Within the band the flames
envelop the figures, here encircling a head or radiating
from it, there flowing into the curve of a leg or an arm.
The figures of *Dante* and his friends connect the flame
band with the band of the cliffs below; the irregular line
of the flame tips connects it with that above. Thus all elements tie together into a decorative pattern. This was one
of Botticelli's objectives. For the drawing was to be an
illustration for a written book, where decorative beauty
in harmony with the text was essential.

To find other great masters of line, let us return to the
Far East — to China. Chinese painting, with brush and
Chinese ink, is a technique peculiar to the East. The ink
is a black pigment, sometimes glossy and sometimes dull,
made from soot and molded into cakes. When the painter
needs some pigment he moistens his cake and rubs it on a
stone until he has a semiliquid. The brushes are made of
the hair of various animals — rabbit, deer, fox, squirrel,
rat's nose — and are of varying length, pliability, and
strength. By understanding thoroughly how to use his
brushes and his pigment, the artist can obtain a range of
tones from richest black to softest gray. The pigment is
applied to paper or silk attached to a frame by rice mucilage
and sized. The artist paints directly upon it, sometimes
with a preliminary sketch for a guide and sometimes with a
slight sketch placed beneath. Seated on the floor, usually,

with his work spread out before him and his brush held vertically in his fist, he paints with his entire arm, guiding its movement by the shoulder as well as by the wrist. He must have his design thoroughly in mind and be very sure of his hand, for once he has placed a stroke on the silk it has become indelible and repainting would mean ruin. Such technique requires long years of training, at least ten or fifteen years for any skill at all.

Skill, however, to the mind of the Oriental is not more important than the attitude of the artist to his work. His whole being must be permeated with the spirit of what he is painting. If it is a tiger, every stroke must reveal the ferocity of that animal. To paint a tiger you must be a tiger. This, to be sure, is more or less true of all artists. Significant works of art are such because the artist has himself lived his own creation. But few peoples have so insistently emphasized the principle as have the Orientals. The following story illustrates this:

It is related of Chinanpin, the great Chinese painter, that an art student having applied to him for instruction, he painted an orchid plant and told the student to copy it. The student did so to his own satisfaction, but the master told him he was far away from what was most essential. Again and again, during several months, the orchid was reproduced, each time an improvement on the previous effort, but never meeting with the master's approval. Finally Chinanpin explained as follows: The long, blade-like leaves of the orchid may droop toward the earth but they all long to point to the sky, and this tendency is called cloud-longing in art. When, therefore, the tip of the long slender leaf is reached by the brush the artist must feel that the same is longing to point to the clouds. Thus, painted, the true spirit and living force of the plant are preserved.[9]

[9] Bowie, *On the Laws of Japanese Painting*, p. 36.

The Oriental technique is wonderfully fitted to convey this sensitive feeling. Take, for an example, a painting of *Bamboo* (PL. 59).[10] The plant is alive, tossing in the wind. The jointed stalk is firm but flexible and the pointed leaves rustle merrily as the wind sweeps in from the left. Each leaf has been painted by one stroke of the brush, broad at the base and tapering to a fine point at the tip. Some of the leaves are near us. These are the darkest, with crisp edges. Others, farther away, are less distinct. The place of each is suggested in space by a gradation in the tone of the ink.

The plant fills the left side and top of the space, leaving an unoccupied area on the right which contains the balancing inscription. This writing is done with the same materials as the painting, producing the same quality and gradation of the brush stroke, thus bringing the same kind of harmony into the painting that Botticelli's drawing does into the book. And just as Botticelli's drawing gave us an impression of the essence of fire, so this Chinese painting gives us not so much a picture of the bamboo as a feeling of it. How little detail is shown either in the stalk or in the leaves! Yet how alive is the plant and with what refreshing gusts the wind sweeps across the paper!

READING

BINYON, R. L., Flight of the Dragon, London, Murray, 1922.
—— Painting in the Far East, N. Y., Longmans, 1923.
BOWIE, H. P., On the Laws of Japanese Painting, San Francisco, Elder, 1911.
TAKI, S., Three Essays on Oriental Painting, London, Quaritch, 1910.

[10] The inscription includes the signature of the artist, "Wu Chên Chung-kuei of Chia-hsing writes and paints." The seals express the approval of those who have judged the quality of the painting. Yüan dynasty (1271–1367 A.D.). Boston Museum.

SOME MASTERS OF LINE AND COLOR

An Egyptian Tomb Painting   The Harlequin
A Persian Miniature   A Madonna of Siena

THE cliffs overlooking the valley of the Nile (Fig. 24) seem to be dotted with dark patches, which on close inspection prove to be openings into rock-cut chambers. Let us go into one of them (PL. 60).[11] What a charming, vivacious room! An unexpected surprise. The gayest color, chiefly red and blue, with some green and yellow, against the plastered wall; an orderly arrangement of these masses of color in more or less horizontal bands with a bright blue and red border at the top and gay zigzags across the ceiling. A second look shows that many of these color masses are figures which are formed by line, as in PL. 61; but the areas formed by the lines are filled with color producing light and dark, which is really difference of color.[12]

Look at them a little more closely. Notwithstanding the curious method of drawing the figures, there is a liveliness and a feeling of reality about them. A banquet is taking place on the opposite wall (PL. 61, not visible in PL. 60). In the upper zone a group of girls are enjoying gifts of fruit and flowers while a little maid adjusts their earrings. The fat blind harper thrums away at the strings, while below a flute-player and a harpist furnish music for the dancer whose supple body moves to the rhythm. Just out of

[11] The *Tomb of Nakht and Tawi*, in the western cliffs of the Nile at Thebes (Fig. 24). About 1425 B.C. Reproductions in color, including details of Pls. 60 and 61, in N. deG. Davies, *The Tomb of Nakht at Thebes*, N. Y., Metropolitan Museum, 1917. A few of the color plates of this volume can be purchased from the museum. (See also color prints of similar paintings obtainable from the Metropolitan Museum and from the Oriental Institute of the University of Chicago).

[12] One needs to keep in mind that often what appears to be light and dark in black and white reproductions is really but a color difference in the original.

PLATE 59

Bamboo in the Wind. Chinese. The reality of the plant life is expressed with a few skillful brushstrokes. (Boston Museum)

PLATE 60

The Tomb of Nakht and Tawi. Egypt. The gay color, the pattern of the figures against the plaster wall, and the zonal arrangement are very decorative. (Metropolitan Museum)

range of our illustration are a man and a woman seated, looking at the scene, while a pet cat beneath her mistress's chair is devouring a fish, her part of the feast. The entire scene is vivacious and convincingly real.

Can this really be a tomb? Those who know say that it is a room in the tomb of the scribe *Nakht* and his wife *Tawi,* a singer in the temple of Amon, as were all ladies of rank. These were average Egyptians socially, intellectually, economically. Hence their tomb would be much more elaborate than that of a peasant, and equally less pretentious than that of a king.

But why is such a scene found in a tomb? Through all social classes in Egypt ran a vivid belief in a future life that lay in the Far West. " To the West! To the West! the land of pleasant life where all that thou lovest is, the fair West who opens her arms to thee that thou mayest rest." For this life the body must be preserved and must be provided not only with necessities and comforts but also with pastimes and luxuries. This could be done if the processes of procuring food, and also scenes of hunting and feasting, were painted in the tomb and magic said over them. The result was that on the walls of the tombs the Egyptian spread a vivid picture of the everyday life that he wished to carry with him into the West. Thus the paintings served a definite function as well as a decorative purpose.

The tomb was chiseled out of the solid limestone cliff and, when the wall was uneven, covered with mud and plaster to give a sufficiently smooth surface for painting. The Egyptian painter was a craftsman who worked very much as did his fellow craftsmen, painting what his patron ordered from the traditional subjects that every one used, but with freedom in detail to make his work vivacious and

convincing, if he was really an artist, rather than dull and stereotyped. He had no shop from which he could buy his pigments already prepared. His blues and greens he secured from copper, yellows he found in the earth, soil stained by iron; red, from cinnabar or soils; black, from burned vegetable or animal matter. From the reeds that grew so plentifully along the banks of the Nile he made his brushes; and from the Acacia tree he obtained the gum arabic with which he mixed his pigment so that it would adhere to the wall. This painting is not true fresco, but painting on a dry wall, either stone or plaster. Hence some binding material must be used, as in tempera painting. For this he sometimes used egg or glue instead of gum arabic. This method of getting color on the wall was the very thing that the Italian painters like Michelangelo avoided — and rightly so. For the dampness of Italy would soon loosen the binding medium and make the color flake off, while the perfect dryness of the Egyptian climate made the method very practical.

On the end wall of the room (PL. 60) the formality of the scheme is due to the fact that here at the door — not a real door but one in facsimile — the spirit comes to receive the offerings brought by the kneeling figures and heaped up in a great pile beneath — bread, wine, meat, fruits, lotus. The entire wall space forms a beautiful scheme of decoration harmonizing in its symmetrical balance and its quiet rhythm with the ceremonial that it represents. On the side walls there is more freedom. Here *Nakht* and *Tawi,* large in size because of their social rank, are pouring oil of incense over the offering which they are making to the sun god, a scene indicative of their piety. Round about, the slaves are harrowing, threshing, storing the grain, and preparing the meat. On this wall is represented

the provision of food both for sustenance and for sacrifice, while on the opposite is the provision of pleasure, the *Banquet Scene* with music and dancing.

The entire scheme of decoration is one of horizontal zones, four, broken in places by the large figures. This zonal arrangement is partly decorative but is also the Egyptian way of expressing depth on a flat surface. The four kneeling figures beside the door, for instance, one above the other, convey to the mind of the Egyptian the idea of one being behind the other, all on one level; the door itself, shown above the pile of offerings, suggests to him the fact that it is behind them. Notice how each figure stands out clearly by itself, with very little overlapping. All are essentially in profile. No one faces you exactly. Part of the body may, but never the head.

Look again at the group of girls in the upper zone. They are wearing thin orange-yellow dresses, broad collar necklaces of beads, bracelets, and large earrings. Their wigs — all Egyptians of rank wore wigs — are held by bright bands. Some have wound lotus blossoms in their wigs; others hold and smell them. You soon notice, in these figures as well as in the standing musicians below, a great similarity — a lack of such differences as always occur in a group of people — and a peculiar method of drawing the figure. The Egyptian, though observant of nature, appears to have little concern about what the figure really looked like to the eye. He had worked out a way of drawing it that illustrated what he thought and knew about it. It consisted of a trunk whose most conspicuous view was the front, showing both shoulders and arms; of legs whose function of carrying the body was most clearly expressed in profile; and of a head whose most arresting aspect was the profile except for the eye, whose front view he saw and

remembered best. Thus he selected the most emphatic aspect of each part of the body and put them all together to form a pattern that meant the human figure. Every one used this pattern but with infinite variations in detail. He could make the pattern stand, sit, run, do anything that the human figure can do. So after we become somewhat accustomed to this pattern, we can enjoy it as much as a more naturalistic appearance. An impromptu dance of *Street Boys,* for example (Fig. 87), who are happy over a

favor bestowed by the king upon some friend, shows what spontaneity can be given a figure drawn in this conventional way. This little scene also illustrates the expression of depth. Three of the boys are above the lower four, each on a line to indicate something for him to stand upon. What the painter means is that all

Fig. 87. An Impromptu Street Dance. (Metropolitan Museum)

seven form a group together upon one level. But not knowing how to do this, he naïvely puts three above, so that all seven are clearly seen. Occasionally we find the Egyptian painter approximating a consistent profile; correct, we say, according to what the eye sees. The harper in the upper zone in PL. 61 and the little maid are examples. But he preferred to use the conventional pattern.

That such a conventional method of drawing the figure can lead to something stereotyped and dead we can also

see in the *Banquet Scene*. The three seated men in the middle zone, exactly alike, are copied mechanically from a stock pattern with no vitality, while the girls above and the musicians below, though drawn in the same conventional way, are full of life.

For comparison, let us look at Picasso's *Harlequin* (PL. 62).[13] Are there any similarities between the Egyptian and the twentieth-century painting? A *Harlequin,* in his costume of entertainer at the comedy, turns pensively from the table at which he is sitting. Is that your first impression? Or does your eye see first a rectangular area of strongly contrasted light and dark masses, through which it is guided by strong rhythms? The painting is just like a building in the exact way in which these masses fit together to construct a balanced, coherent whole. Though each part is clearly defined, still no part exists for itself or could be moved or taken away, any more than columns could be taken away from the *Parthenon* or an arch from *Chartres*.

The means which Picasso used to secure this coherence are the same as those of the Egyptian — line, and areas of light and dark which are areas of light and dark color. As there is no illumination, there is no shadow, and no attempt at producing an illusion of depth. Everything is kept flat. The light and dark masses are sharply separated, and are contrastingly broken and unbroken. The main masses are the head and the ruff, largely unbroken; the costume, broken by the checker pattern; the table, unbroken except for the match box; the ground behind the figure, unbroken except for the vivacious panel at the top.

[13] Pablo Picasso, a painter of Spanish birth (1881 —), usually associated with the French school. The *Harlequin* is from the collection of the late John Quinn of New York. A reproduction in color will be found in the Encyclopædia Britannica, 13th ed., in the article "Painting."

But it is not a matter only of light and dark color masses, broken or unbroken. Fundamental motifs control their shapes. Just as a musician interweaves melodies (tone motifs) with variations into a composition, so Picasso interweaves shape motifs (unit shapes) with variations into this painting — the circle and the triangle. The circle he

Fig. 88. Organizing Curves in the Harlequin (PL. 62). Horizontals are found in the background; verticals and horizontals in the checker pattern of the dress.

suggests in the head, the ear, the flowers, the table, the match box; the triangle, in the ruffs in rapid repetition, in the angle of the arm and the body and of the arm and the table, in the checker pattern, and in the large masses of unbroken ground behind the figure. It is the play and interplay of these motifs that help guide the eye so rhythmically: the circle with its swing and the triangle with its point.

Color too is a guide to the eye. Blue, black, and white are concentrated in the figure; green, red, and yellow in the ground and the table. Yet yellow-red plays into the figure, in the hands and the red lips, and a bluish tone suffuses the green of the ground. So too the textures unite and oppose: the rough pigment of the broken upper ground, the table, the ruffs, and the hands over against the smoother texture in the plain ground and the dress.

These masses of light and dark color are united not only by their interlocking shapes, by their harmonies, contrasts,

and interweavings, but also by the great sweeping lines of organization (Fig. 88). See how, beginning near the upper right corner, a curve sweeps down through the figure and swings strongly to the lower right corner, where the line of the table exactly repeats the line of the figure. From the opposite upper corner a similar curve runs behind the head, is caught and turned by the ruff and shoulder, carried on by the elbow on the table, picked up by the point of the white ruff, the thumb and fingers of the hand in the lower left corner. The curved line dominates, yet is varied by the suggested horizontals of the background and by the verticals and horizontals in the checker pattern and in the uplifted arm.

The balance of these masses and colors is both from side to side and from above and below. Draw a central vertical axis and you will see that the figure and table are largely on your right. Cover the ruff and the hand on your left, that is, the *Harlequin's* right hand, and you will see the necessity of a light mass at that point. Although the figure is placed to the right, a strong movement carries toward the left because the figure is turned in that direction and because the sharp triangle made by the arm and the table points in that direction. Thus movement is a determining factor in maintaining the balance. So too in the balance between the upper and lower parts. The ground at the top broken by the dashing floral pattern balances the lower part of the panel with its strong contrasts and big sweeps of line. Cover the upper part and see how much of the vitality of the painting is lost, how the balance is upset, and how necessary as an accent is the red four-petaled flower.

There are many similarities between the *Harlequin* and the *Egyptian Tomb Painting:* no definite source of illu-

mination; no use of light and shadow, no presenting to the eye an illusion of depth; elimination of detail; simplification of all forms; large areas of unbroken color. Dissimilar, on the other hand, is the attitude toward the figure, notwithstanding the fact that both simplify. The Egyptian used a simplified form because this form was a convention handed down to him. Picasso used a simplified form because he chose to. And the simplification is his own. It is a terse expression of form that includes and suggests an underlying understanding of the figure, of its organization, its capacity for movement, the interrelation of its parts, its existence in space. In the *Harlequin,* how one feels the weight thrown on the right arm, the hunched-up right shoulder, the lowered left, the inward thrust of the left arm! At the same time, the relationship between the parts of the figure, and that between the figure and the table and the ground, were of equal concern to Picasso. To maintain these relationships clearly he did not hesitate to distort. The top of the table and the match box are more circular than elliptical, to maintain the circle motif and to proportion the light mass at that point. The *Harlequin's* left hand is large, so as to afford a large enough proportion of warm color in the midst of the cool blue and white, and to bring the white of the wrist ruff away from that of the neck ruff, and into a definite relation to the light of the table and of the right hand. All through the canvas will be found these variations from natural appearance and proportion for the sake of the unity of parts. In fact, one feels that it was this relationship of parts, all the little subtleties and niceties of organization, that motivated Picasso rather than any interest in a *Harlequin.* The latter was an excuse for the former. Therefore the stronger emphasis lies on the form rather than upon the idea that the form expresses.

Yet one more similarity. How beautifully decorative are both the Egyptian painting and the Picasso! Put the *Harlequin* in a building of the skyscraper type where there are large unbroken areas. How its dominant architectural quality would harmonize!

To emphasize the clear-cut decorative quality of the Picasso, turn for a moment to Renoir's *La Tasse de Chocolat* (*The Cup of Chocolate*) (PL. 63).[14] Though similar in composition, how different in effect! The canvas vibrates and sparkles with color. The pigment is laid on thick and rough, with short strokes. There are no clearly perceptible lines, only vague contours. A mass of blue (the lady's dress) contrasts with a mass of rose (the sofa). How these hues echo and reëcho in broken masses! The blue, in the cup and vase, now lost in the reds, greens, and whites of the flowers, now reappearing in lighter tone in the ground. Likewise the rose, as it plays against the blue, in the nosegay at the breast, for example. It is color rather than line that guides the eye through the canvas. Everywhere are the play and interplay of color, harmonious and contrasting, like melodies in a musical composition, full of grace and charm. Compare one detail, the ruffs at the throat and the wrists. In the Renoir they are indefinite, drenched in light and air; in Picasso they are flat pattern sharply defined by line. Each is right in its own place, for each is one harmonious element in the total unity of the picture.

The *Egyptian Tomb Paintings* and the *Harlequin* are examples of the use of line and color on a large scale in comparison with what we shall now look at — a *Persian Miniature*.

[14] Pierre Auguste Renoir, a French painter, 1841–1919 A.D. *The Cup of Chocolate* was painted in 1879. N. Y., Durand-Ruel Gallery. Color reproduction, *Art News*, May 14, 1927, Supplement.

On the mountainous plateau east of the valley of the Tigris and Euphrates rivers lies the land of Persia. In the dry season the fields are arid and parched, but with the coming of the rains they become carpets of green and vivid colors which vie in intensity with the blue of the immense sky-dome, clear as crystal. Sheep and picturesque shepherds dot every green hillside.[15]

The towns are as full of color as the hillsides after the rain. Brilliantly colored shining tiles cover the mosques and fountains. Gay wares enliven the tiny shops in the narrow streets. At the end of the day the men crowd the little coffee shop and while smoking their long pipes and drinking tiny cups of thick black coffee, listen for hours to the story-teller, who dramatically relates the adventures of Sinbad the Sailor and Ali Baba and the Forty Thieves, or, best of all, the old stories of their own race, such as the romances of the hunter king *Bahram Gur*. Always it is a tale of love or adventure, imaginative, colorful, and told with many gesticulations, and with the singing of musical passages to the accompaniment of a guitar.

But it is not the people alone who love these stories. The kings of old so delighted in them that they employed the greatest artists to write them into books and paint pictures to illustrate them. This was before the days of the printing press, when writing the text was as fine an art as painting the picture to illustrate it. Open one of the royal Persian books (Pl. 78). The flowers of the hillsides and

[15] For illustrated articles on Persia, some with color plates, see the *National Geographic Magazine*, April, 1921; April, 1922; December, 1927. For general background, the Arabian Nights. Color reproductions of Persian painting are available in the Metropolitan Museum Colorprints, *Near Eastern Miniatures*, one of which, "Laila and Majnun in Love at School," is from the same book as the "Bahram Gur in the Turquoise Pavilion." Lawrence Binyon, *Poems of Nizami*, London, Studio, 1928, has summaries of the stories and excellent color plates. [See also the British Museum Postcard Sets (in color), "Persian Painting" (C7), and "Persian and Indian Painting" (C9).]

the blue of the sky have found their way into its pages, intense, clear, sparkling. Here is the great painting of Persia, small but exquisite. Sensitively placed on a gold-flecked page of pale-blue paper (PL. 64) opposite a similar page containing a panel of writing, the little picture stands out like a cluster of jewels in a perfect setting. The intense reds, blues, greens, yellows, and white are areas of clear color untouched by any shadow but enriched by a wealth of minute delicate detail and a lavish glistening of gold. Bright and vivacious, its whole atmosphere suggests romantic adventure.

Such was the experience of the hunter king *Bahram Gur* with the seven princesses. Seeing seven portraits of seven princesses from different lands, he falls in love with them all, and sends his ambassadors to the king of each of the seven lands, asking the hand of the princess in marriage. All seven accept. Each princess he houses in a pavilion tiled in a different color and each one he visits one day a week.

It is the turquoise pavilion, which he visits on Wednesday, that we see in PL. 64.[16] The pavilion is incrusted with gayly colored tiles with geometric patterns or arabesques through which, in the panel above the entrance, runs the inscription, " The foundation of this turquoise dome they have laid and have made a place to entertain the lovers together." Within, *Bahram Gur* and the *Princess* are seated in Oriental fashion on a rug, enjoying a cooling drink from the bottle and cups on the small rug in front of them. In the foreground are musicians and attendants and to the left is a garden with a plane tree and a blossoming fruit tree.

[16] See *A Book of Persian Romances*, p. 255, note 9, of which this painting is an illustration.

The color scheme is based upon blue. Hence the blue of the gold-flecked margin. About this hue is built a design of contrasting and harmonious color. Everything is kept flat; depth is suggested, not presented to the eye. The rug and the floor tiles seem hung on the wall, though the figures are seated upon them. Yet is not the idea perfectly lucid? Everything is in clear silhouette, as in the *Egyptian Tomb Paintings* (PLS. 60–61), with very little overlapping. As there is no illumination there is no shadow, and no attempt to make the figure appear round except as the contours suggest volume. And to what an extent they do! What reality there is in the various figures! And at the same time what quality of line! Unfalteringly it incorporates all detail into a forceful yet delicately drawn contour and then, as if in an exuberance that must find expression, runs off into rapid zigzag (Fig. 89).

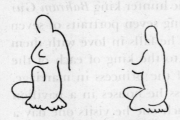

Fig. 89. Sustained and Rapid Movement in Persian Figures (PL. 64).

Charming and irresistible as are the rhythm of line and the jewel-like color, still it is the balanced unity of all elements that contributes most to our pleasure in the little picture. This balance produces a liveliness because of its asymmetry. Compare with it the end wall of the *Egyptian Tomb* (PL. 60) where, quite irrespective of size, the formality of the symmetrical balance produces the opposite effect of quietude. In the *Persian* painting the pavilion alone is symmetrical but is relieved from monotony by the variety in the figure groups. Yet see how the pavilion is adjusted to the panel as a whole. The figure of *Bahram Gur* is exactly on the central axis of the picture and forms an accent because of the dark and

PLATE 61

A Banquet. Detail of Pl. 60 (though not visible). There is a fine sweep of line in these figures which, in spite of the conventional way in which they are drawn, are convincingly real. (Metropolitan Museum)

PLATE 62

Harlequin. Picasso. As flat and decorative as the Egyptian tomb paintings.
The parts are clearly and sharply contrasted by line, and by light and dark
color. (John Quinn Collection)

PLATE 63

La Tasse de Chocolat (The Cup of Chocolate). Renoir. In contrast to Pl. 62 the painting has a vibrant effect. Light and air envelop the figures, blurring the contours and causing colors and forms to melt into each other. (Durand-Ruel)

PLATE 64

Bahram Gur in the Turquoise Pavilion. A Persian miniature. Like Pl. 62, though on a small scale, the picture is a flat decorative pattern based upon line and clear intense color. (Metropolitan Museum)

light, that is, the strong color of his dress and the white of his large turban. The candlestick and the low table also mark the axis, not with mechanical precision but with slight deviation. The figure of the king is further emphasized by the lines and color areas that create movement toward it from the figures in the foreground. How irresistibly the darks of the harpist and her instrument guide the eye up to the figure of the king and unite the two groups! Thus *Bahram Gur* performs two functions in the design: one, as lateral accent in the symmetrical balance of the pavilion alone, and the other as a central accent in the asymmetrical balance of the picture as a whole.

That so strong an element in the composition as the pavilion should be set in one corner, means that equally strong elements must offset it. These are furnished by the more unbroken areas of the tiled foreground, the two standing figures, and the fence and trees against an unbroken sky. Cover the part of the picture at the left of the pavilion and see what a difference there is. Thus the seemingly informal, gayly narrative character of the painting is a matter of a very subtle balance that controls the lines, the color, and the movement.

It is a difficult technique, the painting of these little pictures, one requiring long training and infinite time. The paper was most carefully selected — the Orientals have always been great connoisseurs of fine paper — and polished with a crystal egg until it was glossy and then rubbed with white of egg or soap to give a good surface for writing and for drawing. The colors were mixed with water and some binding medium such as glue, gum, or sugar. It is opacity of the pigment that differentiates this kind of water color, known as *gouache,* from the more

usual transparent treatment (PL. 56B), where the color of the paper is left to form the high lights or show through the transparent washes.

Let us look at one more master of line and color, an Italian. Should an Oriental who knew nothing of European civilization and the Christian religion stand before this little panel (PL. 65),[17] I think that he would muse along something in this fashion: " Here is exquisite feeling directed toward the two figures in the center and here is exquisite decorative beauty as the deep blues, scarlets, and violets harmonize, contrast, and interweave with the shimmering gold that envelops them with its radiance. Once within the frame I am in another world just as I am when I look at our pictures of Buddha. Wherever I look, these masses of color, the gleaming gold, the lines, and the clear-cut patterning all insist upon my coming back to the large seated figure with a child upon her lap; and always with that same tender feeling. Whoever she is, she inspires the feeling." Is the Oriental right? Let us go to Siena to answer the question.

Directly south of Florence, about twenty-five miles as the crow flies, among the rolling olive- and vine-covered hills of Tuscany, lies Siena high up on her triple hill (Figs. 90 and 91). A strong wall with fortresslike gates encircles the hills, winding over their lower irregular slopes. At its base are fountains, orchards, and gardens. Thence the city begins to push itself up the slopes. The red-tiled houses become thicker, jumbled together, and even straddle the narrow winding streets, so eager do they seem to press close to the crest where the three hills meet. Here is the heart of the

[17] *Madonna*, Ambrogio Lorenzetti, a Sienese painter whose dates are uncertain. He died about 1346 A.D. The size of the panel, which is less than 2 ft. high, suggests that it may have been an altarpiece in a small private chapel. It was painted about 1335 and is now in the Siena Museum.

Fig. 90. Italy.

city, above which soars still higher into the sky, as if
defiant of all Tuscany, the slender bell tower of the town
hall and the striking striped dome and tower of the cathedral. In the great days of Siena there were many more

towers, strongholds of the militant nobles, so that the skyline of the hill city must have been boldly ominous.

In the Middle Ages the larger cities of Italy were independent republics, called communes, and included the outlying villages and often the larger towns. Great rivalry, largely over trade matters, brought the communes of Siena and Florence into bitter warfare. Though Florence was ultimately the victor, Siena at first maintained her independence, chiefly, so the chronicler says, because of her

Fig. 91. Siena from the Foot of the Hill. On the left rises the bell-tower of the Town Hall; on the right, the mass of the Cathedral.

faith in " the Gracious Virgin, Queen of Heaven." [18] So the love of the Sienese for the *Virgin* was kin to that of the people of Chartres; and its expression in a painting inspired in them a definite emotion, just as the name of Abraham Lincoln does in an American.

The feeling of our Oriental visitor, then, is right. Everything tends to emphasize the feeling of tender adoration and the exaltation of the central figure. No one needs to know about the story of Siena or of the Christian re-

[18] Read the story of the siege of Siena and the battle of Montaperti in E. G. Gardner, *Story of Siena* (London, Dent, 1902).

ligion to feel that. The heart of the feeling is the heart of the design. The Sienese thought of the *Virgin* as wonderfully majestic. So the painter represents her large and majestic, clothed in a blue mantle, for blue is symbolic of her heavenly love. She is seated on a throne in the center against a glow of gold whose rays reach out to the saints and angels, so that the dark silhouette of her figure makes a strong accent against the gold. The contours of this silhouette are kept simple and unbroken. Notwithstanding the fact that she holds the *Child* on her lap, the two are so compactly grouped that no part of the *Child's* figure extends beyond the contours of the *Virgin's* robe. Thus a conspicuous mass of strongly contrasted dark and light forms our focal point, about which all the elements are balanced.

Fig. 92. Line Organization of the Madonna of Siena (Pl. 65).

See how everything subordinates itself to this balance about an accent. Take the line first (Fig. 92). The figures are so placed that they form a great sweeping curve around the central group and send reverse curves toward the lower corners. The kneeling figures and the carpet provide diagonals, broken in places so as to avoid overemphasis; the standing figures, the crosiers, and the sides of the frame give the stabilizing verticals; the halos and robes of the angels provide the rhythmic curves that swing in and out of the golden rays. Notice how the curves of the top of the frame are one with the lines of the painting. All these lines move inward toward the top and concentrate upon the heads of the central group.

But it is not only the lines that move toward this point of concentration. Look at the lights and darks (Fig. 93). Turn the print upside down or cover it with thin paper to see this more clearly. The darkest areas are the *Madonna* and the kneeling figures. The floor and carpet partake of both dark and intermediate light, for too much of the dark would overbalance the lower part. The intermediate light, or gray, and a little dark play up into the standing figures.

Fig. 93.   Light and Dark Organization of the Madonna of Siena (PL. 65).

Then everything lightens as it rises to meet the highest light behind the dark central figure.

What appears in the print as light and dark, however, is only difference of color that is clear and glowing. The intense scarlet in the robes of the kneeling bishops and the intense blue of the *Madonna's* robe (the darkest tones in Fig. 93) repeat, in small areas, through the carpet and the throne; lighter blues, violets, reds, whites, and gold interweave through all the figures; and the gold ground behind the *Madonna* furnishes the lightest note. What a rhythmic movement, then, of light and dark color and gold to the focal point!

In order to harmonize the lines and colors so as to gain unity and emphasis, Ambrogio had to think out carefully how to compose the figures and objects, how to place each one so that it would perform its function in the design as a whole. We have already noted the strongly emphasized central figure. About it the compact fringe of figures circles not too closely, thus leaving the two in the center somewhat isolated and hence, again, strongly accented.

The bishops kneel, not only because this is an attitude of humility and adoration but because the kneeling figures, by contrast, make the central figure more majestic. Try changing the poses, making the figures in the foreground stand, and see the difference. And finally the entire group is sensitively proportioned and organized to fit the panel, the curving top of the frame and the encircling angels inextricably one. Thus we see Ambrogio using every element at his disposal for the creation of a rhythmic movement to a point of interest. That in itself would make a moving design. But combined with that moving design is a moving idea — the exaltation of a majestic personage that grows out of the most profound feelings of a Sienese. The combination, the inextricable unity of the two, creates a work of art of the highest significance.

This *Madonna* with its exquisite surface of sparkling color and gold, its decorative loveliness and tender feeling, is an excellent example of the tempera technique, as is indicated by the fine brush strokes, the definite contours, and the freedom from deep shadows. Though it is generally flat, still the steps of the throne carry the eye inward; the kneeling bishops and the lower part of the *Virgin's* figure present some illusion of depth. Here then we see that the painter, if he wishes, need not stay on the surface of the canvas but may present to the eye an illusion of space and organize his figures in that space. How he does it, we shall see in our next chapter.

READING

ABBOTT, E., Great Painters, N. Y., Harcourt, 1927.

CAPART, J., Lectures on Egyptian Art, Chapel Hill, University of North Carolina Press, 1928.

MUNRO, T., Great Pictures of Europe, N. Y., Brentano, 1930.

Ross, E. D. (ed.), Persian Art, London, Luzac, 1930.
Schevill, F., Siena, N. Y., Scribner, 1909.

SOME MASTERS OF SPACE

*The Death of Saint Francis   The Last Supper
The Miracle of Saint Mark   The Unmerciful Servant
The Village Road*

The *Death of Saint Francis* (Pl. 66).[19] Impressions crowd hard on each other: massive monumental forms in actual space; men of great dignity, real in their grief; profound calm; a harmony that seems natural and inevitable. How clearly and easily eye and mind grasp the situation! The scene takes place in an open secluded spot between two buildings. There are no onlookers, no landscape with irrelevant details, to detract from the immediate situation. Above, the soul of the *Saint* in the form of his earthly body is carried to heaven by angels. Only one of the group has caught this vision; all the others are preoccupied in their grief.[20]

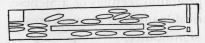

Fig. 94. Ground Plan of the Death of Saint Francis (Pl. 66).

Two groups quietly and solidly flank the two sides while the group in the center kneeling and bending over the bier creates a strong movement toward the head of the *Saint*, the focal point. The symmetrical balance of the sides becomes asymmetrical in the center, thus infusing virility into the monumental dignity. This monumentality is

[19] Giotto, a Florentine painter, 1276–1336 A.D. This painting, a large fresco in a chapel in the Franciscan *Church of Santa Croce*, Florence, was painted about 1325, lay covered by whitewash for centuries, and when discovered in 1841 was almost ruined by repainting.
[20] For Saint Francis, see P. Sabatier, *Life of Saint Francis of Assisi*, N. Y., Scribner, 1927; and *The Little Flowers of Saint Francis*, Everyman's Library.

PLATE 65

Madonna. Ambrogio Lorenzetti. Tender in feeling and beautifully decorative with its intense color, gold ground, and generally flat surface with
strong rhythms.

PLATE 66

Death of Saint Francis. Giotto. A quietly profound feeling harmonizes with a quietly monumental design. There is sufficient consistent depth for all the figures so that the rhythms move in depth as well as on the surface.

partly due to the scale
of the figures (com-
pare PLS. 67 and 69).
Yet there is a natural-
ness about the pic-
ture. Compare it
with the *Harlequin*
(PL. 62) and the
Egyptian Banquet
(PL. 61), in which it
is left to your imagi-
nation to think of the
figure as a mass ex-
isting in space, if you
wish. In the Giotto
how each figure ap-
pears to take its place
easily as a mass in
space! There is room
for each. You feel
that you could walk
in around the group.
Each is presented to
the eye so convinc-
ingly in relation to
the others and to the
buildings that you
can make a ground
plan of the group

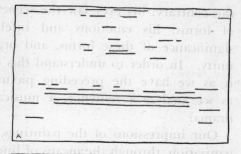

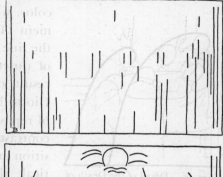

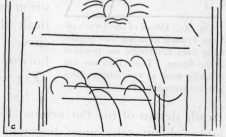

Fig. 95. Some of the Important Organizing Lines in the Death of Saint Francis.
A, horizontal; *B*, vertical; *C*, the emphatic
horizontals and verticals combined with the
emphatic curves and diagonals.

(Fig. 94). In other words, Giotto has been looking at
people and things and has painted them as they appeared
to his eyes. Does this mean, however, that he placed upon
the wall an illusion of what his eyes saw? Not at all. On

the contrary, his eyes saw the scene as a form made up of forms; his emotions and intelligence grasped the significance of these forms, and organized them into a unity. In order to understand this unity, shall we study it as we have the preceding pictures — analyze it just as we analyze a sentence, a musical composition, or a drama?

Our impressions of the paintings are the result of organization, through the means of line, light and dark, and color, with the additional element of space. Let us study the line first. The impression of quietude and dignity is a result of the emphasis that Giotto has placed on the line of repose, the horizontal, with contrasting lines to give opposition and movement: the vertical, the diagonal, and the curve. See how he repeats the horizontal and the vertical (Fig. 95). But the result is too static. Compare the

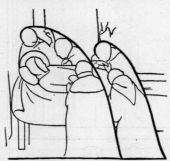

Fig. 96. Detail of the Death of Saint Francis showing how organizing lines determine the position of the figure. These lines are not actually seen as continuous lines but are strongly felt.

façade design of the *Parthenon* (Fig. 21), where the general problem is the same: diagonals and curves are needed. These Giotto concentrates largely in the center, though he repeats them in the sides. Thus the effect of the line organization is consistent with the emotional feeling. Each determines the other. You will notice that these organizing lines are felt when not seen. They repeat, break, and continue, guiding the eye to the point of emphasis and bringing unity into the design. There is as much coherence in the group about the head of the *Saint* (Fig. 96), for

instance, as there is
in a well-formed sen-
tence or paragraph.

However much the
organizing lines ap-
pear to be on the sur-
face, as Figs. 95 and
96 imply, they create
depth and movement
as well. Return to
the ground plan (Fig.
94). The entire
space occupied is
shallow, inclosed, like
a relief, between two
parallel planes — the
frontal plane and the
background (Fig.
97). Within this
space the movement
is not only from side
to side, but also from
the back to the head
of the *Saint* and from
the front to the same
place, which is the
focal point. Each
figure and object is
so placed as a definite
element of the rhyth-
mic movement in
space that no figure or
object or detail could

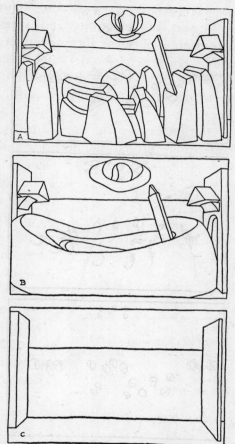

Fig. 97. Depth Organization of the Death
of Saint Francis. The figures have the bulk
of geometric masses, two or three figures often
forming one mass (*A*), and are so placed as to
secure a rhythmic movement about the center
of interest (*B*). This movement is generally
from side to side even in the center where it
bends backward and forward (note the three
quarters positions here), and is concentrated
within the shallow space determined by the
front and back parallel planes (*C*).

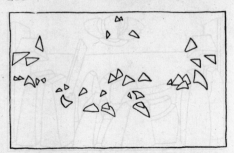

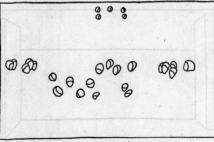

Fig. 98. Unit Shapes (Motifs) in the Death of Saint Francis. Visual motifs, repeated, delight the eye just as aural motifs, the ear.

be altered without disturbing the rhythm and the harmony.

Another way to guide the eye through a picture to the focal point is to repeat unit shapes, as we saw in Picasso's use of the triangle and the circle (PL. 62). Giotto, in creating his forms, constantly repeats, with variations, a triangular shape of curving lines; a spirited pattern made of hand, arm, and fingers; and an oval pattern made by the heads (Fig. 98); and he thereby gains the same effect of rhythmic movement, contrast, and unity as the musician does by the repetition and contrast of several melodies (Fig. 99).

Of light and dark and color we must speak with caution (it is better not to try to deal with the color) because of the repainting.[21] In the original state the contrasts would

21 See note 19, p. 214.

PLATE 67

Miracle of Saint Mark. Tintoretto. A highly dramatic subject expressed by a highly dramatic design with strong movement in depth. Light and dark and color are the chief organizing means.

PLATE 68

A. Flight into Egypt. Giotto. The figures unite with the hills architecturally; that is, every figure and object, every detail in its position and movement takes its place with the nicety of the supporting columns or walls of a building. Try changing a detail and the balance is upset. At the same time the group moves forward, as a unit, urgently.

B. Flight into Egypt. Follower of Giotto. Here the same composition produces a different effect. The group moves, if at all, with uncertainty. The figures and background seem to form two separate units. The terse statement of essentials in A has given way to a loose discursive description especially in the landscape.

not be strong because of the fresco technique. The large area of dark at the top — now much too dark — unbroken except in the center, emphasizes horizontality by its proportions, and contrasts in its quietude with the vivaciously broken area below. The lightest parts appear to be the large areas of the flanking figures, and the halo and open space about the head of the *Saint* which are accented by the darker figure behind. The dark mass of the banner is needed as a strong accent to balance the rapid movement from the right toward the center of interest far to the left. A little use is made of light and shadow to express the mass of the figure, but very little, for the light is diffused, not concentrated as in PLS. 67 and 70. Line, after all, is Giotto's chief means for constructing form.[22]

Convincing evidence of the power and significance of Giotto's painting results from a comparison of A and B in PL. 68. In A the figures and hills tie together into strong simple unities. In the center, the pyramid made by *Mary* and the *Child* fits into the pyramidal mass of the hills behind, keeping the central group isolated and accented. The other figures and objects create balancing units. Yet there is a strong movement of the entire mass to the right, a forward urge, in keeping with the subject matter, that is held firmly by the backward glance of *Joseph* and of the *Angel* and by the stability of the central group.[23] How every detail contributes to the lucidity of the organization, so that a moving design clothes the event with significance! Turn to B. The composition is the same, with minor exceptions. Yet the figures are far from being welded into a coherent unity with emphasis where needed. *Mary* and

[22] Critics from the time of Vasari to the present have remarked on Giotto's great ability in the use of line. See the famous story of his O in Vasari's *Life of Giotto*.

[23] See the same devices to halt movement in the *Parthenon Frieze* (Pl. 51 A).

the *Child* are just part of a group. The entire design is loose and weak, as if it were falling to pieces.

A comparison of Leonardo's *Last Supper* (Pl. 69) [24] with the *Death of Saint Francis* will illumine both paintings. In both we have a dramatic moment: in the Giotto, one of profound quiet; in Leonardo, one of intense excitement in balance with perfect repose. In each painting the artist conveys the impression by means of a form fitting the idea.

In the *Last Supper* we see the twelve disciples grouped about the reposeful Christ in a reposeful room. The disciples, in their reactions to the amazing statement, " One of you will betray me," fall naturalistically into groups of three, each group closely knit within itself and at the same time definitely united with the neighboring group. None press too closely to the central figure, thus keeping it isolated and emphasized as is the *Madonna* (Pl. 69). The room is spacious, with paneled walls and coffered ceiling, and with three windows opening on a quiet landscape.

In organizing this material into a unity, Leonardo has made important use of line (Fig. 99). Long unbroken horizontals in the table are repeated, broken, in the windows and the ceiling. Vertical lines, repeated by means of the paneling and the windows, give balance. The diagonals of the receding room all lead to the focal point, the head of *Christ*. In this quiet framework the figures furnish

[24] Leonardo da Vinci, a Florentine painter (1452–1519 A.D.). On the end wall of the refectory of Santa Maria delle Grazie, Milan. About 1495–98 A.D. Painted in tempera, with oil varnish, on a badly prepared wall, it collected damp and grime, and began to flake soon after it was completed; in 1652, a door was cut through; in the eighteenth century, repaintings occurred; about 1800, when the monks vacated the monastery, the refectory was used to store hay and the painting was seriously injured; in 1908 there began a scientific cleaning, the removal of repaintings, ventilation of the wall to prevent dampness, and binding firmly what remained of Leonardo's work. A large color reproduction is published by the Medici Society of America, Boston, Mass.

great sweeping curves that move in from the sides toward the focal point, inclosing in their sweep many short subordinate curves, all of which meet the outstretched hands of *Christ*. These waves of inward movement are not exactly alike in line or in intensity. For example, at the right of *Christ* (the spectator's right) the uplifted hand and finger which make a strong indication of verticality check the onrushing movement before it can reach the central figure; just as the rapid movement of the cavalcade in the *Parthenon Frieze* was

checked by the figure of the marshall (PL. 51). These curves are concentrated within the narrow rectangle bounded by the table edge and by the upper line of the heads, which are on an approximate level. Outside this

Fig. 99. Death of Saint Francis. The heads (indicated by the solid areas) determine a rhythmic movement that radiates from the head of the Saint. (Kathleen Blackshear)

rectangle there is but one curve, that over the window and just above the head of *Christ* — another means of emphasis upon the center of interest.

In his use of light and dark Leonardo opposes quiet areas of largely unbroken light to the broken animated areas of the central rectangle. The lightest part is seen through the windows. Why at this point? Because the lightest spot in a room is an accent. Here, placed directly above the head of *Christ,* it provides another accent upon the center of interest. The darkest parts are the panels, the space beneath the table, and small irregular areas among

the figures.[25]   Intermediate tones are found on the walls,
the ceiling, the table, and through the groups. This light
and dark is a matter of natural illumination from the left.
Falling upon the right wall, it varies what would otherwise
be a too monotonous balance of the side walls. The figures
are modeled in strong light and shade. Compare these
with Giotto's, where shadow plays but a small part and a
diffused light reveals each standing forth clearly. Furthermore, the strongest light, which is the out-of-doors light

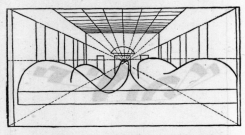

of the landscape,
draws the figure of
Christ, the archi-
tecture, and the
landscape — all re-
poseful elements
— into a rhythmic
unity in deep
space.

Fig. 100.   Line Organization of the Last Supper
(PL. 69).

The use of space
constitutes an important difference between Giotto's and
Leonardo's designs. Although Leonardo's figures are concentrated close to the front, as Giotto's are, they fit pro-
portionately into the room. In the Giotto the portals
are far too small for the people. But Giotto is speaking to your imagination, suggesting buildings, and you
may, if you wish, increase their size in your mind; and
by keeping his figures large he gains an effect of grandeur and monumentality. Leonardo, on the other hand,
presents directly to your eyes the normal adjustment of
the figure to the space. The room recedes naturalistically,
giving a feeling of continuing the actual room in which you

[25] One must analyze this painting with caution, as the Giotto, because of its
ruined condition.   (See note p. 220.)

are standing as you look at the picture (Fig. 100). This feeling, together with the additional impression of depth in the landscape, keeps the eye moving back and forth in the line of vision — that is, at right angles to the plane of the picture — as well as from side to side. In the Giotto the movement is concentrated into a narrow, sternly defined space.

In making these comparisons let us note that neither painting is better than the other. They show different ways of handling the painter's means. Both are of superior quality because the artist has kept his basic design clear,

Fig. 101.   Refectory of Santa Maria delle Grazie, Milan.

consistent, and forceful, has eliminated or suppressed irrelevant detail, and with the dynamic of his feelings and intelligence to guide his hand has created a form which is in harmony with the idea that he wished to express.[26]

To use again our method of contrast to emphasize characteristics, let us look at Tintoretto's *Miracle of Saint Mark*

[26] The life of Leonardo, his primary concern with science, his age and his relation to it, are of unusual interest. There are many books on the subject, reference to which will be found in those listed at the end of this chapter. For Leonardo's famous letter of self-recommendation to the Duke of Milan and for contemporary writers' descriptions of methods and incidents connected with the painting of the *Last Supper*, see O. Sirén, *Leonardo da Vinci* (New Haven, Yale University Press, 1916); also Vasari's *Life of Leonardo*.

(PL. 67) .[27] Here are powerful movement in deep space, dramatic energy, vivid contrasts of light and dark, rich color. They surge through the picture and dominate it. A group of men and women bend excitedly over a quiet, naked figure on the ground. The people are massed high on the sides, all bending toward that form. Down from above sweeps a figure, cutting in its movement a bold arabesque against the sky. Whatever the subject may be, here is a highly dramatic situation — and a highly dramatic design. Briefly, this is the incident. A Christian slave of a pagan Venetian, because of his persistence in worshiping at the shrine of *Saint Mark,* had been brought to trial and condemned to martyrdom. As the executioner lifted his sledge to crash it upon the head of the victim, *Saint Mark* swooped down, split the hammer into pieces, and broke the binding cords.

To create a design that would fittingly express so dramatic an incident, Tintoretto massed strong lights and darks and rich color into what we might almost call a noisy design. Strong illumination, from the observer's right, flecks the strongly massed darks on this side, in the figures of the judge and of the soldiers. This dark mass then swings backward towards the left around the prostrate slave, the highest light and center of interest, and more and more broken by the light, fills the left side. Behind these darks and broken darks and framed in by them on all sides is a light quiet area of sky and buildings across which sweeps the dark silhouette of the *Saint.*

Compare with the Giotto. The one is a design of large quiet areas and reposeful movement; the other, one of broken spotty areas and tumultuous movement: the one has strong quiet rhythms on the surface and in shallow

[27] Tintoretto, a Venetian painter, 1518–92 A.D. The picture, painted about 1548 A.D., is in the *Confraternity of Saint Mark*, Venice.

depth; the other, deep depth rhythms that surge backward and forward in space; the one has diffused illumination and little shadow; the other has a consistent source of strong illumination and hence dark shadows; in the one, clearly differentiated areas of color are marked off by clean-cut lines; in the other, masses of color melt by blurred contours and gradations of tone into a golden glow that ties them into a unity; in the one, the balance is subtly asymmetrical; in the other, notwithstanding the complexity of the groups, far more symmetrical.

We have seen how Giotto used his means to obtain his objective. Let us see how Tintoretto used the same means in a different way to secure a different objective. In the *Miracle of Saint Mark* the outstanding elements of design are light and dark and color. The light and dark areas are partly shadow masses and partly color masses. The darks on the right and on the figure of *Saint Mark* contain much intense red, which is dark; while the lightest areas are intense yellow, which is light. The crowd of people, in their costumes, furnish yellows, blues, and reds, thus breaking the mass into a lively pattern by color as well as by light and shadow. The light of the background is blue and blue-green. Playing through these color masses is a golden light dominating the light areas and controlling the dark, for it bursts through the dark masses now as a high light on armor, now in a turban, a face, or an arm. This golden tone binds into a harmony all the contrasting hues and lights and shadows, producing a dominating tonality that is quite different in its rich effect from that of the Giotto.

This difference is due partly to the difference in subject matter and in the intent of the artist and partly to a difference in techniques: fresco in the Giotto, and indirect oil in the Tintoretto, in which the golden tone is the result of

the yellow underpainting left exposed in places or showing through transparent glazes.

Another comparison to bring out the specific quality of
the Tintoretto might be made with the *Last Supper* (PL.
69). Here too is a dramatic subject, yet expressed in a
much more restrained tone. For though the figures are
excited, a much larger part of the design is given over to the
quieting architectural framework; the contrasts are less
sharp, and the rhythms are more sustained. In comparison,
the Tintoretto is agitated, grandiloquent.

How, on closer analysis, has Tintoretto secured this
effect? The figures of *Saint Mark,* the executioner, and the
slave form a great S-curve across the canvas from top to
bottom, along which the eye is guided not so much by line
as by light and dark. While this curve is a surface pattern
it is also an S-curve in depth. Beginning with the feet of
Saint Mark, it swings backward in the figure, because of
the shadow and of the light about the head; then forward
along his down-stretched arm to the turban of the executioner; back slightly in this figure; then forward into the
light mass of the slave's body. Thus is set up this backward
and forward movement in depth, which, at the same time,
harmonizes with the movement on the surface. In a similar
way another curve sweeps across the canvas from side to
side: down from the judge to the soldiers, around the central group, and up on the other side. But like the other
S-curve, it moves forward and backward as well as down
and up. Organization in space is what one feels most
compellingly.

There is one other line of movement, however, that
hinges upon the turning of the executioner away from the
scene of action toward the judge. This movement is not
only necessary to the subject matter but vital artistically.

PLATE 69

Last Supper. Leonardo da Vinci. A striking contrast of quiet and dramatic elements: a reposeful central figure in a quiet architectural framework is opposed to twelve highly excited persons.

PLATE 70

Parable of the Unmerciful Servant.   Rembrandt.   Effective directness result
from the simple organization of light and dark masses in space.

For the figures are almost all bending toward the slave, so that a contrasting movement is necessary for balance. This is provided by the strong diagonal that runs from the lower left corner through the body of the slave, the movement of the executioner, the dark silhouettes of the three figures in the middle distance, to the judge — a diagonal that is not so much seen as suggested by the light and dark and color masses.

Such strong movement, such agitated rhythms, need stabilizing by more static lines. There is very little of the horizontal — compare the liberal use of this line in the Leonardo — chiefly in the background, where is the greatest amount of quietude, and in the horizontal emphasis in the proportions of the frame; but there is considerable use of the vertical in the architecture and in the groups massed at the sides.

From whatever angle we view the picture, we see and feel highly dramatic action expressed in terms of highly dramatic design. It is precisely what we would expect of Tintoretto, that vehement, impetuous painter; and of Venice, just as Ambrogio's *Madonna* is the natural expression of Siena. Tintoretto was the son of a silk-dyer. Hence his name, which means " the little dyer." Of passionate nature, he wisely chose subjects that lent themselves to dramatic treatment. His home, Venice, was a half-Eastern city, for its ships were constantly sailing to eastern Mediterranean ports and bringing the colorful products of the East to the shops of Venice. Then, too, Venice's own geographic setting was colorful: sparkling water, golden mists, many-hued buildings. Hence the intensity of color, the vivacious contrasts possible in the oil technique, afforded a kind of expression that accorded with the gayety, the love of pageantry, the sumptuousness, of this city of the Adri-

atic. Tempera and fresco might well express the cooler, more intellectual Florentine. Not so with the Venetian. His patron saint was *Saint Mark,* whose winged lion overlooked the Grand Canal and whose colorful Byzantine church was the center of the city's religious life. So when Tintoretto was commissioned to decorate a Venetian interior with scenes from the life of this saint, the result was predestined — sumptuous stuffs, gorgeous pageantry, dramatic movement, rich color.

In the *Miracle of Saint Mark* a certain use of light and dark, color, and space produces a vivid, exciting form. In the *Unmerciful Servant* (PL. 70) ,[28] on the other hand, a different use of the same means produces a form of restraint and imaginative appeal. Out of the warm brown ground a light or half-light emerges, indicating a figure. Redbrowns, yellow-browns, yellows, a little grayed blue — these few hues flow one into another, producing a peculiarly harmonious effect. In the Tintoretto the rich masses of varied warm color stand out sharply against the golden tone and the cool blue. Light binds them together with dramatic appeal. In the Rembrandt the forms quietly melt one into another and into the ground; and a mysterious enveloping darkness binds them together — another kind of dramatic appeal.

Although the figures nearly fill the canvas, there is a feeling of almost infinite spaciousness surrounding them. The broad quiet areas of the ground are not flat dead surfaces but give the impression of great space filled with atmosphere, in which each figure takes its place exactly in reference to the others. You feel definitely that the central figure on the right, for example, is nearer you than the one

[28] Rembrandt van Rijn, a Dutch painter, 1606–69 A.D. Wallace Collection, London. Painted about 1650.

behind it, because of the comparative strength of the light.

Light and dark, then, and the subtle gradations from light to dark of a few closely related hues — these are the means that Rembrandt has used. It is neither natural lighting nor a consistent artificial illumination, but a use of light and dark that is original and personal with this painter. Line — that is, sharply distinguished line as we have seen it in Picasso (PL. 62), in Giotto (PL. 66), in Ambrogio Lorenzetti (PL. 65) — we do not find. Yet Rembrandt was a superb master of line when he chose to use it as his etchings show. And we search in vain for a wide range of color such as we found in the Tintoretto and in Ambrogio. The means of expression are meager. Look at the picture again. Had you noticed that the figures are but three-quarters length? Does it make any difference?

The subject seems to be the parable of the *Unmerciful Servant* (Matthew 18:23–34). On the right is a compact group of three persons, the servant between two bailiffs. He is nervously fingering his cap as he bends forward to hear the judgment of the master. On the left the dignified, imposing figure of the master at a table with books and papers occupies half the canvas, balancing the three on the right and connected with them by the direction of his gaze and by his outstretched hand, a movement repeated by the hand of the servant. To neutralize the strong movement toward the right, the master's other hand turns toward the left edge of the canvas; the light masses of the sleeves, books, and papers hold the attention and balance the strong light on the right. Cover the light mass of even the papers alone and you will find that the picture becomes unbalanced.

The types of people and the costumes are of Holland.
Yet Rembrandt has interpreted the incident on a universally human plane. Because he says so little explicitly
and leaves so much to the imagination he has given the
parable a significance that carries as far beyond Holland as
the *Death of Saint Francis* carries beyond Italy.

To turn from Rembrandt to the *Village Road* of Cézanne
(PL. 71) [29] is to turn from mysterious shadow and forms

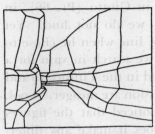

emerging from and melting
into dark, to blazing sunshine
and forms clearly defined in
light. Objects do not blur
and melt within its radiance.
Rather they solidify because of
it, become sharply defined as
geometric solids, even the
masses of foliage. The road in
the foreground filled with sunshine carries you at once, definitely, step by step to the red
house and the poplar tree far
back in deep space (Fig. 102).
Try to stay on the plane of the
canvas. How impossible it is!

Fig. 102. Depth Organization of the Village Road. Two
great planes move rapidly into
the distance at right angles to
the plane of the canvas and
control the design by incor-
porating all objects in the
picture into their sweep. Compare the controlling planes of
Fig. 97 which are parallel to
the plane of the wall.

The insistent impression is of depth, of space in which the
forms stand, each exactly in its own place and related to
all the other forms with the precision of the columns in
the *Parthenon*. This architectural quality dominates the
Harlequin as well (PL. 66), though its forms are essentially flat on the surface of the canvas, however much they
suggest depth to the imagination. In Cézanne the surface

[29] Paul Cézanne, a French painter, 1829–1906 A.D. The *Village Road* is in
Hamburg. Small color print, Artext Prints; large, the Arts Publishing Corporation, N. Y.

PLATE 71

Village Road. Cézanne. Depth, with rhythms in depth, is attained largely by the use of color alone.

PLATE 72

Nine Dragon Scroll, Detail. Chinese. The forms are almost abstract, consisting of conventional symbols for waves. The appeal is to the imagination and the emphasis upon inner meaning — powerful rhythmic movement. (Boston Museum)

is utterly gone and the unity is a unity in deep space. The planes move rapidly back into the distance (Fig. 102) at an angle to the picture plane. Compare the planes in Giotto, which run parallel to that of the wall, rather close together, thus producing but shallow space (Fig. 97).

In Cézanne you see and feel space as definitely as you do upon entering *Santa Sophia* (PL. 11). In this church all movement is to the dome; so in the Cézanne all movement is to the red house and the poplar. A powerful rhythm directly into space reveals itself in the onrushing road, repeated by the roadside grass and the walls. Great curves unite the road, trees, walls, and buildings into a simple, compelling line of direction which recalls again the organization of *Santa Sophia,* with its domes and answering domes, moving to the culmination point. Yet notice how this movement is halted by the insistent verticals in the chimneys, the poplar, the corner of the wall at the left, and the zigzags of the roofs, while the proportions of the frame emphasize the horizontal.

This deep space organization has been expressed largely by color. The surfaces are not as restless as are Renoir's (PL. 63), but are quiet and meet with sharp precision. For example, at the left, if you should look at the actual corner of the actual wall you probably would not see so precise a blue shadow to mark the edge where two surfaces meet. Yet how it does define that corner! Why are the tops of the chimneys red? While they may be red on this house, probably Cézanne made them red because the movement inward here is very strong and needs not only the break in the wall and the chimneys to restrain it for a moment but also the additional help of a little red, a color which advances and thus helps to neutralize a retreating rhythm.

So, too, the red house. Is the house really red? It may be. But again, the rhythm to the focal point has been so powerful that a forward movement is needed for balance. For the balance in such a picture is not only from right to left but also from front to back.

READING

ABBOT, E. R., The Great Painters, N. Y., Harcourt, 1927.

BARNES, A., The Art in Painting, N. Y., Harcourt, 1925.

CHENEY, S. W., Primer of Modern Art, N. Y., Boni, 1930.

FRY, R. E., Vision and Design, " Giotto," N. Y., Brentano, n. d.
—— Cézanne, N. Y., Macmillan, 1927.

GRONAU, G., Leonardo da Vinci, N. Y., Dutton, 1902.

MATHER, F. J., Jr., History of Italian Painting, N. Y. Holt, 1923.

MEREJKOWSKI, D., Romance of Leonardo da Vinci, N. Y., Modern Library, 1928.

MUNRO, T., Great Pictures of Europe, N. Y., Brentano, 1930.

PHILLIPPS, E. M., Tintoretto, London, Methuen, 1911.

TAYLOR, R. A., Leonardo the Florentine, N. Y., Harper, 1928.

VAN LOON, H., Life and Times of Rembrandt van Rijn, N. Y., Liveright, 1930.

WATER AND ROCKS

Northeaster
Nine Dragon Scroll

WATER and rocks. Two interpretations: one (PL. 72) Eastern,[30] the other (PL. 73) Western.[31] Let us look at them not to determine whether one is better than the other but to see how varied art expression can be.

In one Winslow Homer shows us the Maine coast before

---

[30] *Nine Dragon Scroll* (detail), Chinese, Sung dynasty, 960–1280 A.D. Boston Museum.

[31] *Northeaster*, Winslow Homer, an American painter, 1836–1910 A.D. Metropolitan Museum, New York.

a nor'easter, when the waters heave and crash into gigantic breakers against the immovable rocks. The spray dashes against our faces as the great waves thunder defiance at the granite headlands only to slide wearily into the foamy backwash. Two conflicting forces: mighty movement, mighty immobility.

To express this significance the painter has stressed certain elements. Quietude is emphasized by the horizontal: in the proportions of the panel (can you imagine this panel higher than wide?), in the horizon, in the crest of the breaking waves and the rocks at the right. The most arresting movement is the diagonal sweep of both water and rock from the upper left side to the lower right, and in the strongly contrasting light and dark masses in this sweep: the dark immovable rock, the light of the breaking water, and the half-light of the mist.

These three masses are balanced by a similar motif on the right on a smaller scale and by the expanse of sky and sea. Balance too there is between the quietude of sky and rock and the turmoil of the water. The dancing movement in the backwash lightens the awful power of the sea and of the relentless cliffs and provides a transitional movement between quietude and turmoil.

As you turn to the Chinese painting, the first impression is that the forms do not *look* but *feel* like water and rocks. The appeal has not been to the eye primarily, but by way of the eye to the imagination, with emphasis not on natural appearance but upon the essence of the inner life. The shapes have been reduced to symbols with just enough of natural appearance to make them intelligible. In the case of the water, the essence is movement. With what force it rushes over the cliffs between the motionless rocks and recoils upon itself in a single forceful sweep before it breaks

into undulating crested waves, which speed on and half vanish in mists! Movement reduced to its very essence! What rhythm in the sweep and swirl and in the rapid ragged crests! How they play and interplay as the waves race forward in long undulations toward the inevitable crash!

Through the breaking waves and the enveloping mists appear the scaly coils of dragons clinging to the rocks with ferocious claws. To one unacquainted with Eastern thought, the presence of these monsters may be foreboding. Not so to the Oriental, who understands the beneficence of the all-pervading life force that they symbolize.

How did the Oriental accomplish this result? His technical method we have already described in looking at the *Bamboo* (PL. 61). Yet this does not wholly explain. It was rather his attitude toward nature. Instead of following what his eyes saw, he evolved what we may call an alphabet of art forms. Trees, water, rocks, mountains, the plum tree, chrysanthemums — for each of these and for every variety of each he had a formula, just as we have formulas for language, that is, letters and words. When we wish to write or speak we put these together into sentences and paragraphs without thinking about the formulas themselves. So the Chinese painter, having the formulas for certain kinds of rocks and for moving water, combined these formulas into a design whose purpose was not to express the appearance of the rocks and water but the inner feeling of nature.

The actual painting of such a picture might be very rapid, though the preparation was long, as a story of Wu Tao-tzu illustrates. When Wu Tao-tzu was court painter, he was sent by the emperor to paint a certain river landscape of which the emperor was very fond. After spend-

PLATE 73

Northeaster. Winslow Homer. The forms are more naturalistic. The appeal is to the eye and the emphasis upon natural appearance with a hint of inner meaning. (Metropolitan Museum)

PLATE 74

Man with the Glove. Titian. Simplicity and restraint in the use of light and dark, and color, quiet proportions and balance produce an impression of simple elegance and distinction.

PLATE 75

Saint Jerome as Cardinal. El Greco. Dynamic contrasts of light and dark, line, and color with vigorous emphasis give an impression of a vigorous personality. (Mr. Lehman)

PLATE 76

Infanta Marguerita. Velasquez. A charming form to express a charming personality. Every detail — color, textures, deft brushstrokes, the contrasting chair — contribute to the unity of expression: a charming little girl in a conventional setting.

ing some time in this country he returned to the palace and when asked about his sketches replied, " I have it all in my heart." Then, retiring to one of the halls of the palace, " in a single day he threw off a hundred miles of landscape." This story reveals two characteristics of Oriental painters. First, the long mental preparation, the looking and brooding over the subject, the feeling of himself into it until every fiber was permeated with its inner life, its significance. Second, the perfect control over the formulas of art expression. So when the mind and spirit had completed their preparation, the actual painting might be comparatively swift.

In another tale, Wu once visited a monastery where he was rudely treated. So he drew upon the walls a picture of a donkey. That night all the furnishings were knocked to pieces. Finally, after the priests had humbly apologized for their rude behavior, Wu erased the drawing and there was no more trouble. Such stories suggest the quality that we find in Chinese paintings — a reality of inner significance, expressed in terms of symbolic form, the art language.

Thus in Winslow Homer and in the Chinese we see two different approaches to a similar idea. In this expression the Western painter emphasizes natural appearance and suggests inner meaning; while the Eastern stresses inner meaning and hints at natural appearance. Each has been thoroughly consistent.

READING

For explanations and illustrations of the formulas in Oriental painting see H. P. Bowie, *On the Laws of Japanese Painting*, San Francisco, Elder, 1911. For stories of Chinese painters see H. A. Giles, *Introduction to the History of Chinese Pictorial Art*, London, Quaritch, 1918, from which the stories

quoted above are taken; also A. Waley, *Introduction to the Study of Chinese Painting,* London, Benn, 1923. It would be valuable to read Chinese poetry in this connection, for it has much the same simplified form and imaginative character. See L. A. Cramner-Byng, *Lute of Jade,* N. Y., Dutton, 1923; A. Waley, *170 Chinese Poems,* N. Y., Knopf, 1919.

THREE PORTRAITS

The Man with the Glove   Saint Jerome as Cardinal
The Infanta Marguerita

IN portrait-painting a special problem confronts the artist, for a portrait has a definite purpose — to represent the person portrayed. "Represent," we say; which is quite different from taking a photograph, however artistic that may be. Just what, then, does "represent" mean? Let us go directly to our examples to answer this question.

First we shall look at *The Man with the Glove* (PL. 74).[32] Though there may be doubt as to the identity of this youth — he is thought to be a young nobleman of Genoa — there is no question of his aristocracy, of his fearlessness and daring. Aristocracy is revealed in the quiet ease and reserve; fearlessness and daring, in the virility of the pose, the erectness of the head, and in the keen look of the wide-open eyes. The quiet elegance of the dress, the sobriety of the color, and the restrained simplicity of the design are largely responsible for the effective characterization.

The design is organized chiefly in light and dark, and color. Three triangular masses of light are sensitively placed in an almost square area: the face and the linen shirt front, the hand with the pointing finger, and the hand with the gloves. The eye is easily guided from one to another,

[32] Titian, a Venetian painter, 1477-1576 A.D. *The Man with the Glove,* painted a little after 1510, is in the Louvre, Paris.

especially by the narrow V of the linen, whose sharpness is happily softened by the line of the chain and the pendant.

These light and dark masses are interestingly balanced. This is more clearly seen if the print is turned upside down. The largest area of light, made by the face and the shirt front, forms a diagonally moving mass left of the central axis of the area. This is balanced partly by the mass of the gloved hand, together with the half-light in the corner, and partly by the movement toward the right of the head, and of the thumb and pointing finger of the other hand. You may think of the face and the two hands as the corners of a triangle repeating the triangle motif of the shirt front and many triangles that can be found all through the canvas. Contrasting with this virile angularity is the broad sweep of the shoulders and the arms. Note the curve of the head and especially of the ruffles at the throat and wrists, whose rapid movement offers so pleasing a contrast to the broad quiet surfaces of the coat and the ground.

But this organization of light and dark is not a surface pattern. The figure exists in ample space. The darks are by no means a flat, unbroken area. The coat and hair are differentiated from the ground, by color, so subtly that the figure stands out from it plastically and at the same time is beautifully harmonized with it. The light areas of the head and the hands are strongly modeled in light and shadow, but softly fused. You feel light and shade disclosing rounding surfaces. Line (not strongly felt), light and dark, and color combine with extraordinary simplicity. Every detail contributes to this end, so that the canvas is filled with a feeling of harmony.

To return to our question: What does " represent " mean? Titian's problem was twofold: in the first place, to understand the personality of his sitter — a quiet, forceful

aristocrat with eagerness to do and daring to become; and in the second place, to express this personality in paint. A controlling principle seemed to be the elegance and distinction of simplicity, with a few sharp contrasts. It is not so much the expression in the face that makes the portrait so distinctive. Every detail — the pose, the costume, the background, the subtle unobtrusive relation of the figure to the background, the color, the relation and balance of the lights and darks within the space defined by the frame — all these work together harmoniously to create a perfectly unified impression, which is the representation.

Turning to the El Greco (PL. 75) [33] we are immediately in another atmosphere, one of startling dramatic intensity. The figure, though seated, rises majestically toward the top of the space, forming a sharp triangle against the unbroken ground. Interest centers on the light masses of the head and the beard, and of the hands and the book, masses of silver and white set off by the brilliant red and the powerful folds of the cardinal's cape, the intense green of the velvet tablecloth, and the darker green ground. One feels almost immediately the harmony between an arresting design and an intense personality. *Saint Jerome* is here given a typically Spanish interpretation, a Spanish Church Father. The Spaniard, partly by natural temperament and partly through centuries of struggle against the infidel Mohammedans who had intrenched themselves in the Spanish peninsula, was fanatical and bigoted in religious matters. Such a character is emphasized by the determined way in which the left hand rests upon the open book, by the vigorous bend of the right wrist, and by the feeling of

[33] El Greco, meaning *the Greek* (Domenico Theotocopuli), 1545–1614 A.D. Born in Crete, he settled in Toledo, Spain. *Saint Jerome as Cardinal* was painted between 1604 and 1614. Collection of Philip Lehman, N.Y.

finality with which the thumb points to a marginal reference. These movements but repeat the determination and
intolerance in the grim mouth and the piercing eyes. Here
is a relentless upholder of the sanctioned authority of the
Church.

This strongly emphatic characterization is due partly to
the appearance of the *Saint* but largely to the highly individual way in which El Greco has used his elements — his
line, light and dark, and color. Everywhere are strong
contrasts, exaggerations, and vigorous brush work. Lights
and darks meet with cutting edges, making line an important element. Compare this with the Titian, in which
the lights and darks are fused so gradually that line is submerged. In the El Greco the edges form a sharp zigzag on
the right, almost lightning-like in its effect: the point of
the collar, the break of the cape at the elbow, the meeting
of the white sleeve and the red cape, the corner of the table
and of the book — all united in the great sweep of the cape
at the right. On the left the play is more upon the curve
— in the collar, the folds of the cape and of the sleeve, at
the wrist, in the hand. The emphasis upon verticality is
strong: in the elongated proportions of the face, the nose,
in the beard, in the row of buttons. The paint is put on
the canvas in bold strokes which stand out clearly instead
of being fused and blended as in the Titian, strokes which
contribute to the intensity of feeling. Color too plays
its part in the total impression. In the Titian the color
is quiet, restrained, harmonious, for that effect was Titian's
objective. In the El Greco the reds, greens, and whites,
sharply contrasting both in hue and in light and dark, contribute to the effect of dramatic intensity which it was the
purpose of El Greco to express.

To bring out the quality of this head more clearly, com-

pare it with the head of the *Delphic Sibyl* (PL. 54). Make
allowance, of course, for the difference of technique. How
vigorous is the Michelangelo! Yet not electrically so. Its
proportions are very different from the El Greco: its
breadth of surface, its unbroken sweep of line, its emphasis
upon repeated horizontals — in the forehead, the brows,
the eyes, the mouth, the chin — balanced by the vertical
axis so strongly accented by the point in the headdress.
Every detail is a contributing element to a virile serenity
and a consistent unity. Just as consistent is the unity of
the El Greco. But how different! A unity of broken surfaces, agitated irregular lines, strong contrasts of color —
a unity of elements that all contribute toward an expression
of inner fire. The spirit of the Michelangelo is the spirit of
Santa Sophia, of Beethoven's *Fifth Symphony.* The spirit
of El Greco is that of *Chartres,* of the love music of *Tristan
and Isolde.* Each is specific and individual. Yet through
the individual glows the larger concept of the universal
spirit of life.

In *The Infanta Marguerita of Spain* (PL. 76) [34] still another personality emerges. Here is a very attractive little
girl in an overelaborate dress. A general atmosphere of
conventionality, felt especially in the stiff pose and the un-
childlike dress and ornaments, reflects the rigid social conventions of the Spanish court. These conventions were
limitations placed upon the artist. But see what he did
with them. Out of the dress he has made a gay dancing pattern of black against ivory, with soft rose in the bows and
ruching, the flowers in the hand, and the hair bow. The
outstretched hand connects the figure, which is placed
slightly to the right, with the balancing chair which acts

[34] Diego Velasquez, a Spanish painter, 1599–1660 A.D. *The Infanta
Marguerita,* painted about 1655, is in the Louvre, Paris.

as a foil to set off the petite gay figure by its scale, by the severity of its lines, and by its quietly rich velvet upholstery of a darker tone of rose. How much more effective the portrait is because of the chair! Velasquez knew exactly why he put it in. He didn't just happen to do it. The dark background gives an impression not of a flat curtain hung behind the figures, but of a space filled with light and air which envelop the child and the chair. The light is reflected by the silky hair smoothly drawn over the forehead, and filters in and out of the ringlets of soft texture. The round face with the large dark eyes is very delicately modeled by light, light-filled shadows, and color. Everywhere throughout the canvas are brush strokes that are not conspicuously vigorous, like those in the El Greco, but which, on close inspection, look hasty and careless. Stand back, however, and everything takes its place with just the right texture, just the right amount of light, just the right place in depth. What Velasquez saw, he painted — not details, but essentials only.

In all three portraits we can see quite clearly the principle of fitting a form to an idea. The idea is the characterization. The form is a result of a design that will not only adequately express the idea but will also enhance it by contributing its own abstract power of expression. For example, see how fitting in each case is the color used; how fitting is the way in which color unites with line and light and dark to emphasize the restrained simplicity of the Titian, the dynamic intensity of the El Greco, and the childlike charm of the Velasquez.

READING

GRONAU, G., Titian, N. Y., Scribner, 1904.
PEERS, E. A., Spain, N. Y., Dodd, Mead, 1930.

RUTTER, F., El Greco, N. Y., Scribner, 1927.
STEVENSON, R. A. M., Velasquez, London, Bell, 1912.

SUGGESTION

Make a preliminary study for a portrait. Select a person
whom you know. (a) What is the character to be represented? Upon what is the emphasis to be placed? (b) What
form will you use to express the character: shape, size, and
proportions of the canvas or panel; relation of the figure to
the canvas and to the background; organization of line, light
and dark, and color?

PLATE 77

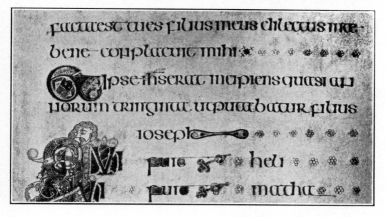

A. Roman Capitals. Carved in stone on Trajan's column, in Rome. Finely proportioned and spaced they have a dignified architectural quality.

B. Half Uncials. Written with a pen held horizontally. From the Book of Kells which contains some of the most beautiful writing of the Middle Ages.

C. Japanese Characters. Made with the brush which sweeps freely from thick to thin line.

PLATE 78

Khamsah (Complete Works) of Nizami. The writing, illustration, spacing, binding — all elements contribute to harmonious unity. (Metropolitan Museum)

PLATE 79

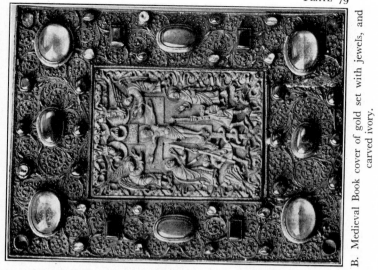

A. Outside of the Cover of the Nizami (Pl. 78). (Metropolitan Museum)

B. Medieval Book cover of gold set with jewels, and carved ivory.

PLATE 80

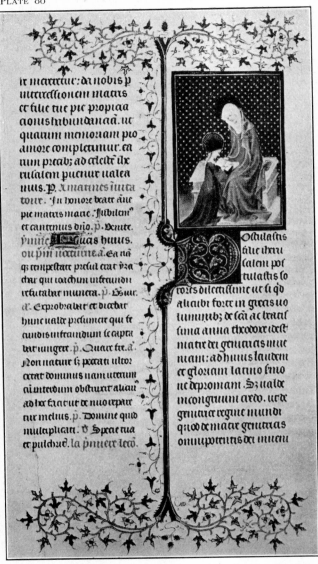

Breviary of the Duke of Burgundy. The columns of writing, varied by the initials, the straight bars contrasting to but united with the delicate curving ivy pattern, the strong accent of the miniature—each of these elements takes its place in relation to the whole; no one obtrudes.

Part Eight

THE ART OF THE BOOK

So COMMONPLACE is the book today that we little realize how recently books have been in great demand or even within the purchasing power of average folk. The printing press, cheap paper, education: these three agencies have made the book today one of the most far-reaching forces in our world.

For perhaps six thousand years man has been writing. From the days when crude picture-writing began to take on the form of letters and words, before 3000 B.C., until about 1450 A.D., when printing began to replace writing by hand in Europe, books were all *manuscripts*, that is, written by hand, as the word denotes, and illustrated by hand. Often they were bound in covers of carved ivory, or of gold with enamels and jewels (PL. 79B).[1] Such books were costly, the rare possession of the few. For the many, the function of conveying ideas was met by songs and ballads, by wall paintings (PL. 66), carvings (PL. 19), mosaics (PLS. 11, 14, 15), windows (PL. 18 and see page 90).

Conveyance of ideas, however, though the function of a book, is not alone a criterion of its quality as a work of art. Is a book most satisfactory when its content alone is satisfying? Even if it is legible and easy to handle? Is there any difference in desirability between the two letters in Fig. 103, which are identical in content? Form as well as content and harmony between form and content are inescapable in a book of quality.

To give a book form calls into play a considerable

[1] A medieval binding of gold with jewels and carved ivory. Tenth century A.D. Cluny Museum, Paris.

number of the arts, whether the book be handwritten or printed. The materials, the writing or the type, the illustration, the binding — each plays its part. Of materials for the text, the best known are *papyrus, parchment, vellum,* and *paper*. *Papyrus* is the oldest. The Egyptian made it from the papyrus reeds that grew abundantly along the Nile by splitting the reed into thin strips, laying these strips in two layers at right angles, and pounding them together into a single sheet. Then he dried it in the sun and polished it with ivory or shell until it was smooth enough for writing. But papyrus was rather difficult to procure, especially outside Egypt. So, according to legend, a king of Pergamon in Asia Minor developed the idea of using animal skins, especially of sheep, goats, and calves, and the material was named after him

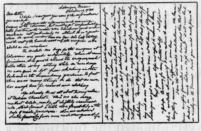

Fig. 103.   A Letter.   The same content expressed in two forms.

pergamentum, or *parchment*. *Vellum* is a very fine skin, chiefly that of newborn calves. By the tenth century a new material for writing had come into Europe from the Orient, a material made from the pulp of fibers — linen or cotton rags. It seems to have been the Arabs who learned the idea from Chinese prisoners in central Asia. This new material soon supplanted parchment and vellum, and by an ironical turn received its name, *paper,* from papyrus, the material which parchment in its turn had supplanted.

Writing fulfills man's need of recording and conveying ideas and thus has always had a definite use. At the same time its form has often lifted it to the plane of an art, that is, *calligraphy*. How different in different parts of the world are the forms of letters! And how dependent each form has been upon the materials with which the writing is done: Japanese characters made with a brush on silk or paper (PL. 77C); Roman capitals carved with a chisel in stone (PL. 77A);[2] letters made with a turkey quill, held horizontally or obliquely, on vellum or paper (PL. 77B[3] and Fig. 104).

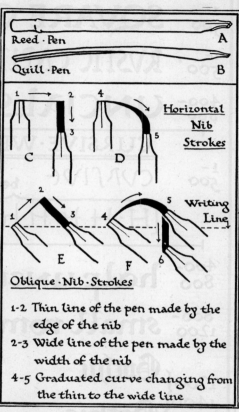

1-2 Thin line of the pen made by the edge of the nib

2-3 Wide line of the pen made by the width of the nib

4-5 Graduated curve changing from the thin to the wide line

Fig. 104. Pens and Their Strokes. (Ernst Detterer)

Generally speaking, there are two kinds of writing, *formal* and *cursive*. The *formal,* before the days of the print-

[2] Carved on the base of the *Column of Trajan*, Rome. 4½ in. high. About 114 A.D.

[3] From the *Book of Kells*, from the monastery of Kells in Ireland. About 700 A.D. Trinity College, Dublin.

FORMAL·WRITING

A·D.		
1– 500	SQVARE CAPS	I
1– 500	RVSTIC CAPITALS	II
400– 800	UNCIALS	III

CURSIVE·WRITING

| 1– 500 | CVRSIVE becomes [H·H·H·h·h·h] | |

400– 800	half uncials	IV
800– 1200	small roman	V
1200 {	Gothic	VI
1400 {	Gothic	VII
1400	small roman	VIII
1400	Italics	IX

ing press, was used for inscriptions, often carved in stone, for books, and for many documents, but has now been replaced by printing. The *cursive* has always been and still is the everyday handwriting, the running hand, which the word cursive means. That this evolved from formal writing, because of the materials and the instruments used, and because of the need of rapidity, we can see in the evolution of the form of almost any of our letters, H for example (Fig. 104).[4] The chisel predestines the straight line; the pen, quill, or brush, the curve.

For thousands of years, then, books were written by hand (Fig. 105), many of them the world's finest books. When the German bookmakers began to stamp the letters with type, they left spaces for the elaborate initials and decorations to be added by hand after the printing was done (compare PLS. 80 and 81). When printing was first introduced into Italy from Germany, it was scorned by book-lovers, who still demanded for their libraries volumes made entirely by hand. The Duke of Urbino is said to have had a library in which " every book . . . is of faultless beauty, written by hand on parchment, and adorned

---

[4] To see the same kind of an evolution in Egyptian writing, see J. H. Breasted, *Ancient Times*, Boston, Ginn, 1916, p. 44.

Fig. 105. Book-hands. The letters which we use today both in writing and in printing are derived from the capital letters of the Romans (PL. 77A). I. Though written with a pen these large letters are close kin to those of PL. 77A. II. These letters are better adapted to the pen and are more compactly spaced. III. Uncials (from the Latin word meaning inch-high) have a still more rounded form. Compare the A and U with those in I. IV. Half-uncials (PL. 77B) are a development, in smaller size, of the uncial. Note how the pen tends to connect the letters. V. The small roman is a further development of the half-uncial. Compare the "n" with that in IV. VI. Gothic (sometimes called Old English) is the roman made angular and heavy. In Italy and Spain it retained the round form (VII). VIII shows a smaller, lighter form of V; and IX, a slanting more cursive form with a tendency to connect the letters. (Ernst Detterer)

tue tcõ. Tibi enĩ ac liberis tuĩs reposita
sunt de hostijs salutaribus filiox̃, israe-
hel: eo cp̃ armũ z pedus z adipes quĩ
remãtur in altari·eleuauerũt coram 1

the extreme usefulness of the works printed
in the famous city of Venice, especially of
those which are from the excellent workshop
of Master Nicolas Jenson, the Frenchman. 2

The whole duty of Typography, as of Calligraphy, is to communicate to the imagination, without loss by the way, the thought or
image intended to be communicated by the
  3
dono puro di Dio e felicità di natu-
ra, benchè spesso provenga da lunga
esercitazione e abitudine, che le piu 4
difficili cose agevola a segno che in
  5

ver a difference in design which sets it distinctly apart from
all sans serifs of similar appearance, for a new idea has been
embodied in this type. It has not been developed from a prototype. It has assumed a similarity to the sans serif letters

Fig. 106. Type Face. 1. Gothic type of the
Forty-Two Line (the so-called Gutenberg) Bible
(PL. 81), about 1450 A.D. See Fig. 105, VI.
2. Roman type of Nicolas Jenson of Venice,
1470 A.D. See Fig. 105, VIII. 3. Type of
William Caslon, London, 1720 A.D. 4. Type of
Gianbattista Bodoni, Parma, 1818 A.D. In comparing 3 and 4 with 2, notice that the difference
is a matter partly of spacing, partly of thin and
thick strokes (the thin stroke is particularly emphasized in the Bodoni), and partly of the terminal strokes of the letters called serifs. 5. Futura
type, modern German, marked by the absence of
serifs and by a uniform width in the strokes.
Notice the blackness and strength of 1 as contrasted
with 2, 3, and 4; and the blackness and boldness
of 5. Which of the five is the easiest to read?
(Ernst Detterer)

with miniatures.
There is not a
single printed
book in the
collection. The
Duke would have
been ashamed to
own any such." [5]
How surprised
this duke would
be, could he
spend half an
hour in one of
our fine libraries!
Printing, then, at
the outset, was
but a labor-saving
device.

It was not long,
however, before
some of the
printers realized
that the printed
book, the entirely
printed book,
could possess a
quality compar-
able to that of the
hand-made book.

[5] F. P. Lippmann,
Drawings by Sandro Botti-
celli for Dante's Divine
Comedy, Berlin, 1896, p.
14

At first the type face was copied directly from the written letter — *gothic, roman, italic.* But in writing there is a dash, a life, with many small variations and flourishes. The quill, as it moves from letter to letter, naturally makes beginning and finishing strokes called *serifs,* which seem to finish the letter and to carry the eye more easily from letter to letter. In metal type the serifs are more precise and uniform than in handwriting. Sometimes they have been abandoned altogether, as in the modern *futura* type of Fig. 106.

In addition to serifs, thin and thick strokes furnished the typesetters a problem. In writing, the strokes of the pen naturally vary according to the way the instrument is held and the direction of its movement. In type, there is no reason for this differentiation and its use is a matter of giving variety to the form of the letter, and it is also important in distinguishing type faces (Fig. 106). Thus the type-designers came to the realization that letters of metal used mechanically call for a different form from those written by hand, although they are the same A,B,C,D.

The book is not, however, a matter of letters alone, whether written or printed, but of letters grouped into words and words into sentences and paragraphs which create a pleasing form if placed with pleasing proportions and spacing in relation both to each other and to the entire page.

The book has had various forms. There is the long scroll of the Egyptian, Greek, and Roman (Figs. 107 and 108), one long page with a stick at each end for handling it and rolling it up. Sometimes the writing was continuous the long way and sometimes was broken into columns so as to prevent so much rolling and unrolling. This practice led to the idea of cutting the scroll into sheets the width

of the columns and sewing them together along one edge. Thus evolved the *codex,* the present form of the book.[6]

Fig 107. Scroll Form of the Book. In reading one hand unrolls while the other rolls (Fig. 108).

Whatever the form of the book and however clear and beautiful the writing may be, there has always been a tendency to enliven and enrich the page with embellishment and to elucidate the contents with illustrations: initial letters, borders, engravings, paintings. Then the question rises: Do the initials and borders embellish? Does the text explain the illustration? Does the illustration illustrate? Does it take its place as one contributing element in the design of the book as a whole, like well-designed sculpture or ornament of any kind in a building, or does it exist for itself? These questions we shall consider in the examples that we shall look at.

Finally, there is the binding of the book, obviously a protective measure. Its character depends on the material of which the book is made and on the way it is to be used. While a Japanese book of thin rice paper, which naturally lies flat, needs but

Fig. 108. Roman Youth Reading a Scroll. (After Clark)

a light paper cover to prevent soilure, a medieval European book of thick vellum, which tends to curl, must

[6] It may prove interesting to find other forms of the book, such as the Babylonian clay tablets, Roman double-hinged tablets, or those of the Far East.

be held firmly by stout boards tied or clasped together. The unsightly appearance of the boards and their large unbroken spaces led the bookmakers to concentrate decoration here and, in the case of finely decorated and illustrated books, to make the outside worthy of the inside (PL. 79). This was particularly true of religious books, the Bible and Books of Prayer in the Christian churches and the Korans in the Mohammedan mosques. The great enemy of the wood-covered book, however, is the bookworm, which invades not only the cover but the pages as well. This disadvantage led to a search for some other stout material, which was found in cardboard. At first this too had its own disadvantage, for it led to the destruction of many fine books. For, as paper was not as plentiful as it is today, old books were in demand to make cardboard, in the layers of which have been found pages of some fine lost books. With the extension of the use of paper lighter and more flexible material such as leather, textiles, and papers have supplanted the stouter stuffs.

Fig. 109. Roman Methods of Storing Scrolls. The tabs contain the titles. (After Clark)

In binding a book another consideration confronts the maker: How is the book to be used? How stored? Roman scrolls were kept in boxes or on shelves (Fig. 109). In this matter of storing the codex obviously has an advantage over the scroll. Many of the fine religious books with jeweled covers had but little handling, for they were kept on a lectern, used only in the service, and considered as

precious as the vessels on the altar. Early books were bulky and not well enough sewed to stand on end. They were laid on their sides on shelves or in cupboards (PL. 81A), and often had metal corners and pieces to protect the sides. The preciousness of books often led to chaining them (Fig. 110). Still in some old library, as at Merton College in Oxford, you can see volumes with their chains, or at least the holes in the stout cases for the fastenings.[7] Finally, the advance in methods of sewing the leaves and binding them securely between their protective coverings led to the practical present-day method of placing the title on the back and stacking the books vertically.

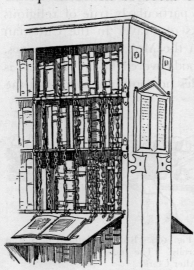

Fig. 110. Method of Storing Books in the Middle Ages. Bound in stout covers and straps they were frequently chained to their cases. See also PL. 82. (After Clark)

READING

HERBERT, J. A., Illuminated Manuscripts, N. Y., Putnam, 1911.

IVINS, W. M., Jr., A Guide to an Exhibition of the Arts of the Book, N. Y., Metropolitan Museum, 1924.

JOHNSTON, E., Writing, and Illuminating and Lettering, London, Pitman, 13th ed., 1923.

MORISON, S., Type Design of the Past and Present, London, The Fleuron, 1926.

POLLARD, A. W., Fine Books, N. Y., Putnam, 1912.

---

[7] See J. W. Clark, *Care of Books* (Cambridge University Press, 1909), for many illustrations of books kept flat in presses, and chained to shelves.

Many inexpensive illustrations, both in color and plain, can be secured in the British Museum Postcard Sets.

SUGGESTIONS

The field of the book offers many opportunities for the play of judgment and taste, and for creative endeavor.

1. Study books from the point of view of unity of design in the entire book.

2. Make a collection of different kinds of type face, noting in each case its use and your opinion of its suitability for this use.

3. Illustration. Find examples (a) where the illustration harmonizes with the letterpress and takes its place as one element in the whole; (b) where the illustration is more emphatic than the text, or does not harmonize with it.

4. Design a complete book. Select a piece of literature and determine the complete design from the beginning: size, writing or type, page layout, illustration, title-page, binding, cover design. Material gathered for Art Appreciation courses, or in fact for any course, may well serve as content. For suggestions see L. L. Winslow, *Elementary Industrial Arts,* N. Y., Macmillan, 1922, Chap. I.

A BOOK OF PERSIAN ROMANCES

THIS book is an ornament on the page of time.

The merit of the book is suited to the quality of reader.

For each small detail of it the artist has procured limpid gold. . . .

In wisdom the book is deeper than the pearl of pure water.

It is the perfect verse of an intimate friend.

Sometimes the tongue of the love-lorn lover speaks;

At other times a charming word from the lips of the beloved is unveiled;

It scatters sweetness over the memory of Khusrau and Shirin.

It describes the story of Laila and Majnun as a pearl of pure water. . . .

Beyond measure and great is the amount
Of the beautiful writing on its rose leaves. . . .

May these beautiful pages and their unparalled script
Grant light to the pupil of the eye of the writer;
And with it sweet virtues and comfort.
The veil is raised from his face, in hope
That from the Asaf of the time he may obtain a glance and
    may gain
From that glance everlasting joy.
By the gift of God may the prosperity of his fortune be ever-
    lasting;
And may the prayers from the lips of the people be accepted.[8]

Thus speaks the artist in words of gilded leather, clear
against the blue panels of the inside cover. It is not only
a poetic table of contents and introduction but also an expression of the artist's own feeling of the lofty quality of
his work. And we enthusiastically share his feeling as we
open the book and see the writing, the illustration, and the
binding all brought together into an orderly balanced harmony (PL. 78). The quiet spaciousness of the margins, relieved by flecks of gold, sets off the beauty of the writing,
the flashes of intense color and gold in the miniatures, and
the intricate richness of the cover.

The book contains the five romantic poems of *Nizami,*
a famous Persian poet.[9] Of these is the Bedouin love story
of Laila and Majnun, illustrated in PL. 78, the Romeo and
Juliet of Persia; and the romances of the hunter king,
Bahram Gur (PL. 64). Each poem is written on a differ-

[8] A. V. W. Jackson, *Catalogue of Persian Manuscripts,* N. Y., Columbia
University Press, 1914, p. 59.

[9] *Nizami* lived 1140–1203 A.D. The book page measures 12¾ in. by 8¾ in.,
and was written 1524–25 A.D. Metropolitan Museum, N. Y. A similar
Nizami, in the British Museum, is published with fine color reproductions by
The Studio, London.

ent-colored paper — light cream, yellow, pale blue, pink, dark cream — and each is introduced by a chapter heading of intricate design which harmonizes in hue with the hue of the paper on which the poem is written.

Throughout the book, the materials and craftsmanship are of the finest quality, and every detail has had the most scrupulous care not only in itself but also in its relation to the whole. The paper is heavy and of unusual texture, the writing — in this land where writing was one of the fine arts — of the highest quality. In the concluding lines is the modest statement that the work was " finished with God's help by the hand of the poor and obscure Sultan Muhammed Nur," who, we well know, was one of the most famous calligraphers of the day.

Opposite the writing is the illustration, sometimes with a few lines of text. It forms a panel of the same width as the text, though of different height, thus observing harmony of margin together with variety. These illustrations (PL. 64) are vivacious and sparkling in color: clear, intense red, blue, green, yellow, gold. Because there is no shadow the flat areas of color have a particularly decorative quality.

The binding of the book, when closed, gives an impression of quiet richness and elegance — brown leather, embossed and gilded (PL. 79A). The field, which consists of a landscape scene with a decorative tree, deer, birds, monkeys, and conventional cloud forms, is framed by a broad border containing alternately large and small panels. As you pull out the flap and open the book, you are surprised and delighted. For the inside of the cover, though designed to harmonize with the outside in its general composition, flashes with color. Here the gilded cut-leather medallion on a blue ground is surrounded by a deep-red field; and in the borders by green and blue panels, through

which run, in gold letters, the inscriptions quoted at the opening of the chapter. This color harmonizes with the color of the miniature, carrying out the same note of gayety.

Such intensity of color and richness of detail are possible without being gaudy if given space and if proportioned to the whole. Just as the rich detail of the interior of *Santa Sophia* demanded not only the scale of the building to relieve it but also a strong emphasis on the major elements of the design, so in the *Persian Romances*, the strong accents of color and the elaborate detail are relieved by the contrastingly quiet broad margins, which are unbroken except for the flecks of gold. All the parts are clearly defined, proportioned, and balanced. Appearance and atmosphere harmoniously reflect the gayety of spirit of the romantic tales. Content, too, is part of the larger whole. Can you think of a form that would better fit the content?

SOME PRINTED BOOKS

ABOUT 1500 A.D., in the Piazza Manin in the heart of Venice (Fig. 90), not far from San Marco and its great library, you would pass a house on which was this notice:

Whoever you are, you are earnestly requested by Aldus to state your business briefly and take your departure promptly. Then you can be of service even as was Hercules to the weary Atlas. For this is a place of work for all who enter.

To waste time chattering was not for Aldus Manutius. Too large a task it was to which he had set himself. Not many years before there had come into Italy from the north a new idea, the possibilities of which grasped the imagination of the keen-witted Italians — the idea of movable type, which made printing practicable. The basic idea in printing, that is, stamping a number of impressions from

one form, was not novel. The Chinese had used such a device long, long before. In Europe block books already

existed, in which letters, together with the illustration, were cut in the wood block (Fig. 111), and the impressions from these blocks bound together into book form. But the idea of cutting letters separately so that they could be moved about to make words and sentences and the idea of casting the letters in metal — these two ideas originated in northern Europe about 1450, and books printed with movable type began to appear about this time. The novelty of the method is apparent

Fig. 111. A Page from a Block-Book, the Biblia Pauperum (Bible of the Poor). Center, Christ Rising from the Tomb; left, Samson and the City-Gates; right, Jonah and the Whale. Printed, probably in Holland, about 1450 A.D. British Museum, London.

by its specific mention in the colophon [10] of a *Psalter* (the first printed book which is dated) printed by Fust and Schöffer of Mainz (Fig. 112), which reads in translation:

The present book of Psalms, adorned with beautiful capitals and clearly divided with rubrics has been thus fashioned by an ingenious invention of printing and stamping and was dili-

[10] A *colophon* consists of a few lines at the end of a book which give the title, perhaps the name of the writer or illuminator, the place of writing, and the date — information now placed on the title-page. Today a colophon is a sort of publisher's trademark.

gently brought to completion, to the glory of God, by Johann Fust, a citizen of Mainz, and Peter Schöffer of Gernsheim in the year of our Lord 1457 on the vigil of the Feast of the Assumption [August 29].

These earliest printed books, such as the *Forty-Two Line Bible* (Pl. 81),[11] bear a far greater resemblance to

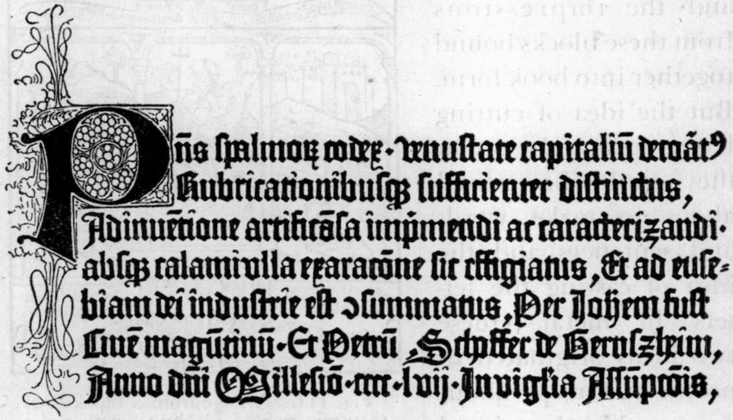
Pñs spalmorũ codex · venustate capitaliũ decoratꝰ
Rubricationibusqȝ sufficienter distinctus,
Adinuētione artificiosa imprimendi ac caracterizandi ·
absqȝ calami vlla exaracōne sic effigiatus, Et ad euse-
biam dei industrie est ꝯsummatus, Per Johem fust
Ciuē maguntinū · Et Petrū Schoffer de Gernszheim,
Anno dñi Millesiō · cccc · lvij · In vigilia Assūpcōis,

Fig. 112. Colophon of the Psalter of Fust and Schöffer.

medieval manuscripts than to printed books. Let us turn for a moment to one of these manuscripts. Pl. 80 shows a page from a *Breviary*,[12] in which the writing, in the gothic hand (Fig. 105), is in two columns. The capitals, some in red, and the gold initial give a vibrant effect to the columns, while the miniature provides a strong accent of red

[11] A page from a Bible so called because there are forty-two lines in a column. Printed at Mainz, 1456 A.D. It is sometimes called the *Gutenberg Bible* because it may have been printed by Johannes Gutenberg, who is credited by some with the invention of movable type. A color reproduction of a page in the New York Public Library can be found in the Encyclopædia Britannica 14th ed., article "Printing."

[12] Called the *Burgundy Breviary* because it contains the arms of John the Fearless, Duke of Burgundy and of his duchess, Margaret of Bavaria. French, early fifteenth century A.D. British Museum. For a color reproduction see J. A. Herbert, *Illuminated Manuscripts*, N. Y., Putnam, 1911, Frontispiece; and British Museum Postcard B 277.

and blue, like the accenting glass at *Chartres*. The figures against the checkered ground make a decorative pattern whose charm and grace find an echo in the charm and grace and in the color and gold of the ivy borders that bind all parts together. There is a unity in the writing, the borders, the illustration, and the initial — a unity of spirit and of form.

Most of these beautiful handwritten books of the Middle Ages were made by the monks in the monasteries (PL. 82).[13] As there was no store where a book could be bought, it was ordered of the monastery. Six months to a year was not too much time to allow, for the book was all written by hand, decorated and bound by hand.

As we compare the *Forty-Two Line Bible* with the *Breviary,* we see more resemblance than difference. The printed letters, to be sure, reveal a certain precision and regularity not found in handwritten letters, though their shapes are the same. The material is the same, expensive vellum, and the guide lines are ruled as for writing. The text was printed to save time and labor, and space was left for the initials and decorative borders to be added by hand. In general, the conception of the book has not changed. There was still, as in the manuscript, no title-page. Any information as to title, author, printer, or date was placed in the colophon. These early books are called *incunabula,* books " in the cradle." Yet how beautifully they are printed! There is a fine quality in the strong, angular gothic type, in the blackness of the ink, and in the splendid massing on the page.

[13] From a French manuscript written in 1456 A.D. by the secretary of Philip the Good, Duke of Burgundy. National Library, Paris. For the place of the monastery in the Middle Ages and the attitude of the monks toward their work, see H. Gardner, *Art Through the Ages*, N. Y., Harcourt, 1926. Chap. XIII, and the references there given.

In Italy, at the time of this invention of movable type, the recovery of ancient literature — the writings of Homer, Plato, Sophocles, Virgil, Ovid — was the passion of the day. To rescue these treasures, to preserve them, and to increase their use — that is, to make cheaper editions than those written by hand — was the ambition of Aldus. And not-

Fig. 113. An Early Print Shop in Venice. (After Ongania, *Early Venetian Printing Illustrated*)

withstanding the opposition of nobles like the Duke of Urbino, the curiosity and eagerness of the age decided the success of the printing-press. It was an arduous task to which Aldus put himself. He wrote:

I have made a vow to devote my life to the public service and God is my witness that such is my most ardent desire. To a life of ease and quiet I have preferred one of restless labor. Man is not born for pleasure which is unworthy of the truly generous mind but for honorable labor. Let us leave to the vile herd the existence of brutes. Cato has compared the life of man to the tool of iron: use it well, it shines, cease to use it and it rusts.[14]

[14] W. Roberts, *Printers' Marks*, London, Bell, 1893, p. 218.

With this spirit, why was the task arduous? Because the necessary materials for printing could not be purchased and the methods of the craft were unknown. If Aldus was to succeed, he must be a pioneer. He designed and cast his own type, made his own ink, taught his helpers as he was learning himself through experience (Fig. 113). He could obtain paper from a mill at Fabriano in central Italy. In fact the possibility of securing good paper, cheap in comparison with the cost of vellum or parchment, was a vital factor in the development of bookmaking.

Fig. 114. Anchor and Dolphin. Aldus' printer's mark.

Thus we do not wonder at the sign on Aldus' door. And is not his famous printer's mark (Fig. 114) significant — that dolphin and anchor to which were added the words *Festina lente (Make haste slowly)*? And the result? From the Aldine Press came books which were cheap, compared with the manuscripts, as well as beautiful — as beautiful as any ever made.

Although the Greek and Latin classics occupied Aldus chiefly, still he printed Italian works also. One of these we may take as an illustration (Fig. 115), a romance of the day, the *Hypnerotomachia Poliphili (The Strife of Love in a Dream of Poliphilus)*. Here is beautiful organization of beautiful elements. A complete break has been made with the manuscript. Every part of this book is adapted to the process of printing. The illustration and text form a unit that is so placed on the page that it leaves amply satisfying margins, and every element keeps its place in one plane, the plane of the page. The unity results from both the harmony and the contrast of three

parts: the *woodcut*,[15] a paragraph printed in capitals, and a paragraph which begins with one line of capitals and then, with the help of the initial, makes an easy transition to lower-case letters.[16]   The illustration, being linear, partakes of the nature of the type. It is the charming variety among similar elements that gives character to the unity. Cover the initial and see how the elements fall apart. The L and its floral ornament together form a compact square which makes a break in the rectangle of the paragraph and creates an accent at that point. The patterning of the surface of this square echoes the patterning in the illustration above and serves the printed page as does a small area of one hue,

Fig. 115.   Page from the *Hypneroto-machia Poliphili*.   Printed by Aldus in Venice, 1499 A.D.

green for example (see page 90), when it helps balance a larger area of the same hue.

In Florence, some of the most charming examples of early printing are the pamphlets of romances, plays, and religious tracts. Fig. 116, for example, reproduces the first page of a

[15] A *woodcut* is printed from a block of wood on which the design is drawn and then all the surface cut away, with knife and chisel, except the lines of the design, which are left standing in relief. The block is then inked and an impression made in which only the lines are visible, the parts cut away being represented by empty spaces.

[16] A term applied to small, in distinction from capital letters.

PLATE 81

Forty-two Line Bible. Though the text is printed and the letters, therefore, more regular, the general appearance of the page is similar to that of Pl. 80.

PLATE 82

Monk in Scriptorium (Writing-room). Around him are scrolls, and books with stout covers and straps. (J. C. Couderc, *Les Enluminures des Manuscrits du Moyen Âge de la Bibliothèque Nationale.* Paris, Éditions de la Gazette des Beaux-Arts)

romance in which, as in the *Hypnerotomachia*, there is a charming unity of illustration and type and a pleasing relation of this unity to the page. In the woodcut there is a particularly fine sweep of line and a consciously balanced decorative effect (cf. Fig. 111). The two figures are accented, each by an arch, but the group has variety because the youth stands forward and is larger; the lady stands toward the back and is smaller. The entire effect is from the use of line alone, without hatching for shadow — a maximum of expression with a slight means. Its strong border and the initial B furnish major accents; the first line set in capitals, a minor one. In few books is there a finer balance of all parts and a closer unity than in early Italian printed books.

Perhaps no kind of illustration has been more satisfactory than the woodcut, because the character of this medium

Fig. 116. Title Page of the *Story of Two Lovers*. Florence, xvth century. (Metropolitan Museum)

is closely related to that type and therefore peculiarly harmonious. For the design of the woodcut stands in relief just as the type face stands in relief, so that the two can be printed together; and has a crispness of line which is harmonious with the crisp linear quality of type.

Somehow one feels, in turning the pages of these books, how eagerly these early printers were using the medium of printing as something precious, something to be used not alone for the conveyance of ideas, but for the creation of a form which should enhance the ideas conveyed. Literature, like music, is a language and implies an audience. A musical composition does not exist, except for the composer, without the interpreter. So the piece of literature does not exist, except for the writer, without its interpreter, the bookmaker. The great bookmakers have always taken the author's work that is the content and created a form that will interpret it, just as the violinist or pianist interprets the composer's work. This implies that there must be harmony between the form and the content.

Today when the world is flooded with books as never before, the principles of the ages, in spite of much mediocrity, still hold. Let us look at three books of unusual quality. In the *Moby Dick* (Fig. 117) there is a largeness that permeates the entire design and bespeaks a largeness of spirit in the content of the book. In the illustration, how effective is the scale of the figures in relation to the houses! It is this scale even more than the vigorous stride that conveys the impression of adventure, of conquest over circumstances. But it is not the illustration alone that gives this impression. All the elements of the page contribute and are linked into as close a unity as we found in the *Hypnerotomachia* (Fig. 115) , and by the use of the same principles. The woodcut, the capitals of the chapter title, the initial N, and the fine large type, the comparative size of the capitals and the lower-case letters — each is a contributing element. See how they are related and united! How the vigorous N serves as the needed accent in the lower half

CHAPTER XIII   WHEELBARROW

NEXT morning, Monday, after disposing of the em-
balmed head to a barber, for a block, I settled my
own and comrade's bill; using, however, my comrade's money. The grinning landlord, as well as the
boarders, seemed amazingly tickled at the sudden friendship
which had sprung up between me and Queequeg—especially as
Peter Coffin's cock and bull stories about him had previously so
much alarmed me concerning the very person whom I now com-
panied with.

⊲ 86 ⊳

Fig. 117. Page from *Moby Dick* by Herman Melville. Illustrated by Rock-
well Kent. Printed at the Lakeside Press, Chicago, 1930. (Lakeside Press)

JOSEPH CONRAD : THE MAN

BY

ELBRIDGE L. ADAMS

A BURIAL IN KENT

BY

JOHN SHERIDAN ZELIE

Together with some Bibliographical Notes

NEW YORK

WILLIAM EDWIN RUDGE

1925

JOSEPH CONRAD : THE MAN

Ever since I came upon "The Nigger of the Narcissus" in tranquil ante-bellum days I had been under the spell of Conrad's art. "Typhoon," "Lord Jim" and "Chance" were read with increasing beguilement, and then "Nostromo," that most astonishing creation of the imagination. One felt that here, indeed, was a magician who could conjure up the very spirit of some Eastern river and make one smell the rank stifling jungle or feel the motion of the ship as it drives before the hurricane. Nothing quite like these stories was to be found in the entire range of English literature. One was prepared to agree with Galsworthy that such writing "is probably the only writing of the last twelve years [he was referring to 1896–1908] that will enrich the English language to any great extent." But what sort of man, one won-

3

Adams.   Designed by Bruce Rogers at the Printing House of William Rudge, House of William Rudge)

AND GOD SAID LET THE WATERS
UNDER THE HEAVEN BE GATH—
ERED TOGETHER UNTO ONE
PLACE AND LET THE DRY LAND
APPEAR AND IT WAS SO + AND
GOD CALLED THE DRY LAND
EARTH AND THE GATHERING
TOGETHER OF THE WATERS
CALLED HE SEAS AND
GOD SAW THAT
IT WAS
GOOD

Fig. 119. *Genesis: The First Chapter*. Woodcuts by Paul Nash. Printed

at Nonesuch Press, Soho, London, 1924.   (Nonesuch Press)

of the page! Cover it and see how the unity vanishes.
See also how effectively the diagonal bar of the N is broken
by white lines. Make this bar solid black and see if it does
not jump out of the page toward you.

In the *Joseph Conrad: The Man* (Fig. 118) the same
principles are evident. It is again the beauty of the page
organization, vigorous yet tranquil. Look at the headpiece.
On each side of the blazing disc of the sun are birds and
palm trees symmetrically balanced. The motifs used to
form them combine to form dolphins which swing the
movement to the right, while reverse curves guide a
countermovement to the left. Every detail relates to Conrad's writing and at the same time is a harmonious element
in the page design. The diagonals of the slanting capitals
in the title continue the movement of the dolphins and of
the waves above and thus serve as a transition to the initial
and thence to the body of the printing. The same motifs
combine in the title-page, with the beautifully differentiated and beautifully spaced letters and words to produce
the same mood. Thus results harmony, for every element
contributes to the larger whole.

In the *Genesis* (Fig. 119) it is perhaps the boldness
of the design that impresses one primarily. There is a
monumental quality in every part: in the letterpress, the
illustration, the page layout, the binding. The elemen-
tal simplicity and grandeur of the design interpret the epic
grandeur of Genesis. What elements contribute to an expression of this spirit? The type face is all in capitals that
have a stern simplicity, for they have no serifs. A letterpress in such severe type, to be effective, requires great
spaciousness. Hence the unusually wide margins. A
similar quality in the woodcut and a similar placement on

the page bring unity and harmony between the two pages. And again a similar quality greets you as you close the book and see its cover of black paper of a velvety texture and devoid of ornament except for the gold lettering at the top and bottom of the sides and on the back.

THE ART BOOK   371

the page bring unity and harmony between the two pages.
And again as you close the book and lay it down, the book
and see its cover of black paper of a velvety texture and

Part Nine

THE ART OF WEAVING

DID you ever try to imagine what our world would be
without the weaver? Take away the products of this
craftsman — the coverings of our floors and of our furniture, our hangings, our blankets, our woven clothing. It
is difficult to imagine a world without textiles. Go where
you will and you find them. And you ask why this is
so? As we saw in the case of buildings, the craft rises
out of a definite human need, primarily the need of protective coverings.

But it is not only this need that makes the art so vital.
What pleasure the color and texture of fabrics bring into
everyday life! Soft colorful hangings or a warm note in
carpet and upholstery can transform a cold room into a
place of charm. The gay hues of present-day clothing make
our drab cities much more stimulating. What delight in
the texture of smooth satin, soft velvet, warm wool, cool
muslin! What rhythm, balance, harmony, there is in a
fine textile, just as in a fine painting or a fine building! It
may be a silk woven by a complicated power-driven loom
or a damask made by the hands of a patient weaver of the
East, a lustrous velvet, a boldly designed rug that helps
protect the hogan of the Navajo from the winter wind, a
great tapestry large enough to cover a wall or a Dacca muslin
of India so delicate that if it is wet and spread on the grass
it looks like dew. Infinite in variety though textiles may
be, still it is their rhythm, balance, and harmony that bring
them into the plane of art.

And further still, with some peoples there is often a
meaning, a symbolism, in their textile designs that springs
from their deepest feelings. The Persian carpet provides

the Persian, imaginatively, with a garden, his chief joy, when winter deprives him of his real garden. The Navajo weaves into his rugs designs that are symbols of the harvest and as much a supplication for rain and good crops as are his prayers. Thus the art of weaving is a great art. That it is vital and universal is seen by the many allusions, both literal and figurative, in all literature, to spinning, weaving, the loom, the warp, the weft.

The craft goes back to prehistoric days, thousands of years ago. During this long time, the great majority of textiles have been made with infinite patience, by hand. It is only within the last one hundred and fifty years that the machine has entered. As in early printing, the machine at first was merely a labor-saving device. By an ironical twist of meaning the word *manufacture,* from the Latin words "to make by hand," now denotes the making by machinery. The infinite delightful variations and irregularities of hand weaving, so charming in Persian rugs, for example, have been imitated in machine-made rugs, often with grotesque effect. To do this is obviously a disrespect for the craft. Those irregularities represent the human element. In the machine there is no human element. Its very nature demands a regularity, a precision. When faithful to its own principles, that is, when the designs are adapted to the machine idea of weaving rather than to the hand idea, then the machine has a capacity for creating fabrics of high quality. No one would want to do away with the machine. With all the unfortunate results to society of its discovery and application, at the same time it is one of the greatest agencies to make life easier for man in this modern complex civilization. The problem is to make the machine man's servant and not his master. The handmade textile requires time and leisure, the machine-

made fulfills present-day demands for quantity and rapidity. Either process may or may not produce a beautiful textile.

Whether by hand or by machinery, weaving means making a fabric by interlacing threads. Before seeing how we can manipulate these threads, shall we stop to consider where we can get them? Threads are to the weaver what clay is to the potter, pigment to the painter, words to the writer, or tones to the musician — a medium of expression. Nature provides the raw material for the most important threads in animal fibers, such as wool, hair, silk; and in vegetable fibers, such as flax, cotton, hemp. Important from the mineral realm are the precious metals, gold and silver. This raw material the craftsman must procure or raise, clean, spin into thread, dye. Each step in preparation of material is a vital process, demanding as thoughtful care as the weaving itself.

With his material prepared, how does the weaver produce a textile? To a *loom* he attaches longitudinal threads, the *warp*. Through these he interlaces a transverse thread, the *weft,* or *woof.* These three are the fundamentals: loom, warp, weft (Fig. 120). The warp reaches the entire length of the fabric and must be strong and pliable, for it is the ground upon which the artist works, as is the panel or canvas to the painter, or the block of stone to the sculptor. The weft is the versatile instrument, with which he can do many things. It is sometimes called *filling,* for the weaver literally fills the space left unoccupied by the warp.

Let us see what some of these things are. Shall we first make a plain cloth with a simple weave? On our loom we have strung the warp threads and are now ready to work with the weft, which is attached to a shuttle. Immediately we see a problem. In interlacing the weft we go

over one warp thread and under the next, entirely across the loom; and then we return over and under the alternate warp threads (Fig. 121). This is a tedious process. Hence, many ages ago the weaver worked out the problem of making a *shed* through which he could shoot his weft at a single throw. By various devices he attached the even-numbered warp threads so that on a vertical loom he could bring them all forward and shoot the weft behind them but in front of the odd-numbered warp strings. For the second throw he would bring all the odd-numbered warp threads forward so that the weft would run behind these and in front of the even-numbered ones.

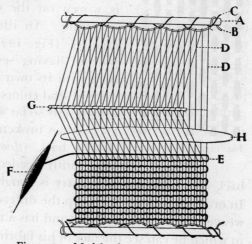

Fig. 120. Model of a Loom. The warp is strung on loom strings instead of loom bars (compare Fig. 129) in order to give the warp threads greater play and to relieve them of strain during the weaving. *A*, loom bars; *B*, loom strings; *C*, binding strings which hold the loom strings to the loom bars; *D*, warp; *E*, weft; *F*, spindle which carries the weft; *G*, rod to which alternate warp threads are attached and which, when brought forward, forms a shed through which the spindle has just shot a weft thread (for the sake of clearness the rod to which the other threads are attached is not shown); *H*, weave sword, a piece of polished wood to push the weft up against the part of the fabric already woven. (After Crawford, *Peruvian Textiles*, N. Y., American Museum of Natural History)

To make a plain cloth means to interweave the weft on this over-one-under-one principle entirely across the width of the fabric, so that in the finished

textile both warp and weft show. Muslins and linen handkerchiefs are good examples of this weave.

Let us next try a weave where one weft does not run the

Fig. 121. Plain Cloth Weave.

entire width of the loom, although it is woven on the over-one-under-one principle. An illustration of this is *tapestry* (Fig. 122). Here the purpose of having several weft threads, each with its own shuttle, is to introduce several colors. Each weft thread is used only so far as its color is needed and is then broken off or left hanging on the back (*floated,* as the weaver says) until needed again. Thus the back of a varicolored tapestry is rough-looking (Pl. 84). In order to pick up and drop the different weft threads the weaver sits behind his loom and has a mirror in front of it in which he can see the face of his fabric (Fig. 123). Another characteristic of tapestry is the fact that the weft is combed down tight and entirely covers the warp, making a firm fabric with a *rep,* that is, a ribbed surface. The fact that the weft thread stops when the color stops in the design is likely to leave slits in the fabric. Sometimes these slits are left, as in Pl. 87; sometimes they are sewed together, as in

Fig. 122.   Tapestry Weave in Three Colors.

Pl. 88; sometimes the weft threads interlock, thus avoiding slits, as in Pl. 86 and Fig. 132.

In the *twill* and *satin* weaves, the weft runs the entire width of the warp, but instead of the over-one-under-one principle, the thread may run over-one-under-six or over-

five-under-one, thus exposing longer strands of the warp or the weft (Figs. 124 and 125). This exposure is of advantage in making silk fabrics, where a smooth texture can be obtained by leaving uninterrupted a smooth fiber. Combining a satin weave with a *plain cloth* weave — that is, to weave part of the fabric in the satin weave and part in a plain cloth weave, thus creating parts that contrast in texture — produces what is known as a *damask* (PLS. 83 and 88B). The fabric is reversible, the part that is satin weave on the face being plain or twill cloth on the back and vice versa. This weave is used in linen damask.

One method of enriching any weave is to *brocade* it (PL. 88). This implies the use of an additional weft not essential to the body of the fabric but inserted as a part of the weaving proc-

Fig. 123. Loom for a Large Tapestry. (Müntz)

ess, where needed, thus obtaining additional color and texture. Where gold and silver are used in weaving it is usually by brocading. These additional threads are floated or cut on the back, as in tapestry.

Pile fabric is made by an additional weft. Pile weaving recommends itself for carpets because the hard usage to which floor coverings are subjected calls for something dur-

able. That is the great advantage of pile. It can at the same time stand hard wear and protect the woven ground.

Fig. 124. Twill Weave. Each weft thread passes over one and under six warp threads in such a way as to give a diagonal rib (rep).

What do we mean by *pile?* The loom is strung with a warp that is tough and pliable and usually a band is first woven of plain or tapestry weave. Then the weaver twists short bits of thread, usually woolen, about the warp threads (Fig. 126), going across the width of the loom and using the colors which his design calls for. This is called *knotting*. The knotted threads stand up at right angles to the warp and weft and form the pile. When the weaver has gone across the loom with a row of knotting he puts in one or more rows of weft and then combs both the pile and the weft down firmly. Though his fingers work with amazing rapidity, the carpet grows slowly. For in fine carpets it takes from fifty to one hundred or even several hundred knots to make a square inch. After he has woven a considerable amount he trims the uneven ends of the pile with his shears, leaving them short or long. In a pile surface the pattern will not be clear-cut in its outlines as in other weaves because of the movement of the pile; and the longer the pile, the more irregular will be the contours of the pattern.

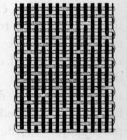

Fig. 125. Satin Weave. The weft threads pass over one and under six but not so as to form a diagonal pattern.

Figs. 121, 122, 124, 125: From N. A. Reath, *Weaves of Hand-Loom Fabrics* (1927) by permission of the Pennsylvania Museum of Art.

PLATE 83

Face (A, *top*) and Back (B, *bottom*) of a Fragment of Brocaded Damask. On the back the light and dark are reversed and the brocading threads floated. (Art Institute of Chicago)

PLATE 84

Face (A, *top*) and Back (B, *bottom*) of Sewed Tapestry.
A firm weave with the rep showing clearly. The figure
(a bishop) is well simplified to meet the demands of the
medium. (Art Institute of Chicago)

Another pile fabric is *velvet*. In this weave extra warps or wefts, in addition to those needed for the foundation weave, are looped at right angles to the surface and left as loops or cut (Fig. 127), in either case produc-

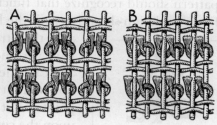

ing a pile, as the knot-ting does in carpet.

With the weaving process in mind shall we ask the question: How does the process affect the design? The very fact of a shuttle passing over and under warp threads at right angles imposes a defi-nite limitation. How

Fig. 126. Two Methods of Knotting. In *A* both ends of the knots, which form the pile, come between two warp threads; in *B* the ends are evenly distributed, one for each space. The drawing is greatly en-larged, for in good carpets there are from fifty to several hundred knots to the square inch. (After Tattersall)

different this is from the freedom with which pigment is applied to a surface by means of a brush! (Fig. 128). In weaving you are making the surface and decorating it at the same time and the character of the decorative pattern must harmonize with the method of making. In the actual doing you cannot forget warp and weft at right angles,

Fig. 127. Velvet Weave. (After Reath)

creating a flat surface. Geometric patterns are effective. When the forms of nature are the basis of the design they are highly simplified.

The character of the design must needs harmonize with the weight and texture of the fabric. A pattern that is suit-

able for a heavy woolen rug is by no means suitable for a soft silk damask. Purpose also controls the design. If the fabric is to lie flat on the floor or hang flat on the wall, its pattern should recognize that function. If it is to hang in folds, its design should permit the breaking of the pattern, and the strong play of light and dark with no unpleasant effect. In any case the art of the weaver does not attempt to imitate the art of the painter but depends for its effects upon the contrast, rhythm, and harmony of color masses, and upon texture.

Fig. 128. Bird Motif in Textile and Pottery Design. *A*, from a Peruvian textile showing the form adapted to weaving; *B*, from Amerindian pottery, showing the free sweep of brushwork.

READING

HOOPER, LUTHER, Hand-Loom Weaving, New York, Macmillan, 1920.

REATH, N. A., The Weaves of Hand-Loom Fabrics, Phila., Pennsylvania Museum, 1927.

TATTERSALL, C. E. G., Notes on Carpet-Knotting, London, Victoria and Albert Museum, 1920.

SUGGESTIONS

1. It is difficult to understand textiles without actual examples to handle and to examine. Make a collection to illustrate at least such important weaves as plain cloth, twill and satin, damask, brocading, tapestry, velvet, pile carpet. Have two pieces of each, to show both sides; or fold over a part; or mount in a mat so that both sides can be seen.

2. Have samples of cotton, wool, silk, velvet, pile carpet of various textures, tapestry, etc., to handle for texture. Feel with the eyes closed so as to concentrate on the sensation of touch.

3. Visit Oriental rug stores or departments, where it is often possible to see knotting done.

4. Unquestionably the best way to understand weaving is to do it. Small looms are easily procurable. (a) String the loom and weave a plain cloth to get the feeling of warp and weft; (b) one weave like the satin, which is one over and several under, or vice versa; (c) one weave where there are several weft threads, one for each color as in tapestry, and where the weft threads are combed down to cover the warp. Many suggestions, as well as illustrations, of the technique of weaving will be found in the books listed below.

5. Find designs, in fabrics or illustrations of fabrics, which you think are good textile designs and also some which you think are not. In each case explain the reason for your opinion.

6. Make original designs for different kinds of textiles: a soft silk, a pile carpet, a linen damask, a tapestry. In each case distinguish, in the character of the design, between the textures. Select motives from geometric, floral, bird, and animal forms, or from any suitable motives taken from everyday life. Actually weave the design; one unit if it is a repeat pattern, or one detail.

TAPESTRIES OF PERU

BEFORE the Spanish conquests in South America there lived in the highlands and along the shores of what is now Peru peoples of primitive culture who made everyday things of high artistic quality, especially pottery and textiles. We have, as yet, far too little knowledge of these people. But we do know that the women, with the simplest kind of a loom (Fig. 129), with wool from their llamas, vicuñas, and alpacas, with cotton and a few vegetable dyes, wove ponchos, decorative bands for clothing and saddles, pouches, and other articles that today are unsurpassed in the quality of their craftsmanship and of their design.

Let the pieces reproduced in PL. 85 serve as examples.

In the lower piece [1] the motif of the central band appears to be an S-shape but is really made up of straight lines. This figure is regularly repeated, yet how free from monotony! See the infinite variety of detail within the motif. Three bands form the body of a strange creature in three colors, rarely repeated in the same sequence. The head is sometimes light and sometimes dark. In the narrow border is another motif of steps and spirals. Here the small slits in the weave — for this is slit tapestry — accent the blocklike broken ground and the spirals repeat the spirals of the central motif. At regular intervals the spiral is strongly accented by a white ground, which marks an insistent rhythm, while the intermediate spirals, hardly perceptible in the reproduction without the color, give a vibrating, elusive character to the ground in contrast to the quiet un-

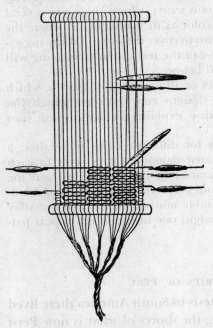

Fig. 129. Small Peruvian Loom. The warp is strung on bars and the weaving of slit tapestry begun but not yet beaten down by the smooth stick already inserted between the warp threads for the purpose. Notice that three colors are being used and hence three shuttles; the two along the side are for the selvage. (American Museum of Natural History)

[1] Width, 6 in. The warp and white areas are cotton; the rest, fine vicuña wool. 75 to 105 weft threads to the square inch. Both pieces are in the Boston Museum.

broken ground of the central band. These harmonies, variations, and contrasts of color, pattern, and rhythm produce a distinctly pleasing form.

The curious creature in the central band seems to be a composite of various forms, bird and animal, and possibly conveyed a definite meaning symbolically, as do many of the motifs in primitive art, though that meaning is often quite unintelligible to us. Form alone, then, is the source of our pleasure. How delightful and ingenious it is! For the expression is terse yet inclusive of essentials. In the bird form, for example, which is frequently used, so patternlike has the figure become that two birds are interlocked to form a striking motif (Fig. 130). In the upper example of PL. 85 the animal figure has been seen as an angular geometric pattern sensitively placed within a diamond shape.

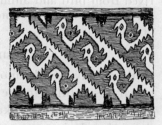

Fig. 130. Peruvian Textile with Interchangeable Bird Motif. Turn the drawing upside down and the same bird form appears in dark. (After a piece in the Metropolitan Museum)

Here too the slit-tapestry weave and subtle variations of color produce an elusive vibration of surface that is particularly pleasing.

The majority of these Peruvian textiles are tapestry weave and many are incredibly fine. Weaving was an almost universal craft among the women, who could spin the cotton into a warp that was smooth and even enough to form an even rep and at the same time strong enough to carry the wool weft and withstand the beating of the weft to make a firm weave. So fine a thread was spun for the weft that examples have been found which contain nearly three hundred and eighty weft threads to the inch.

READING

MEANS, P. A., Ancient Civilizations of the Andes, N. Y., Scribner, 1931.

—— Peruvian Textiles, N. Y., Metropolitan Museum, 1930.

SUGGESTION

Study the designs in Peruvian textiles, especially those derived from bird and animal life. From the bird and animal life of your own environment create textile designs in the style of the Peruvian.

SILK FABRICS

Is there any textile more charming than silk? To the touch so soothing, to the eye so lustrous. Now so soft that it hangs in long unbroken folds. Now so heavy and rich that it breaks into masses of high lights and deep shadows. In few textiles are there such possibilities of rich effects, so that silk has always been highly prized wherever known.

The derivation of the word leads us to the source of its discovery, China. *Seres* was the name given the Chinese by the Greeks and Romans. *Sericum* was a garment of silk, whence is derived the word for silk in all the European languages. To the Romans *serica* were considered a great luxury, for they were enormously costly, even for the wealthy Romans of the days of the luxurious clubs. Their ideas about the fabric and about the people who made it were equally hazy. The patterns were so unfamiliar and puzzling that the Roman weavers appear to have unraveled the fabrics and rewoven them with Western designs.

Silk is one of the fibers produced by insects for nests or webs or protective covering during the change from worm to moth. Its strength and brilliance are the qualities that make it so valuable. To expose such a fiber as much as is

practical, so that it can reveal its possibilities, is the reason why silks are usually woven in the twill or satin weave (Figs. 124 and 125). Most of the silk used in weaving comes from the mulberry silk-moth, which was discovered in China many centuries ago. Just how, we do not know. The Chinese themselves have legends about it; of the empress who, they say, invented the loom and who cared for the precious silkworms herself and gave directions to the gardeners about the cultivation of the mulberry trees.

The Chinese, with their natural conservatism and their geographic isolation, probably made the finest silks for many centuries before they discovered how lucrative was traffic in this fabric with the lands in the West, lucrative even though it entailed months of caravan travel across deserts or hazardous sailing over unknown seas.[2]

With the Chinese and also with the Japanese the designs of silk fabrics have always been traditional and full of meaning. As an example we may look at a *Japanese Obi* or broad sash, which is worn over the kimono (PL. 88A).[3] On a restrained gray-green ground a repeat pattern is made of bamboo tops in grays and ivory, each leaf outlined in gold. These tops alternate in direction with each row and make an insistent rhythm over against wavering pine branches brocaded in gold. There is distinction in this restrained harmony and refined elegance. The design is the same in principle as in a musical composition in which the sustained rhythm of a melody rings in a cello out over a wavering pattern in the violins. Thus color and rhythm charm the observer. A delightful pattern the weaver has seen in the pine and the bamboo. This alone may suffice for our enjoyment. Not so for the Japanese. To him the

---

[2] In this connection the travels of Marco Polo will be found interesting.
[3] Eighteenth or nineteenth century A.D. Art Institute of Chicago.

pine and the bamboo, because they are evergreen, are symbols of long life. Did we not see him planting these trees in his garden? Here, then, meaning attaches itself to design. And when a Japanese sends such an *Obi* as a gift to a bride or as a votive offering to a temple, he is sending a gift which is doubly significant because form is infused with meaning.

The same principle of rhythmic design we see in an *Italian Brocaded Damask* (PL. 88B),[4] in which a pattern of buff, brocaded in silver, is woven against a ground of green. This pattern is made up of pairs of parrots and gazelles balanced with striking symmetry about heart-shaped palmettes. The birds and the animals form alternating rows, with floral motifs filling the intervening spaces so that the ground is filled but not crowded. The large areas of the figures furnish the strongly accented rhythm, the broken palmettes the wavering movement, and the two are held together by the green ground. Though the figures are flat patterns they are infused with a surprising amount of reality — the grace of the gazelle and the asperity of the parrot. Yet no compromise has been made with the requirements of textile design. Even the terminal of the gazelle's leg has become an arabesque and the bird's plumage a geometric pattern. Almost inevitably the birds, animals, and palmettes interlock, with the help of scattering arabesques, to fill the space!

SUGGESTION

Color reproductions of fine silks, damasks, and brocaded fabrics can be found in the *Encyclopædia Britannica*, 14th ed., in the article " Textiles "; and in the *Near Eastern Textiles* of the Metropolitan Museum Colorprints. In these study particularly the color schemes and the designs from the point of view

---

[4] Sicilian, twelfth century A.D. Metropolitan Museum, New York.

PLATE 85

Two Pieces of Slit Tapestry. Above: an elusive vibrating ground with strong accents in the animal motif alternating in light and dark. Below: an unusually fine tight weave with strong rhythmic movement through unit shapes and color. In both pieces the adaptation of the figure to the requirements of weaving is particularly sensitive. (Boston Museum)

PLATE 86

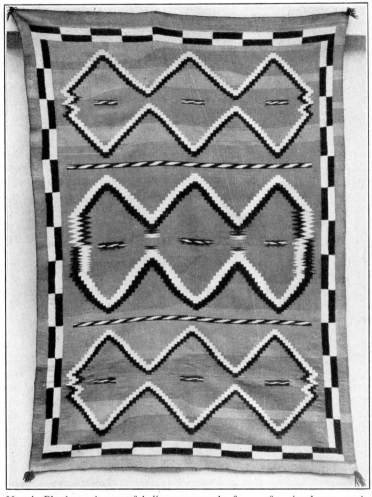

Navajo Blanket. A powerful directness results from a few simple geometric motifs used boldly on a large scale with strong contrasts — an expression of primitive life. (Metropolitan Museum)

PLATE 87

Persian Animal Carpet. A subtle richness results from the intricate
interweaving and contrasting of numerous motifs both geometric
and naturalistic, from the soft texture, and from the abundant yet
sternly controlled detail — an expression of a wealthy luxuriant
court. (Metropolitan Museum)

PLATE 88

A, *top*. Detail of a Japanese Gold Brocaded Obi. (Art Institute of Chicago)

B. Detail of an Italian Silver Brocaded Damask. (Metropolitan Museum)

Both these designs are well adapted to silk weaving and with the brocadings of gold and silver convey an impression of elegance.

of suitability of motif to weaving and the influence of the process on the pattern.

A PERSIAN CARPET

WE have already visited Persia and looked at the fine books of the wealthy shahs (PL. 82). Books were one of the most aristocratic of the arts of Persia. Carpets, on the other hand, belong to all the people. They are found alike in the palace of the shah, the tent of the nomad, and the home of the merchant. Almost every one has a share in the craft — in the raising of the sheep, the shearing, the spinning, the dyeing, or the weaving.

Conditions of life foster a need for rugs. The mountainous plateau of Persia is subject to great contrasts of climate and the Persian builds his house to secure as much comfort and pleasure as he can in view of these contrasts. In the torrid summer, stone, stucco, and glazed tile protect against heat and glare. Into this house of cool, hard surfaces the soft texture of the carpet on the floor, wall, or chest brings a happy contrast, especially as the Persian house has but little furniture. In the cold rains and snow of winter both the stone palace and the shepherd's hut need warm coverings — a need met by firmly woven rugs. Pile weaving appears to have originated in the need of the nomad shepherd to find a warm, serviceable covering for the floor and walls of his tent-house.

Besides this protective purpose, carpets were used as gifts, dowries, or indemnities. In the home or on the desert the prayer rug served as a sanctuary. The wealth of the family might consist of carpets, or of great skill in dyeing or weaving, which father would transmit to son, generation after generation.

Not only did everyday life in Persia require carpets, but also the land provided the materials for making them. Persia is a great sheep-raising country and has developed shepherds with extraordinary skill in producing just the quality of wools required. Clear springs furnish running water for the washing of the wool, and the tropical sunshine, heat, and light for drying and bleaching. Nature provides the colors beyond the white and black of the sheep's wool and the warm neutral of the camel's hair: blue from the indigo plant; red from madder root or the dead bodies of insects living on the oak trees; yellow from Persian berries. The silk that was used for the sumptuous carpets of the shahs came originally from China and was introduced thence into Persia, which was on the great trade route between eastern and western Asia. Though silk, linen, and cotton are used in these carpets, wool is the most important material.

As Persian rugs, both large and small, come from all classes of life, so the impressions that they create vary. Those of the shepherd which he uses in his tent or on his saddle are smaller, of tougher texture, bolder design, and stronger contrasts of color. Those of the palace and mosque, often large enough to cover floors and walls, are of softer texture, more delicate and subtle in color and in design. These great royal carpets were woven by court weavers. A court or a mosque had, as part of the establishment, highly skilled weavers who were among the great of the day, as were the calligraphers and miniature-painters. They were given all the time they needed and all the materials, no matter how costly. The shahs were enormously wealthy and seemed to take delight in spending enormous sums on fine carpets and fine books.

Such a *Persian Carpet* is the animal rug reproduced in

PL. 87.[5] Color, movement, and texture — that is what one sees and feels. Deep somber hues with light accents are so massed that you are aware of rhythms of both line and color guiding the eye through the carpet. See how the eye moves over the central rectangle and thence into the borders, which emphasize the proportions of the carpet, keep the movement within the area, and definitely mark it off from its environment. The texture is firm and fine — four hundred and eighty-four knots to the square inch — making possible a delicacy of decorative motif impossible in a coarser weave.

What are the large elements of the design that are responsible for this rhythmic movement? There is first a central rectangular field of rich warm red with five strong accents in the five pairs of fighting lions and gazelles, the lions yellow, the gazelles black spotted in white. From these accents a more rapid and more delicate movement glides through the field, guided by the other animals, by the light peonies with silver threads, and by the spiraling stems.

This movement of line and color is held as a unit by the second element — the group of borders. First a light narrow band which holds the red ground of the inner field firmly by the strong contrast of the ground color yet harmonizes with it because it uses the same hues. The broad border has a deep-blue ground through which runs rapidly, very rapidly in comparison with the more suave movement of the central field, two running motifs: one, strong and bold, of the red of the inner field; the other, light and delicate, like the spiraling stems. Both enclose a light peony which serves

[5] Of wool. 10 ft. 10 in. by 5 ft. 10 in. From the royal tomb-mosque at Ardebil, in northwestern Persia. About 1520–30 A.D. Metropolitan Museum, New York. An excellent color reproduction of a detail is published in postcard form by the Metropolitan Museum.

as an accent, a stable point about which the movement
glides. The outer finishing border has a red ground contrasting with the blue of the broad border and recalling
the central field, and a quiet floral motif, thus quietly and
harmoniously but definitely terminating the design. You
notice that the color in the ground is not a perfectly uniform tone but varies just a little, producing a vibrating
quality like that of *Gothic Glass* (see page 90) .

The motifs with which this design is carried out are
partly geometric and abstract and partly from the world
of nature — plants and animals. While there is a surpris-
ingly realistic feeling about them, at the same time they
are perfectly flat patterns, each playing its part in the composition to fill the space without crowding and without
overlapping, and united in the big rhythmic movement
partly by their relative position and partly by the slender
stems that swing through the rectangle. Look closely at
any detail and you will find that although it is repeated
again and again, there is a great deal of subtle variation in
form, or spacing, or color, that does not interfere with the
rhythmic movement of the design, but which adds enormously to its interest and vivacity.

READING

Bode, W., and Kuehnel, E., Antique Rugs from the Near
East, N. Y., Weyhe, 1922.
Dimand, M. S., Handbook of Mohammedan Decorative Arts,
N. Y., Metropolitan Museum, 1930.
Encyclopædia Britannica (14th ed.) , " Rugs and Carpets."
Pope, A. U., An Introduction to Persian Art, London, Davies,
1930.

SUGGESTIONS

1. Lay a piece of tracing paper over the reproduction or,
better, over a photograph or the postcard detail and trace the

spiraling movement in the central field. Note just what part the animals, flowers, and stems play in guiding the eye through the field. Do the same for the movement in the borders.

2. Find examples of handmade pile carpets or rugs at home, in stores, in museums. Make sketches of the big basic parts of the design. What colors are used? How are they repeated, harmonized, and contrasted? What motifs are used? Are they the same in the field and in the border? What is the texture? Do you think that the texture and the motifs harmonize?

A NAVAJO BLANKET

As you stand on the brink of the Grand Canyon, on a clear afternoon, at Navajo Point, you see at your feet the gigantic gorge of the Colorado filled with pinnacles all blue and rose, with violet shadows already filling the lower gulches. Far down within the chasm below winds, like a tiny thread, the river that carved it. To the east, the cañon of the Little Colorado makes a snakelike crack in the level plateau. Beyond stretch miles and miles of flat country over which hangs a golden mist that blurs half-visible masses of turquoise-blue, mauve, rose, green — a living opal. Far to the northwest rise the dim blue peaks of the sacred mountains. This is the land of the Navajo and Hopi Indians (Fig. 131).

It is a bold land, in scale and in ruggedness, in contrasts of burning heat and biting cold, a land of desert aridity and floods from an occasional cloudburst, of barren soil that is rich wherever rain or a spring gives it the needed moisture. It is not a land where life consists of little pleasantries and sentimentality, but where necessities are wrung by hard effort from a forceful, stubborn nature. Yet it is a land of great natural beauty. The vastness of earth repeats the immensity of the dome of the sky. Profound calm envelops the land. By day the dry air, stimulating

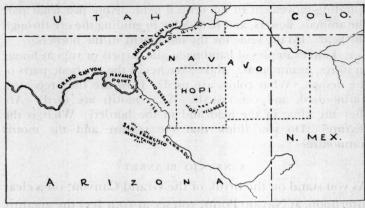

Fig. 131.   Land of the Navajo and Hopi Indians.

even in the heat, quivers with brilliant color; by night the
sparkling stars reach down to touch the earth.

The Navajo felt all this.   Listen to one of his songs:

On the trail marked with pollen may I walk,
With grasshoppers about my feet may I walk,
With dew about my feet may I walk,
With beauty may I walk,
With beauty before me may I walk,
With beauty behind me may I walk,
With beauty above me may I walk,
With beauty all around me, may I walk,
In old age wandering on a trail of beauty, lively, may I walk,
In old age wandering on a trail of beauty, living again, may I
walk,
It is finished in beauty.[6]

Is it not inevitable that so forceful a nature should dominate the Navajo's thought, belief, and expression?   That
his designs should be boldly vigorous?   And that in them
he should be expressing what is most vital in his life?   That

[6] Matthews, W. *Navaho Myths, Prayers and Songs*, Berkeley, University Press,
1907.   (See the inscription in Fig. 61, p. 104.)

in red he should see the sunshine; in white, the early morning light; in blue, the cloudless south; and in black, the
storm clouds of the north?   A common motif in his pottery
and textiles, for example, is the step pattern (PL. 86),
usually interpreted as a rain-cloud symbol.   And when, in
this step pattern, he uses black and red, he seems to be
using these colors not only for their contrast, but because
of their meaning: sunshine and rain bring harvests.   While
some of his decorative motifs may be used for their form
only, it seems probable that many are as symbolic, as significant in meaning, as are his songs and his dances.

For towns you will search in vain, because the Navajo is
a nomad.   His songs suggest that his real home is the wide
out-of-doors.   Yet, in a protected place near a spring you
will find a winter *hogan,* a hut of logs and mud to serve as
a storage place for his corn, and as a warm sleeping-place
in bad weather.   Perhaps it is near a shelving cliff to shelter
the flocks, for the Navajos are shepherds.   In summer this
hogan lies deserted when the family moves from place to
place to find the sparse pasturage, carrying all their house-
hold belongings with them.   In the lee of an overhanging
rock they make a home, or in a light summer hogan.[7]   One
of the hut poles will serve as one side of a very simple loom
of logs.   Seated on the ground before it, the Navajo woman
— for most of the weavers are women — during the long
summer days will weave the tight coverings to protect the
family against the winter winds of the high plateau.   The
sheep furnish the wool, black, white, and gray.   Add a few
vegetable dyes for some of the wool, and the material is
complete for many of their rugs.

Look at a group of Navajo blankets and rugs.   It is their
bold simplicity that first catches the eye.   Their austere

[7] See p. 310, note 6.

power was born of a clean air, a rugged out-of-door life in a land of brilliant color. Everywhere are straight lines and angles. Not a curve in sight. And sharp meeting of contrasting color; black, white, red. What the eye sees and the effect that this produces are at almost an opposite pole from those of the royal *Persian Animal Carpet* (PL. 87), where everything suggests the easy luxury of a wealthy

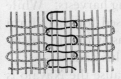

Fig. 132. Interlocked Tapestry Weave. (Crawford, *Peruvian Textiles*, N.Y., American Museum of Natural History)

court. In the *Navajo Blanket* of PL. 86 [8] a step border of black and white frames the inner field of vibrating rose, which is divided into three parts, each containing a double zigzag pattern made of the step motif. Notice how the central division is wider, the step pattern larger; and how the large zigzags terminate in groups of small rapid zigzags, with fragments of the same motif in the field. As the step or terrace figure symbolizes the rain clouds and the zigzag the lightning, we may see here not only a design of barbaric dignity and boldness in harmony with the life that it serves; a useful protection because of its firm tight weave; motifs suited to tapestry weaving; superb color — not only these qualities may we see, but an inner meaning, as potent a supplication for rain-bringing storms as the ceremonial chants. In one of the legends we read, " I wish good and beautiful black clouds, good and beautiful thunderstorms, good and beautiful gentle showers."

In order to give the blanket a firmness to stand hard usage and to protect adequately, the Navajo uses the tapestry weave, not slit or sewed, but interlocked (Fig. 132). Look closely at a Navajo rug and see how the line separat-

[8] Nineteenth century. Metropolitan Museum, New York.

ing two colors, sharp though it looks, is really wavering as the black penetrates the red or white for one warp thread. The loom is most primitive. Two upright poles with an upper and lower beam between form a frame to which the warp beams are lashed. The weaver squats in front of the loom on a rug or an animal skin and when the work is completed beyond the reach of her arms loosens the top lashes, lowers the upper warp beam, and winds the woven section around the lower beam.

READING

HEWETT, E. L., Ancient Life in the American Southwest, N. Y., Bobbs-Merrill, 1931.
JAMES, G. W., Indian Blankets, Chicago, McClurg, 1914.
MATTHEWS, W., Navaho Legends, Boston, Houghton, 1897.

SUGGESTIONS

1. It is quite possible to weave some of the Navajo patterns on a small loom and to carry them out in the interlocked tapestry weave. The books listed above will give illustrations of the important motifs.

2. Design an original blanket or rug, using the terrace, zigzag, diamond, or cross motif.

Part Ten

THE ART OF POTTERY

WHAT a familiar figure is the potter with his clay and his potter's wheel! Every age and every land have known him. Literature frequently alludes to the potter's wheel and to clay in the potter's hands. Sometimes his vessels are only useful containers. Or they may not only serve their purpose but at the same time delight us with shape, texture, and color, as do the wares of Persia.

Can you not see the old Persian craftsman bending over his wheel? A green turban is wound about his head. This color means that he has made the sacred pilgrimage to Mecca, the holy city of the Mohammedans, a hazardous journey by caravan across wide deserts — the event of a lifetime. Thus he is marked as a man of importance among his friends. But for more reasons than that. Because of his great skill in making the richly colored vessels so loved by the Persians, not only is he in the employ of the shah, but also, like his friends the carpet-weaver and the calligrapher, he is one of the notable men of the land.

He may well be intent upon his work, for a message has lately come from the shah. A ewer is to be made as a gift to a prince who, a courier has reported, will pay the shah a visit some weeks hence. The ewer is to be of the finest shape and color, the shah has said, and is to carry an inscription that will convey his felicitations to the prince. So the potter is bending over his clay thoughtfully. Many a vessel he has made for the shah, but this one for the prince must surpass them all. A mass of clay he places in the center of the wheel and thoughtfully he turns the disk. His fingers feel a shape forming. A little pressure, here inward, there outward. How the soft clay responds to the

slightest touch! He stops and looks. No, it is not quite right. Shape and proportions are his greatest concern. Yet, this is to be a ewer. Will it stand firmly, hold a sufficient quantity of liquid, and pour easily? Are its outlines pleasing, and will the surfaces display to best advantage the rich color with which he intends to cover them? Is the handle strong, easy for the hand to grasp and at the same time harmonious with the shape and contour of the body?

The shape is now finished but is not ready for the glaze, because the clay is too coarse to provide a good surface. The potter coats it thinly with fine white clay, on which he paints a floral design in black, together with the inscription, and then covers all the surface with a thick transparent blue glaze to reveal the decoration beneath and to set off the shape of the ewer. This blue is his secret, which he has worked out after many experiments. How will it look after it is fired? Eagerly he removes it from the kiln and looks with delight at its somber richness, at an intensity of color that he had hardly hoped for, as the rounding, slightly irregular surfaces catch and reflect the light. Yet even this is not enough for the prince, the old potter thinks. Again he calls upon his skill to add a final subtle touch. Another glaze he makes of copper, which he paints very lightly over the ewer. A gentle firing and again he holds the vessel to the light. At first it looks just the same. Then, with a slight movement of his hand, there appears a flash of intense coppery red and gold. With the slightest movement it disappears and only the blue remains. Now it reappears. How surprised and delighted the prince will be, says the potter to himself, when he discovers unexpectedly these fugitive flashes. The ewer is finished. With low obeisance he places it on the carpet before the shah. "May the work of a humble servant be pleasing to your Majesty."

What do we mean when we say that such a ewer is an example of *pottery,* or of the *ceramic* art, as it is called, from the Greek word for earthenware? It is the art of clay: clay shaped and subjected to heat. It may be sun-dried in hot dry countries or baked by fire — *fired,* as we say. With the exception of flat pieces such as tiles, it brings us very close to sculpture and architecture, the three-dimensional arts. For most of the potter's wares, though small in comparison, are like statues or buildings in that they depend for their effect upon shape, proportions, and organization of mass.

In pottery there are four fundamental processes: the preparation of the clay; the shaping; the decorating; the firing. The preparation requires cleaning and kneading, or *wedging,* to remove foreign materials and to secure a smooth texture. The shaping can be done in several ways. A mass of clay can be shaped by hand. Or it can be rolled into coils with which the vessel can be built up. Or it can be pressed or, if thin enough, poured into molds. This last is the present-day method for quantity production, for a large number of pieces can be made from one mold. The great method, however, by which the finest wares have been made, a method discovered early by different people separately in different lands, is the use of the potter's wheel. By this device the potter can turn the mass of clay by mechanical means and have his hands free to shape it (Fig. 133). He then lets it dry until it is leather-hard, replaces it on the wheel, and with his tools *turns* it, that is, smoothes and refines the shape, molds the lip, the base, and adds the handles.

The shape is then ready for the third step, the decorating and glazing. An important use of pottery is to hold liquids. Yet clay is porous. A primitive method of making the ves-

PLATE 89

A. Persian Jar. Here is a sculptural quality in the unity of the masses. (Metropolitan Museum)

B. Persian Dish. The motifs of decoration are particularly fitting to pottery and to the specific shape. (British Museum)

PLATE 90

A. Pitcher from Bokhara. (Art Institute of Chicago)

B. Italian Majolica Vase. (Victoria and Albert Museum)

Though the Italian vase shows great skill technically it lacks the fine unity seen in Pls. 89, 90A, and 91, particularly in the upper part where the contours are jerky and disconnected and the decoration too obtrusive.

sel impervious was to rub some waxy substance into the surface. But early the potter learned a more permanent method, *glazing*, that is, coating the vessel with melted glass, or glaze. At the same time he saw that with glaze he could also hide a rough clay base, secure texture, and by adding pigment to the molten glaze, obtain his most powerful decorative element, color. The glaze may be painted or sprayed on. Or if the vessel is not too large, it may be dipped into the glaze. Some kinds of clay when fired at a high temperature become vitreous like porcelain, and hence impervious, and if they are glazed it is for decorative purposes only. Glazing, though perhaps the most important, is not the only kind of decoration used by

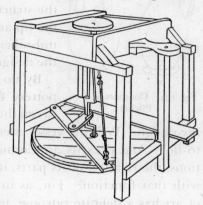

Fig. 133.   Potter's Wheel.

potters. A design may be molded in low relief, or incised, or painted. These methods of decoration are often combined with glazing: painting beneath a transparent glaze; painting over a glaze; relief covered with glaze. To make both the clay shape and the decoration or glaze permanent is the purpose of the firing. Sometimes one firing is sufficient. Or several firings may be necessary. Or one heavy firing and then a light one, as in the case of the Persian ewer.

Ceramic wares depend for their effect largely, as we have said, upon shape, proportions, and color. The maker of the *Pitcher* in Fig. 134A felt this. The firm contours have a quality which they impart to the entire vessel. The base is finely proportioned to lend a feeling of strength and the

handle is an integral part of the whole, its contour joining that of the body and the lip in an unbroken line. Compare it with the *Pitcher* in Fig. 134B, whose wavering fantastic contours weaken the sense of structure. One feels as if it were falling to pieces. Slight irregularity in contour

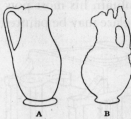

may have a pleasing effect if it is controlled by lines that emphasize the structure, as in PL. 90A, where the lip and the base with their firm unbroken lines accent and finish the design with a clear directness.

A   B

Fig. 134. Contours of Two
Pitchers.

By no means least important in pottery design is the relation between the function of the vessel and the design. Will the vessel adequately do what it is made to do? And does its appearance — its shape, its proportions, the relation of its parts, its decoration — harmonize with that function? For, as in a building, when a work of art has a definite purpose, much of our pleasure in it comes from a feeling of harmony between its appearance and its purpose.

Let us visit the shops of some of the world's great potters and see how they have solved the problems involved and produced vessels that have delighted many people. As we have begun our travels in Persia, shall we stay a little longer to visit a potter at Rhages (Ray, Rayy, Rai, Raiy)?

A PERSIAN JAR

Rhages, the site of whose ruins is a few miles south of Teheran, was one of the old capitals of Persia and once an important ceramic center. In the *Rhages Jar* of PL. 89,[1] we

[1] Height, 5½ in. Twelfth to thirteenth century A.D. Metropolitan Museum, New York.

see a low broad shape with a sculptural compactness that determines and is determined by an ellipse (Fig. 135). The animal handles are true clay forms so adjusted to the function of a handle that it is difficult to tell where the animal ends and the handle begins — an excellent example of the sensitive adjustment of form and function. You feel with equal conviction the idea of animal and the idea of handle. Furthermore, they are so placed that they not only serve adequately to lift the jar but also serve to fill the space made by the tapering shape and thus to produce the organizing contour, just as Giotto's figures are grouped so as to produce a sweeping line of organization (Fig. 96).

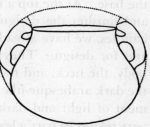

Fig. 135. Organizing Lines of a Persian Jar (PL. 89A).

By comparison with a less successful design (PL. 90B) we may realize better the unity and harmony in the Persian jar. In the *Medici Vase* the handles are disjointed excrescences rather than integral parts. The inner as well as the outer contour is jerky. The masks obscure rather than elucidate the unity between the body and the neck. Contrast with this the simplified contour and clear expression of parts in the Persian jar. In the *Medici Vase,* again, the ornament overloads the vessel, conceals the structural form, and seems to exist for itself rather than as one element within a unified design. In the *Rhages Jar,* on the contrary, the decoration accents the structural parts and unifies them into clear whole, without obtruding itself.

Let us look at this a little more closely. As with much of the Persian pottery, the jar is covered, because of the coarse clay, with a *slip,* here ivory white, which furnishes a

ground for the painting in blue, turquoise-green, purple, brown, and brick-red. The narrow bands of Arabic letters and arabesques accent the two main parts of the jar, the body and the neck, and their relative proportions. In the broad band between, dumpy mounted figures, freely painted, fill the space as they gallop around the jar and add another horizontal movement that emphasizes the low broad shape. Below, arabesques parallel to the band of letters seem to indicate the direction of the surface toward the base. At the top a row of brush strokes accents the lip and finishes the design as a frame does a picture. The handles, we have already said, function equally for utility and for design. They are so placed that they unite the body, the neck, and the lip; and their surfaces, broken by the dark arabesque-like motifs, have about the same movement of light and dark as the body. Thus, structurally, part relates to part, clearly and harmoniously; and decoration insistently stresses these relationships.

The free, sketchy character of the painting may at first seem puzzling. Consider, however, the irregularities of the clay shape, and the fact that pottery, with the exception of some flat pieces, has curving surfaces. When figures are used, most of them are seen foreshortened. Under these circumstances may it not be more effective merely to suggest the figure to the eye and to the imagination than to express it more naturalistically where the foreshortening is disturbing? In the *Rhages Jar* the horsemen appear equally well, both as decorative masses and as horsemen, whether seen directly in front or foreshortened. And how refreshing is their spontaneity! These galloping riders are real, and undoubtedly they delighted the Persian because they recalled to him his favorite pastime.

An excellent example of suitable ceramic design both

as to form and color is found in a piece from Rhages or possibly from Rakka, another important ceramic center of Persia. Here we have a shallow platelike dish (PL. 89B) [2] the inside of which is nearly filled with a harpy figure, that is half bird and half woman, combined with spiraling motifs to maintain the balance and to fill the area. Turn the dish as you will and see how beautifully the figure fills the space. What movement in those sweeping lines, now in unison with the outer contour, now in opposition to it! The border, contrastingly, presents a more rapid movement, like the border on the *Persian Animal Carpet* (PL. 91). Here the eye is carried both by the six strong accents and by the rapid minor accents of diagonal strokes of alternating color. Thus each of the two parts of the dish has a decoration that suits it in scale; the interior, one of larger mass and bolder rhythm; the border, one with smaller scale and more rapid movement. How effective are these insistent straight strokes in a design all curves!

A simple color harmony controls the design; blue, green, and manganese (a purplish brown) on an ivory ground. In the border the strong accent consists of a green disc surrounded by blue and the straight strokes of alternating manganese and blue. The central figure employs the same hues, partly in larger areas and partly in small accents to carry the rhythm. The figure is incised so that the color fills the incisions, producing dark lines. How delightfully the eye is caught by the larger masses of green in the center, enticed into the border by the accenting discs, and then lured back by the spirals which again bring it to the central mass!

[2] Diameter 16.75 in. Eleventh or twelfth century. British Museum, London. An excellent color reproduction is found in the British Museum Postcard Set, C 14, "Islamic Pottery of the Near East."

SUGGESTIONS

1. The British Museum Postcard Set referred to on p. 303, footnote 2, contains fifteen excellent color reproductions, with a brief description of Near East pottery. Additional reproductions in color are found in the Metropolitan Museum Colorprints, *Near Eastern Ceramics,* and in the *Encyclopædia Britannica,* 13th ed., " Ceramics," or 14th ed., " Potteries and Porcelains." Secure as many examples as possible and study both the shapes and the decoration, and the relation between the two.

2. A study of handles. Find examples where handles seem an integral part of the design and where they are excrescences. See suggestions under " A Greek Cup."

A PITCHER FROM BOKHARA

NORTHEAST of Persia in Turkestan lies the province of Bokhara, a mountainous land that is bitterly cold in winter, in turn deluged with rain or buried in snow; in summer intensely hot, parched, and dusty. These extremes produce a vigor in the people that finds expression in their arts; in the particularly firm weave of their rugs, for example, which serve at the tent door as a protection against the biting winds. A *Pitcher* from this land (PL. 90A) [3] shows this characteristic strength in its shape, proportions, decoration, and color contrasts. It consists of three parts clearly distinguished and closely united — body, neck, handle. The body is nearly spherical and the neck of similar proportions, for its height and its diameter are nearly equal. Three incised lines clearly separate the two parts, while the unbroken contour unites them. The slight flare of the lip brings the contour of the neck into harmony with the curve of the body and forms a finish, like a border on a rug, as does the inconspicuous base of equal

[3] Height, about 10 in. Seventeenth century A.D. Art Institute of Chicago.

diameter. The handle is proportioned similarly to the other two masses. Its contour repeats the contour of the body and it is so attached that it unites the two parts firmly and also functions easily for the hand in pouring. Every detail of the shape, proportions, and contour tends to a clear enunciation of the parts, and at the same time ensures their indissoluble, satisfying unity.

Is this true of the decoration also? Perhaps its most striking characteristic is the bold vigor that results partly from its character and partly from its strong contrasts. This vigor of decoration harmonizes with the vigor of shape and proportions. The strongest part of the decoration is on the strongest mass, the body. The motif is taken from the pomegranate plant. Root, leaves, and flowers form a curving pattern that repeats the curve of surface and of contour with a countercurve in the leaves that not only balances the strong movement but also repeats the shape of the handle. There is no attempt to give a naturalistic appearance of the plant but only to see in it a flat pattern that is peculiarly adaptable to the curving surface that it decorates. The ornament on the neck is equally fitting, for the vertical lines accent the shape, while the curves emphasize, by inverse curve, both the lip above and the body below. The repetition of this motif, on a small scale, near the handle is another happy way of bringing unity between the two parts. The light brush strokes on the handle serve to break the plain surface and are not emphatic enough to overaccent. These decorative motifs stand out clear and strong because of the color. The pitcher has a yellow slip and a yellow-orange glaze, against which the decoration on the neck and handle is painted in black. The pomegranate is outlined in the same black and the areas are filled with green, blue, and red.

A GREEK CUP

CONTRASTING with the *Bokhara Pitcher* of sturdy vigor is a *Greek Cup* of slender grace (PL. 91A).[4] Its outline is clear-cut and its colors, coppery red and black, give it a quality of distinction.

The ordinary beverage of the Greek was water and wine mixed. Hence a vessel in great demand was the *mixing-bowl* with a wide flaring rim, large enough for pouring the liquids in, for mixing them, and for dipping in ladles, pitchers, and cups. The commonest shape of cup was the *cylix*, a shallow, saucer-like vessel with two handles, set on a stem (Pl. 91A). The Greek drank from it, holding it either by the stem or by the handle, and hung it up by the handle. The cup consists of four parts — body, handles, stem, and base — which flow one into another, in contrast to the *Bokhara Pitcher,* in which the parts are clearly separated though harmoniously united. From the body the handles seem to grow by some inevitable law and their contours merge so imperceptibly into that of the body that the entire contour of the cup is a continuous curve of unusual quality. The proportions are as pleasing as the contours. The base is wide enough for stability, in proportion to the width of the body, and the stem thick enough as the supporting member, high enough for pleasing proportions, and at the same time well adjusted to the hand holding it. The entire cup is potted with thin walls so that it will be light in weight, even when filled.

From its decoration, this cup is known as *red-figured ware* because the figures are reserved in red-ochre color, while the ground is filled in solid with black glaze. This red ochre was added to the cup after it was shaped on the

---

[4] Fifth century B.C. Metropolitan Museum, New York.

PLATE 91

A, *top*. Greek Cylix (Cup). The parts flow one into another with an unbroken contour. (Metropolitan Museum) B, *center*. Greek Cylix. The copper-red figures form flat decorative masses against a velvety-black ground. C, *bottom*. Hopi Jar. Bold in shape and decoration. (Bureau of Ethnology, Smithsonian Institution)

PLATE 92

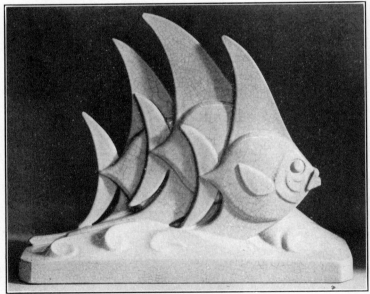

A, *left*. Chinese Flower Pot. A simple vigorous shape covered with a rich
glaze of many-toned violet. (Art Institute of Chicago)

B, *right*. Modern Jar. As simple and rugged as A. The contrasting textures
are effective. (Metropolitan Museum)

C. Modern Decorative Piece. Of the nature of relief, in contrast to the
three-dimensional quality of A and B, with strong rhythms from side to side.
(Metropolitan Museum)

wheel, turned, and dried. For though the color of the clay had a reddish tint, it did not have the depth of tone to contrast well with the black. The design was sketched in with a blunt instrument, then the contours and details were painted in black, and finally the ground was covered with black glaze. Then the cup was fired.

The decoration of a cylix was usually confined to the broad undersurface of the body and to a small circle in the center of the inside. With the exception of the borders the decorative motifs were chiefly scenes from everyday life or from the Greek myths, and thus employed human figures. Yet this was so done that the first and last effect remained one of decorative fitness. The subject, however, did not become purely abstract decoration. For the Greek, life centered about himself — man. " Man is the measure of all things." His gods were very human. His buildings and his sculpture, as we have seen, have to do with the same subjects and represent the very fiber of his life.

The *Theseus Cup* in PL. 91B [5] is an illustration. *Theseus,* one of the Greek heroes, is seen in two of his labors, hobbling the fire-breathing bull of Marathon and wrestling with the tyrant Cercyon, who put to death every stranger who could not vanquish him in a wrestling match. Notice how the figures and objects are so composed that they easily fill the space. Each, no matter what the natural proportions, rises to the rim. Flat, with very little detail and with no use of light and shade, they are reduced to a pattern in one plane silhouetted against the strongly contrasted black ground. The two trees, part of this pattern, suggest a woody country. The rest of the environment is left to the imagination. For the potter does not forget that he is decorating a flat clay surface, breaking up its broad

[5] Fifth century B.C. Louvre, Paris.

expanses into a lively pattern. Instead of moving about the cup, as the riders do in the *Rhages Jar* (PL. 89A), the figures are balanced on two sides of the tree and so posed that the organizing line is a sweeping curve that repeats inversely the contour of the cup (Fig. 136) and the curved plane of its body, thus bringing harmony between the shape and the decoration.

The potters' quarter in Athens (Fig. 16), called the *Ceramicus,* must have been a busy part of the city. It was a large section lying both inside and outside the *Dipylon Gate.* The cups, pitchers, bowls, jars, and other objects that the potters made were not only for home use but for export to all lands about the Mediterranean Sea. This was one of the most important industries in Athens, and its products were not primarily or-naments, decorative though they were, but were the ordi-nary utensils of everyday use. There must have been many potteries in the *Ceramicus,* among which there appeared to be commercial rivalry. One of these was run by a man named Euphronios, who signed the vessels that came from his shop " Euphronios made me." The *Theseus Cup* at which we have been looking probably came from his shop. A rival shop was that of Euthymides, who, on one jar be-side the usual signature, added, " as never Euphronios did."

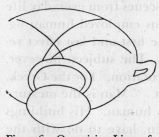

Fig. 136. Organizing Lines of a Greek Cup (PL. 91B).

Thus in looking at Greek pottery we are looking at the common objects of everyday life, articles of a far-reaching trade. This is a democratic art in distinction to Persian pottery, which was made under aristocratic patronage. Quality in everyday objects of trade is determined by pub-

lic demand. So when a democratic art reaches as lofty a plane as does Greek pottery, it is a clear index to an artistic spirit that infused the entire fabric of its civilization. On the same principle the beautiful way in which the Japanese ties a winter covering about his shrubs (Fig. 69) reveals an artistic spirit permeating his entire life.

SUGGESTIONS AND READING

1. A study of proportions. Find illustrations of several Greek cylixes and analyze the proportions of body, stem, and base. Examples are given in *Shapes of Greek Vases,* N. Y., Metropolitan Museum.

2. The influence of function upon shape. Greek pottery offers excellent examples of a strong influence. See H. Gardner, *Art Through the Ages,* N. Y., Harcourt, 1926, Figs. 56–61; and *Shapes of Greek Vases.*

3. Find illustrations of Greek myths on Greek pottery.

4. For an interesting account of the Greek potter, his craft, and his place in Greek society, see E. Pottier, *Douris and the Painters of Greek Vases,* N. Y., Dutton, 1916. A general reference book is E. Buschor, *Greek Vase-Painting,* London, Chatto, 1921.

A HOPI JAR

SHOULD you go into the National Museum in Washington and look at the bowls and jars from Arizona, especially those from Sityakti, you would probably see in them simple, rather uneven shapes, warm color — yellow, red, brown, black — and a bold decoration. What looks like a geometric band with striking contrasts of line and color encircles the body or covers the shoulder (PL. 91C), emphasizing the low broad proportions; or a puzzling figure (does it suggest a bird?) boldly decorates the inner surface of a shallow bowl (Fig. 137). Were the potters who made these vessels as vigorous a people as the bowls and jars imply? They were the Hopi of the Painted Desert.

Above the undulating floor of this desert plateau rise flat-topped spurs of rock on which are perched the towns of the Hopi Indians (Fig. 131). Unlike their wide-ranging neighbors, the Navajo, the Hopi have settled homes because they are primarily farmers. This Peaceful People (the meaning of *Hopi*) built their homes high on the mesas as a protection against warlike tribes. Like barren cubes of stone set compactly together, they seem at a distance to be a normal growth of the barren rocky headland. No trees soften their masses or suggest refreshing shade. Austere they stand in the blazing heat of summer and the cold of winter. Come nearer and they remind you of an apartment house three or four stories high but spread out over the ground, large enough to house the whole population, perhaps three or four hundred people. And always, in the midst, an opening in the ground, with a ladder protruding, the entrance to the *kiva,* the underground council chamber and place for the secret parts of their religious ceremonies.[6]

Fig. 137. Design upon the Shoulder of a Hopi Jar (PL. 91c). (After Fewkes)

At the foot of the mesa lie the gardens, perhaps some trees if a spring is near. These gardens they had to protect as best they could from raiding tribes intent upon capturing their corn, beans, and melons. This desert land is rich if water can be found. But even with a minimum amount the Hopi have always been skilful farmers — dry farmers, depending upon deep planting and thorough cultivation

---

[6] Models of Navajo hogans and of Hopi villages, houses, and ceremonials can be found in such museums as the American Museum of Natural History in New York and the Field Museum of Natural History in Chicago. Photographs can be obtained from the museums

to mature crops from seeds that have been adapted to this environment after centuries of experiment.

In such a land, the vital needs of the community, water and crops, are reflected in religious practices. All manifestations of nature are deified — clouds, lightning, sun, dawn, fire, animals, insects — and have magic power. As innumerable as the deities are the festivals, religious dramas enacted largely by the dance, through all of which runs the eternal quest for rain.

An evidence of a settled rather than a nomad life among primitive people is pottery. With nomad tribes something less fragile must serve for everyday use. As the women among the Navajo were the weavers, so among the Hopi the women were the potters, the makers of the necessary vessels for everyday and ceremonial use. The clay, which was found near each mesa, was not shaped on the wheel but rolled into coils about eight inches long. With these the potter built up her jar, flattening a piece of clay into a disc for the bottom, or starting at once with the coiling, perhaps using a basket as a mold until the shape was well started. When she had completed the shape she smoothed away the traces of the coils with a gourd and then polished the jar both inside and outside with smooth stones. Vessels made by coiling tend to be heavy with thick walls. So it is surprising how thinly potted are the bowls and jars of these Hopi women who shaped and decorated their vessels with the most primitive implements and fired them in the open with the most meager fuel, so used as to extract all its potentiality.

The *Hopi Jar* in PL. 91C has a broad shallow shape with a continuous, unbroken surface and contour, and with no base to enable it to stand firmly. Upon the broad shoulder, the strong part of the jar, is concentrated a bold design

(Fig. 137) which at first appears to be a mass of unintelligible shapes yet is held sternly within two concentric bands, and is strikingly decorative. The strong black band is broken abruptly at one point. This break, a convention found in all Hopi art, is known as the *lifeline*, which like a gate offers a means of escape for the spirit and if closed would mean the death of the maker or bad luck for the clan. About the neck are triangular dentations — seven on one side and three on the other — conventionalized feathers, which may indicate that the jar was used to bring ceremonial water from the sacred spring. The complicated design consists of terraced rain cloud, feather, and other motifs (not understood), and an unusually naturalistic bird form.

Fig. 138. Man-Eagle Design on a Hopi Bowl. (After Fewkes)

No doubt the bird represents some mythical character, for Hopi legend is full of birdlike beings. Chief among these was *Man-Eagle* (Fig. 138), a creature who swooped down from his home in the heart of the sky and carried off women and maidens to devour. Finally the war god *Youth,* whose bride *Man-Eagle* had kidnapped, penetrated the monster's abode with the help of *Spider Woman* and *Mole,* and not only recovered his bride but converted *Man-Eagle* into a beneficent being.

To us, who cannot enter fully into all this life meaning, the enjoyment of the jar comes from what our eyes see — rich color and bold patterning, placed sensitively on the strong part of the shape, enhancing its structural form, and a feeling of stern dignity that carries us into the stimulating air and broad reaches of space and a life of bold vigor.

Such a jar is at home in the barren interior of the stone
Hopi house or in the ceremonies of the stone village.   In
our crowded cities it seems suffocated.

READING

HODGE, F. W., Handbook of American Indians, Washington,
   Bureau of American Ethnology, 1910.
HOUGH, W., The Hopi Indians, Torch Press, Cedar Rapids,
   1915.

CHINA AND TODAY

As you look at a collection of Chinese Sung pottery, what
do you see?   A sweeping glance reveals two characteristics:
simple shape and one-color glaze.   In general there is a
feeling of restraint and sobriety.   To be sure there is great
variety of shape, color, and texture.   Here is the singu-
larly delicate Ting bowl, potted thin, covered with an
ivory-white glaze.   If there is any decoration beyond the
glaze it is inconspicuous incising or low relief.   Or here is
a small vase of a rare imperial ware, simple, elegant in its
proportions, as thin as an eggshell and covered with a misty
blue glaze.   Or here is a *Chün Flower Pot* (PL. 92A).[7]
What dignity and grandeur!   The simplicity of the shape,
the sturdy proportions, the powerful contours, the thickly
potted walls, and the thick glaze of blues and violets —
every part of the pot contributes to a unity of effect.   There
is always sobriety and distinction in these Sung wares,
which are dependent upon the shape of the mass, its proportions, and its contours, all of which are brought out by
a uniformly colored surface.

   [7] Chinese *Flower Pot.* Chün ware of the Sung dynasty (960–1280 A.D.).
Height, 10 in.   Note the finely designed carved wood base which sets off
the pot.   Buckingham Collection, Art Institute of Chicago.   Color reproduction of a pair of these Chün flower pots, in Encyclopædia Britannica, 13th ed.,
article "Ceramics," Pl. II.   See also Encyclopædia Britannica, 14th ed.,
article "Potteries and Porcelains," for color plates of many Chinese wares.

Technically the Chinese rank among the master potters. To secure a vessel that is hard and impervious without the help of glaze is one objective of the potter. This the Chinese discovered in *porcelain*. True porcelain is made of *kaolin*, a fine white clay so called from the hills near a Chinese pottery where it was found. It is mixed with stone that contains glass, and fired at a high temperature, which transforms the mixture into a fabric that is not only hard and impervious but also translucent and resonant. Glaze is used not for practical purposes, but as one element in creating a fine form.

In our *Chün Flower Pot* the broad shape and the wide lip are necessary for a flower pot. How firmly it stands! It is potted thick, is heavy. You can see its heaviness with your eyes; you feel its weight, though you do not lift it; its roundness, though you do not touch it. These feelings are conveyed by the proportions, by the movement of the surfaces and of the contours. The height of the neck is the same as the height of the body but the addition of the foot gives a slight accent on the vertical. The diameter of the lip is the same as the diameter of the body. Note the rhythmic variation in the diameters of the parts; from the narrow foot, to the wide body, to the intermediate neck, to the wide lip. Similar rhythms of surface and of contours strengthen each other.

The color, the only decoration, emphasizes the shape, the proportions, and the contours. Over a base of gray runs a thick glaze of rich violet and blue-violet, with many streakings, bubbles, and tiny pinholes which give depth and vibration to the color like the streakings and bubbles in the windows of *Chartres*. This single hue brings the parts into a close unity and its richness sets off the pot sharply against its environment. It is this complete unity

and harmony of all the elements that constitute the art in
Sung pottery — sensitively felt shapes of great simplicity
and dignity; thin or thick potting according to shape and
function; great restraint in decoration, chiefly a glaze of
one hue, which is delicate or rich as is consistent with
shape and function.

Our knowledge of the finest Chinese wares has come to
us rather recently. But their influence is seen in the work
of many of our best potters today. It is not that they copy
the Chinese. Rather, they see that the operation of certain
practices produces the finest results. Pottery, they realize,
is like sculpture in the round, and even like a building,
in that its success depends upon the organization of a mass
into a form which pleases the eye with its proportions, balance, harmony, and at the same time serves the function
that it was created to serve.

A jar recently exhibited in New York (PL. 92B) [8] reveals an affinity with the Chinese. Its sturdy shape and
proportions give it rugged vigor. The potting is thick.
Like the *Chün Flower Pot,* it *looks* its weight, just as the
delicate Ting ware *looks* its lightness. The decoration is
a matter of bold contrasts of surface texture, an extraordinary smoothness opposed to incision and crackling. Two
bands emphasize the two main parts of the jar, the body
and the neck. The more powerful, with its incisive angularity, is on the larger body; the more suave, all curving, on
the smaller neck. Yet see how the triangles incorporate
the curve in the wavy lines of their sides, and how they
inclose three irregularly curved motifs which repeat a like
motif above.

[8] *Brown Stoneware*, a fabric which is fired at high temperature and has a
body of intense hardness. Designed by Émile Lenoble, a contemporary
French potter. Exhibited at the International Exhibit of Ceramic Art, Metropolitan Museum, N. Y., 1928–29.

Another piece with a cream glaze, crackled (Pl. 92C),[9] illustrates a tendency toward purely decorative ceramics with no other function except to provide a pleasing mass of color and texture. Out from a solid base rise flat crescent masses with great rhythmic sweeps of unbroken line, interwoven with the circular motif of the body of the fish. These forms recede in definite shallow planes like a relief carved in stone, so that there is a slight movement in depth in addition to the strong movement from side to side. With its vigorous rhythm and its architectural character, how decorative it is when placed against a ground and in a spaciousness where these qualities can display themselves!

READING

Illustrations of the technical process — wedging, throwing, coiling, turning, firing, glazing — will be found in:

BINNS, C. F., The Potter's Craft, N. Y., Van Nostrand, 1910.

COX, G., Pottery for Artisans, Craftsmen, and Teachers, N. Y., Macmillan, 1914.

RICHTER, G. M. A., The Craft of the Athenian Potter, New Haven, Yale University Press, 1923.

WINSLOW, L. L., Elementary Industrial Arts, N. Y., Macmillan, 1922.

SUGGESTIONS

1. The best understanding, as in weaving, comes through actual making. Construct simple shapes on the wheel and also by coiling. Keep in mind the purpose of the vessel, the relation of the form to the purpose, and the relation of the decoration to the form. Experiment on thin and thick potting, their relation to the form and its use.

2. Find ten or a dozen pieces of pottery whose use is known.

[9] *Cream Stoneware, Crackled.* From the Manufacture Nationale de Sèvres, France. Exhibited as the jar in Pl. 92B. (See the illustrated catalogue of this exhibit, published by the Metropolitan Museum, N. Y., October, 1928, for other examples of contemporary potters.)

Show how their use has determined any elements in their design. Find examples where use and design harmonize and where they do not.

3. Find examples of porcelain; of glazed pottery with no other decoration; of painted decoration; of incised; of relief.

Part Eleven

ART IN EVERYDAY LIFE

We are all potential artists — almost all of us. There are but few who seem entirely wanting in capacity for understanding or creating; many have considerable ability; a few become great artists. It is a matter of degree. Art and the way of art exist for most of us — not only exist but permeate all life, today as well as yesterday. Today life is most complex and its activities and contacts, however much they differ in number and breadth with the individual, are varied and pressing. With this immediate present we are concerned primarily.

A current opinion, far too common, holds that art is a luxury, a monopoly of wealth, a matter of museums, something to be indulged in only in one's leisure, and quite inessential to and divorced from one's daily activities. How far from the truth! It *is* true that to understand a great painting one must look at it long and contemplatively; that to understand a sonata one must hear it, undistractedly, many times. Few poems reveal all their beauty and meaning in one reading. Real understanding requires concentration of eye or ear, feelings, and intelligence. Granted, however, that great art is relatively rare and requires contemplation and leisure for its true appreciation, still art and a way of art permeate the world in which we live.

But what, you ask, has a *Skyscraper* or a *Navajo Blanket* or Leonardo's *The Last Supper* to do with my everyday life, my humdrum seven days a week? To be sure, our study of some of the arts has been restricted to the work of great masters, often of foreign lands, and far-away ages. But in them all, as we begin " to see what we know how to look for," we begin to discern certain qualities and char-

acteristics so constantly recurrent that we conclude that they are the result of some fundamental, universal principles. What words have we used constantly in our discussion, whether it be of buildings or statutes or paintings, of books or textiles or pottery? *Unity, variety, harmony, rhythm, balance, contrast, proportion, emphasis.* What words do we use in discussing music, the dance, literature? Are they not the same? Are there not, then, some guides to point out the way to art in everyday life?

Let us be specific. The way we look at things may or may not be an art. Recalling our discussion in the first chapter of seeing as the artist sees, consider the view framed by your own window — a yard, a street, a lake bordered by woods, a group of roofs. Can you apply to it the words we have just mentioned? Is it lacking in contrasting lines and masses, or colors? Would you shift the position of some objects, imaginatively, or by shifting your own position can you obtain a better balance? Everything in the view has a form.[1] When we look at these forms as artists, we re-form them. Is this not what we have seen the artist doing in all his works that we have studied? We have found him nowhere imitating what he sees, but everywhere taking the forms that he sees as his raw material and out of them creating new forms that are more beautiful, more real and significant than the originals. Sometimes the new form is close to the original; sometimes far removed, as we saw in our chapter on " Water and Rocks." To see everything as form or a group of forms and with imaginative insight to re-form these forms into something which has harmony, unity with variety, balance, rhythm — this is to see the world as an artist. Thus everything we see, from the small objects about our rooms to skyscrapers and mountains, we

[1] See p. 5, footnote 1.

see, if we are artists, as forms and unities of forms which give us a far greater sense of their reality and significance than any exact copy of their appearance can give. To see significant aspects of commonplace things (Fig. 69) [2] is to transform what is mediocre, if not ugly, into something that is lovely and worth our while.

She had a sensitivity that was very wide, eager and free . . . it lighted on small things and showed that perhaps they were not small after all. It brought buried things to light and made one wonder what need there had been to bury them.[3]

Do not the same principles hold in what we hear? In our music? As I sit writing on my porch some one on the road below is whistling a melody. He repeats it again and again. The monotony becomes irritating. Ah! He changes the key. This change brings in a pleasing variety. The whistler is the potential artist creating through the medium of tones a form for his melody. I listen for him to create a still more complex form, perhaps by the addition of another melody. In imagination I hear him interweave and contrast these two melodies (each a form) and unite them into a harmonious form which is the entire song. Just as the weaver of the *Navajo Blanket* selected two motifs, the step and the zigzag, which he varied and united into the harmonious form which is the work of art. Thus the whistler and I are two potential artists working together: one an artist in understanding because the ear can hear forms; the other an artist in creating because he can use forms. The eye too, to a limited extent, reinforces the ear in the comprehension of a musical form if one looks

---

[2] See Walt Whitman's description of a ride on a Brooklyn ferry and in a Broadway street car quoted by William James in *Talks to Teachers*, "On a Certain Blindness in Human Beings," N. Y., Holt, 1901.

[3] V. Woolf, *A Room of One's Own*, N. Y., Harcourt, 1929, p. 161.

at the score.[4] The pattern which a simple folk-melody
makes on the printed page contrasts in appearance as well
as in sound with that of a theme which consists of a group
of melodies in much the same way in which the simple
boldness of the *Navajo Blanket* contrasts with the complex
richness of the royal *Persian Carpet*.

To see and to hear as an artist is a necessary foundation
stone for doing things in an art way — creative activity.
For this too most of us have some capacity, if it is not left
latent. Let us consider a few of our daily activities. Can
we be creative artists in their pursuance? Can we make
out of them works of art? We might select four, almost
at random: writing letters, furnishing our rooms, selecting
our clothes, and using our leisure.

Can letter-writing be an art? Are not some letters more
pleasing than others? Why? Probably for at least two
reasons. First, because the letter presents to the eye a
pleasing form (see Fig. 103). The writing is legible and
is thoughtfully spaced with ample margins; and page follows page in a logical, harmonious way. The effect of the
form is an enhancement of the content. A pleasing form
alone arouses in the recipient an emotional response. But
how much greater the response if, in the second place, the
content too has a pleasing form! To write a letter, in fact
any kind of literature, one starts with an idea, which he
expresses through the medium of words. Words are to
the writer what stone is to the builder or sculptor, tone to
the musician, pigment to the painter, or clay to the potter.
By means of words he creates a form for the conveyance of
his idea. The better the form, the more forceful the expression, provided the idea is worth expressing. He may

[4] See T. W. Surette and D. G. Mason, *Appreciation of Music* N. Y., Gray,
1924, vol. 1, p. 32.

elaborate the idea, add other ideas for emphasis or contrast, just as the musician contrasts his melodies (musical ideas) or Leonardo, the figure of Christ (an idea of repose) with those of the disciples (an idea of agitation).

In any kind of literature as well as in the letter, the visual form of the printed words bears a direct relation to the form of the content, just as does the visual score to the audible form of the music. The grouping of words into paragraphs and the separation of paragraphs by space devices is a simple illustration of how the eye assists the mind to grasp a break in the thought.[5] Many poems by Carl Sandburg[6] will afford a more complex illustration in which the grouping of the printed words on the page creates as definite a pattern of light and dark as do the light and dark colors in the Sienese *Madonna* (Fig. 93). In both cases the purpose and result are the same: a form presented to the eye reinforces the idea presented to the mind. Thus we see that the fundamental principles of music and painting (we might carry the comparison further) are the fundamental principles of letter-writing also — in fact of any kind of writing, from the simple memorandum to a complete story or drama.

To turn to our second activity, do we find these principles at work in the furnishing of our rooms? Every one lives in an abode. Does he enjoy it or dislike it? Does it have a feeling of " rightness " about it? Or is he indifferent to it? To which of the two types illustrated in PL. 28 does your room belong? Is it overloaded with furnishings that are largely useless, and irritating in their demand of

---

[5] Compare a page of a modern book with a classical manuscript in which all the letters are capitals and follow each other with no punctuation and no paragraphing.

[6] See E. Rickert, *New Methods for the Study of Literature*, Chicago, University of Chicago Press, 1927, Chapter VII.

time for their care? Or is it reposeful and harmonious, a place in which one really likes to live?

Interior architecture, as we saw in our chapter on " Some Interiors," is a complex art with many branches, involving the purpose of the room; its space design by the placement and proportions of walls, ceiling, and openings — the permanent elements; and the furnishings and people — the changeable elements. Its ultimate character is dependent upon not one but all of these elements; working in accord, if harmony results; at cross purposes, if discord results.

For many of us our room is already built. It may be furnished or partly so. If it is ugly to start with, is our objective hopeless? By no means. The room may be small and disproportionately low; a door and windows break three sides and leave the fourth a long monotonous wall surface. Let us consult, imaginatively, our sense of balance. If the room is too small, a quiet, inconspicuous, lightly broken wall treatment of retreating color will add a feeling of spaciousness; while an advancing color and a wall paper of strongly contrasted light and dark would make the room appear even smaller. If it is too low, an emphasis upon verticality (as in the hangings and other furnishings) and a suppression of horizontality (as in the avoidance of horizontal moldings and borders) will increase the appearance of height. The *Parthenon* (PL. 7) is long and low, but the insistent verticals of the fluted columns create a balance and a feeling of " rightness." *Chartres* (PL. 17) is very vertical, hardly held in restraint by horizontals. Here too is " rightness." Both are " right." Behind the design lie the purpose and the people with their ideas and feelings. Balance for the Greek was different from balance for the Gothic. One must not be dogmatic. Each must determine for himself what constitutes balance

in his own room. But balance there must be; without it everything collapses.

What then of the monotonous wall space? It may be needed to balance the broken walls of the other sides, just as the reposeful spaces about *Day* (PL. 43) were needed to balance the intense restlessness of the figure. If, on the other hand, the wall still remains monotonous and over-balances with its unbroken space, the furnishings (perhaps a picture or hanging) can be used to break the large area and establish a balance.

In the furnishings, the first question is that of function: what is there in the room that has no use in function or design? What can be eliminated without sacrificing efficient use and pleasing appearance? Having reduced the furnishings to the necessary minimum with a modicum for that which delights by indulging the personal tastes of the owner (for too much impersonality is as bad as none), one may then consider each piece, first as a form and then as related to the other forms and to the form of the room as a unit. A good chair, for instance, *looks* its use. The supporting parts are proportioned to the weight; the back and arms are related to the seat so as to insure comfort. The materials fittingly harmonize and contrast. The upholstery, in pattern, color, and texture, depends upon the material of the frame: massive wood, woven reed, light metal. The construction of a good chair is dependent upon the same guiding principles as the *University Chapel* (PL. 3). In both it is a matter of materials, the way in which they are used, and the purpose for which they are used, subject to the creative sensitivity of the artist who can proportion and balance, contrast and unify. In the *Chapel* the thick stone walls, the great windows, the relative open and solid stone areas of the tower, the relative proportions

of all parts — every detail presents itself to our eyes as a contributing element to the unified and harmonious whole; and the visual impression of strength and aspiration dignifies every event which takes place in the building. It is true that the *Chapel* gains in majesty and power through its size. A fine chair, though small in comparison, is as architectural in principle and may appeal to some as strongly as the *Chapel.*

To return to our room, though the chair may be fine of itself, does it belong in the room? Have you not seen a chair look ugly in one place and " just fit " in another? Study that chair, not in itself but in its relation to its surroundings, and you will probably find the explanation. Its form or some details of its form — its materials, their color or texture, its shape, size, or proportions — clash too dissonantly or harmonize too mildly with the table, for example, or with the room as a whole. Our objective, the harmony of the whole, is a stern master. Yet by it every piece of furnishing in a good room — furniture, hangings, wall decoration, rugs, pictures, ornaments, lighting fixtures — is measured. Each is a form of a definite material — wood, stucco, tile, metal, textiles, glass — subject to its own guiding principles of material, function, and design, and each is also a contributing element to the whole.

If we can make of our rooms works of art, can we not do the same with ourselves in our personal appearance? Just as we began with what was given us, in making a work of art out of our room, so in the matter of ourselves we begin with what nature has given us. It may or may not be beautiful. We re-formed the ugly room into an attractive one by infusing into it, by means of the furnishings, qualities of balance, proportion, unity, and harmony in accordance with our own personal interpretations of those qualities.

In the same way the physical self is re-formed by clothing into something attractive or unattractive in proportion as the garments are selected to secure these qualities. Have you watched people on the street with this observation in mind? How often does a tall gaunt person wear garments that accent verticality! And the stout person, those which emphasize horizontality! A pale type — pale complexion, light eyes and hair — often selects a pale uncontrasted color when it should have a color that in hue and intensity brings in the needed contrasting strength. Some types need brown; some, blue. Not the prevailing style but suitability to myself. My physical self and my personality (ideas to be expressed) are the basic forms to be re-formed and hence set forth in their essential qualities, not obliterated. Each article of clothing is partly a form in itself and largely a contributing element to the whole. How attractive is a hat in a shop window! How ugly on me!

One more activity we mentioned for discussion — the way in which we use our leisure. Here too can we see the way of art? It depends upon whether we see life itself as an art — a balanced, unified, harmonious whole. If we do, then we know that variety is essential for this harmony.

After all, there is not only variety, but also unity. The diversity of the Many is balanced by the stability of the One. That is why life must always be a dance, for that is what a dance is: perpetual slightly varied movements which are yet always held true to the shape of the whole.[7]

The great wall of the *Egyptian Temple* is more unified when broken by carving and color. The rapid zigzag motif of the *Navajo Blanket* brings in so refreshing a contrast to the more austere step pattern that the unity of the entire design is greater. In Leonardo's *Last Supper* the reposeful

[7] H. Ellis, *The Dance of Life*, Boston, Houghton, 1923, p. viii.

room and the poiseful central figure would be uninterest-
ing were they not set over against and united with the restless, moving masses of the disciples. Is there a work of art
which does not illustrate this principle of variety in unity?
If life, then, is a work of art, may we not see in leisure a
vitalizing variety to the main business of life? May we not
look upon leisure as a form and ask whether the character
of the form is such that it exists partly for itself and partly
for the intensification which its contrasts bring to the larger
whole? The pattern of life may be like that of the *Navajo
Blanket:* simple and forceful; or like that of the royal *Persian Carpet:* complex and rich. It is a difference not of
value but of kind. One thing, however, is certain: neither
the *Navajo Blanket,* nor the *Persian Carpet,* nor any kind
of life is a work of art without wisely placed, balanced
variety. As for life, the activities of our leisure time form
one of the chief sources of this variety.

There is a tendency, in these days of specialization, to
pigeonhole our activities — work, play, religion, civics, art
— and when engaged in one, to banish all others to their
tight compartments. An illustration of the possibility of
breaking down these partitions is the late Prof. A. A.
Michelson, one of the world's great physicists, who, when
asked why he persisted in his attempt to measure the
velocity of light even more precisely when the present
measurement was an acknowledged absolute, said that it
" amused " him. A profound scholar, relentless in his demands for accuracy, found " amusement " in his work.
Fittingly he has been called the " scientist-artist."

If we conclude that it is possible to look at everything
with the artist's vision and to pursue all activities in accordance with art principles, let us restate what is involved.
Life is the raw material of the artist, as it is of every one's

living. The artist, in the first place, as he looks out upon the world, sees things, people, and incidents as forms and grasps their significance, both outward and inward, and the significant aspects of commonplace things, in proportion as he has within himself the capacity to perceive and feel such significance. In the second place, he creates an appropriate form in appropriate material for a convincing expression of this significance. In the third place, he is a craftsman grounded in the technique of his craft. Some of these activities he pursues consciously, some subconsciously. No one of them is *a priori,* nor are they to be isolated. Each acts on and is inextricably fused with the others. They do not account entirely for the artist. Other forces are at work — social, economic, religious, geographic. But these three are distinguishable and essential wherever we find great art. There is, it is true, a difference in degree between profound, imaginative, universal art and the art of our daily activities — but not in kind. We are all potential artists.

READING

BEST-MAUGARD, A., A Method for Creative Design, N. Y., Knopf, 1926.

BUERMEYER, L., The Aesthetic Experience, Merion, Penn., Barnes Foundation, 1929.

DIMNET, E., The Art of Thinking, N. Y., Simon and Shuster, 1930.

ELLIS, H., The Dance of Life, Boston, Houghton, 1923.

GOLDSTEIN, H. I., and V., Art in Everyday Life, N. Y., Macmillan, 1926.

LETHABY, W. R., Form in Civilization, London, Oxford Press, 1922.

MEARNS, H., Creative Youth, Doubleday-Doran, 1929.

SPALDING, W. R., Music: An Art and a Language, N. Y., Schmidt, 1920.

INDEX

The diacritical marks used are those found in Webster's New
International Dictionary.

Abstract, building, 143; design, 157; form, 105; idea, 175; sculpture, 156

Accent, 19, 24, 41, 100, 103, 150, 168, 201, 207, 211, 262 ff., 289, 301, 303, 314

Acropolis (à-krŏp'-ȯ-lǐs), 32 note

Adobe (à-dō'-bĕ), Indian, 13, 14

Alabaster, 68

Alphabet of art forms, 234

Altar, 36, 38, 68, 72

American Colonial. *See* Craigie House; Powel House.

Amphitheater, 26 note, 27

Apse, 70, 72, 86, 97, 98, 100

Arabesque, 205, 224, 286, 302

Arcade, 25

Arch, pointed, 75, 81, 84, 96; round, 30, 65, 66, 81

Arch system, 27, 28 ff., 56, 84

Architecture, 14; interior, 116, 323

Armature, 145, 146

Automobiles, 5, 14, 135

Axis, 18, 49, 81, 109, 128 f., 155

Background, 67, 141, 217, 225, 227, 238, 241

Bahram (bäh'-ràm) Gur (gōōr), 204 ff., 254

Balance, 7, 81, 82, 85, 90, 142 f., 157, 162, 166, 173, 201, 211, 229, 232, 233, 237, 240, 254, 263, 272, 308, 319, 323 ff., 326; asymmetrical, 126, 128, 147, 206, 214; symmetrical, 18, 115, 147, 151, 196, 206, 207, 214, 225, 270, 286

Bamboo in the Wind, 178, 193, 234

Banquet Scene, Egypt, 194 ff., 215

Baptistery (băp'-tĭs-trĭ), Florence, 94, 95; doors, 95

Barrel vault, 57 f.

Basilica (bà-sĭl'-ĭ-kà), plan, 70

Baths of Caracalla (kăr-à-kăl'-à), 52, 56, 69, 71, 95; plan, 55

Beethoven (bā'-tō-vĕn), Ludwig (lüd'-vĭg) von, 240

Berries, 288

Bible, Forty-two Line, 258, 259

Binding, 243, 244, 250, 254, 255, 270

Bird-form, 280, 283, 286; Hopi, 312

Birth of Athena (à-thē'-nà), 158 note

Bodhisattva (bō-dǐ-sät'-và), 164 f.

Body color, 187

Bokhara (bȯ-kä'-rä) pitcher, 304 ff.

Book covers, 243

Book-hands, 247 note

Book of Kells, 245 note

Border, 194, 250, 282, 290, 294

Botticelli (bȯ-tǐ-chěl'-lǐ), Sandro, 180, 190 f., 193

Brass, 145

Breviary (brē'-vǐ-à-rǐ), Burgundy, 258, 259

Brick, 26 note, 27, 30, 57, 60 note, 61, 146 note

Bridge, 12, 20, 114

Brocade, 277

Bronze, 2, 66, 95, 121, 145

Bronze-casting, 145, 168

Bronze-crowned Delphi (děl'-fĭ), 169

Brunelleschi (brōō-nĕl-lĕs'-kĭ), 94 note, 95 ff.

Brush, 180, 247

Brush strokes, 185, 186, 193, 213, 241, 302

Brush work, 239

Buddhists (bōōd'-ǐsts), 164, 189 note

Buffalo and Maize, 104

Building systems, 28, 38, 50, 56 ff., 65 f., 85 f.

Buttresses, 85

Byzantine (bǐ-zăn'-tǐn or bǐz'-àn-tǐn) art, 61 note

Cahokia (kà-hō'-kǐ-à) Power Plant, 113, 114

Calendar (Chartres), 83

California, gardens, 129

Calligraphy, 245, 288

Capitol, Washington, 136 ff.

Carbon, 182, 196

Carpets, 188

Carving, 145

Carvings, 51, 82 ff.

Cathedral of Florence. *See* Santa Maria del Fiore.

Cedar, 48

Cement, 27, 66, 67

Cenotaph, 108

Centaur (sĕn'-tôr) and Lapith (lă'-pith), 174

Center of interest. *See* Focal point.

Centering, 28

Ceramic (sĕ-răm'-ĭk) art, 298

Ceramicus (sĕ-ră-mī'-kŭs), 308

Cézanne (sā-zän'), Paul, 179; Village Road 230 ff.

Chalk, 180

Chapel, University of Chicago, 11, 21, 150, 324 f.

Characterization, 7, 171, 239

Charioteer, 168 ff.

Chartres (shär'-tr') Cathedral, 15, 37, 40, 74 ff., 94, 95, 96, 105, 115, 129, 143, 199, 240, 259, 314, 323; façade, 81, 82; plan, 86; windows, 86 ff.

Chiasmus (kī-ăz'-mŭs) in sculpture, 167

Chicago Plan Commission, 133

Chicago Tribune Tower, Saarinen (sär'-ĭ-nĕn) design, 23 note

Chinese painting, 178, 191 ff., 232 ff.; pottery, 314 ff.

Chippendale, 119

Chisel, 247

Chün (chōōn) flower pot, 313 ff.

Church of San Lorenzo, 154, 156

Church of Santa Croce (krō'-chĕ), 214 note

Cinnabar, 196

Circles, 64, 65, 97, 98, 200, 218

Cire-perdue (sēr'-pär-dŭ') method, 171 note

Clay, 145, 146 note, 274, 298 f.; 321; modeling, 145 f.

Clerestory (klēr'-stō-rĭ), 73, 74.

Cloister of Saint Paul's, 68, 71, 72

Clubhouses, Roman, 52, 55

Codex (kō'-dex), 250

Coffering, 59, 68, 220

Coherence, 100, 172, 178, 199, 216

Coiling, 311

Coins, 27, 169

Colonial Home. *See* Craigie House; Powel House.

Colonnade, 35, 37, 48

Colophon (kŏl'-ŏ-fŏn), 257, 258

Color, 41, 44, 47, 61, 66, 68, 75 f., 86, 87 ff., 92, 112, 200, 202, 203, 206, 208, 212, 224 ff., 228, 231, 238 f., 240, 254 ff., 280, 288, 289 f., 294, 296 ff., 299, 302 f., 305, 306, 309, 313 f., 323, 326

Colosseum (kŏl-ŏ-sē'-ŭm), 26 ff., 44, 54, 56, 58, 71, 72, 84, 95, 99, 102; plan, 29

Columbus Memorial (Whitney), 149, 150, 154, 158

Column of Trajan (trā'-jăn), 245 note

Columns, 38, 40, 49 ff., 56, 63; engaged, 31; free-standing, 31

Concrete, 20, 21, 26 note, 27, 57

Cone, 4

Consistency, 24, 43, 116 f., 235, 240

Contest of Athena and Poseidon (pŏ-sī'-dŏn), 41

Contour, 12, 24, 43, 60, 101, 167, 171, 173, 299, 300, 305, 306, 313

Contrast, 12, 58, 86, 88, 90, 98, 118, 125, 172, 200, 224, 227, 238, 239, 261, 277, 280, 282 f., 289, 294, 315, 319, 324, 326

Convention, 126 f., 163, 197, 202, 240, 312

Coördination, 74, 152

Copper, 297

Core, 145

Cornice, 25, 30, 31, 42

Cotton, 53, 244

Course, 38

Craigie (krăg'-ĭ) House, 15, 113 ff., 125, 127, 129, 130; plan, 115

Cramps, 26 note, 38

Cross, Greek, 97, 109; Latin, 81

Crown, 65

Cube, 65, 66, 98, 310

Cup, Greek, 306, 307

Cursive writing, 245 ff.

Curved line, 6, 21, 29, 40, 56, 57, 60, 84, 91, 95, 98, 99, 111, 119, 156, 157, 159, 163, 166, 170, 176, 180, 201, 216, 226, 231, 237, 270, 303, 306

Cylinder, 3, 6, 10, 11, 25, 98, 114

Cylix (sī'-lĭks). *See* Cup, Greek

Daily News Building, Chicago, 17 ff., 104; Plan 18

Damask, 118, 120, 277, 286

Dance, 147, 198, 293, 311

Dante (dăn'-tĕ; It. dän-tā), 190 f.

Dark. *See also* Light and dark.
Day, (Michelangelo), 154 ff., 172, 173, 324
Death of Saint Francis (Giotto), 214 ff., 222, 229, 230, 231
Decoration, 83, 112, 116 note, 301, 305, 307
Delphic (dĕl'-fĭk) Sibyl (sĭb'-ĭl), 183, 240
Demuth (dĕ-mūth'), Charles, 187
Depth, 5 note, 10, 174, 190, 198
Design, 13
Details, 6, 7, 39, 51
Diagonal line, 12 note, 40, 57, 115, 150, 157, 163, 172, 180, 215–16, 227, 270, 278
Dimensions, three, 141, 156, 157, 298; two, 174, 178
Diorite, 144, 151 note, 154
Dipylon (dĭp'-ĭ-lŏn) Gate, 35, 308
Discord, 14, 323
Distortion, 202
Divine Comedy, drawings (Botticelli), 190 f.
Dome, 3, 5, 64, 65, 92 f., 94 ff., 106 ff., 110, 291
Dome on pendentives, 65
Donatello (dŏn-ȧ-tĕl'-lō), 95
Dowels, 38
Dragons, 234
Drapery, 90, 156, 160, 163, 165, 167, 177
Drum, 97 note, 102
Duomo (dwō'-mō), Il. *See* Santa Maria del Fiore.
Dyes, vegetable, 293

Earth colors, 196
Egg, 184, 196, 207
Egypt; Map, 44; Tomb painting, 194 ff., 201, 203, 206, 215
Egyptian Temple. *See* Pylon Temple.
El Greco. *See* Theotocopuli.
Elgin (el'-gĭn) marbles, 32 note
Ellipse, 301
Emphasis, 73, 100, 102, 126, 210, 219, 256, 319, 326
Entablature (ĕn-tăb'-lȧ-tŭre), 42
Essence, 190, 193
Exaggerations, 239
Expression, 145, 157, 178, 181, 321, 328

Façade, 40, 45, 46, 47, 49
Fenestration, 25

Fibers, 274
Figure, human, 67, 81 ff., 84, 143, 146, 147, 165, 198, 307
Filling, 274
Finder, 170
Firing, 297 ff., 307, 314
Flavian (flā'-vĭ-ȧn) Amphitheater. *See* Colosseum.
Flight into Egypt, 219
Floated, 276
Florence, 92, 93
Focal point, 64, 73, 110, 133, 136, 157, 220 f.
Foreshortening, 302
Form, 5 f., 74, 112, 180, 202, 216, 220, 223, 228, 233, 241, 243, 245, 256, 264, 301, 319 ff., 324, 326, 327, 328
Formula, 234, 235
Fountain, 18, 63, 129
French style, 119
Fresco, 179, 182 ff., 196, 225, 228
Function, 10, 14, 19, 21, 27, 49, 84, 89, 104, 243, 300, 301, 324
Furniture, 118 ff., 121 f., 324 ff.

Gable, 38, 40, 41 note, 74
Garden, California, 129 f.; Craigie House, 116, 125; Italian, 127 ff.; Japanese, 121, 125 ff., 130, 309; Taj Mahall, 107 ff.
Genesis, 268 ff.
Geometric, 11, 51, 98, 143, 150, 217, 230, 279, 283, 286, 309. *See* Circle; Cone; Cube; Cylinder; Hemisphere; Pyramid; Rectangle; Sphere; Square; Triangle.
Gesso (jĕs'-ō), 184
Gill (ḡĭl), Eric (Gravestone), 176
Giotto (jŏt'-tō), 94 note; Death of Saint Francis, 214 ff., 222, 225, 229, 230, 231, 301; Flight into Egypt, 219
Glass, 21 note, 24, 67, 76, 84; Gothic, 78 ff., 85, 86, 87, 88, 89, 188, 290, 314
Glassworking, 87 f.
Glazes, 186, 226, 297, 298 f., 305, 306, 307, 313, 314; glazing, 299
Glue, 196, 207
Goat (Chartres), 83
Gogh, Vincent van (Sunflowers), 186 f.
Gold, 36, 61, 66, 91
Gothic style, 95, 96
Gouache (g-wäsh), 207
Gravel, 29

Gravestone (Eric Gill), 176
Groin vaulting, 58
Gropius (grō′-pĭ-ŭs), Walter, designs, 21 note
Guilds, 79, 87, 89
Gum, 184, 207
Gum arabic, 196
Gutenberg (goō′-tĕn-bērg) Bible. *See* Bible, Forty-two Line.

Halo, 162, 163, 211, 219
Hare Pursuing a Monkey, 189
Harlequin (här′-lĕ-kwĭn), (Picasso), 199 ff., 215, 230
Harmony, 6, 7, 12 ff., 21, 61, 84, 87, 97, 99, 154, 159, 163, 193, 225, 237, 238, 243, 254, 270, 272, 280, 301, 308, 319, 323 ff.
Harpy figure, 303
Hatching, 185
Heberton (hē′-ber-tŏn) House, 130
Hemisphere, 65
High lights, 168, 208, 225
Hippodrome, 63
Hogan (hō′-gŏn), 272, 293, 310 note
Homer, Winslow (Northeaster), 232, 235
Honey, 184
Hopi (hō′-pē) jar, 309 ff.
Horizontal line, 19, 20, 21, 25, 40, 71, 72, 81, 90, 95, 99, 111, 114, 115, 157, 172, 176, 180, 201, 216, 219, 231, 240, 323
Hue, 181, 183, 203, 262, 314, 326
Hypnerotomachia Poliphili (hĭp′-nĕ-rō-tō-mä′-kĭ-á pŏl-ĭ-fē′-lē), 261 ff.

Ideal, Greek, 39
Illusion, 5 note, 178, 190
Incising, 299
Inconsistency, 95
Incunabula (ĭn-kŭ-năb′-ū-lá), 250
Indian Warrior (Mestrovic), 171 ff.
Indigo plant, 288
Infanta (in-fän′-tá) Marguerita (mär-ger-ē′-tá) (Velasquez), 240 f.
Ink, 180, 191, 193, 259
Inlay, marble, 73, 112; silver, 48; wood, 120
Inscriptions, 51, 71, 112, 193, 297
Interior decoration, 44 note; 116, 325
Interpretation, 264, 325
Iron, 8, 26, 42, 89
Irregularity, 4, 43, 72, 273, 300, 302, 315

Istanbul (ĭs′-tan-bul) (Constantinople), 59 ff.
Ivory, 36, 144, 243

Japanese Garden, 125 ff., 130
Japanese House, 120 ff.
Japanese painting, 189 ff.
Japanese Saint, 162 ff.
Jewels, 80, 86, 88, 108, 243
Joseph Conrad (Adams), 266 ff., 270
July (Chartres), 79, 83
Justinian (jŭs-tĭn′-ĭ-án), 60 note, 62 ff.

Kaolin (kā′-ō-lĭn), 314
Karnak (kär′-năk), 49 note
Keystone, 28, 29
Khafre (käf′-rā), 151 ff., 158 ff., 173
Kings and Queens of Judah (Chartres), 83, 84
Kiva (kē′-vá) (Hopi), 310
Knotting, 278, 279
Koran (kō′-ran), 108, 112, 251

Lacquer, 121
Lantern, 94 note, 96, 100
Lapis lazuli, 182
Last Supper (Leonardo), 220 ff., 226, 318, 322, 326
Law-givers, 103
Lead, 38, 60 note, 61, 88
Leather, 2, 251, 255
Leisure, 38, 55, 273, 326, 327
Leonardo da Vinci (lā-ō-när′-dō dä vēn′-chē), 185, 220 ff., 226, 318, 322, 326
Lifeline in Hopi art, 312
Light, 9, 10, 12, 228, 230, 241
Light and dark, 12, 17, 33, 40, 41, 68, 90, 111, 147, 180, 199, 212, 216, 218, 233, 236 ff., 322
Light and shadow, 10–11, 12, 31, 33, 74
Lime, 29, 183
Limestone, 76 note, 96, 144, 195
Line, 12, 17, 21, 31, 40, 51, 57, 64, 67, 75, 76, 90, 114, 127, 150, 157, 160, 161, 178, 180, 189 ff., 194, 199, 201, 203, 206, 211 f., 216, 219, 220, 229, 239, 263, 289, 308. *See* Curved, Diagonal, Horizontal, Vertical.
Linen, 184
Lintel, 28, 38, 50, 51, 56; system, 28
Longfellow House. *See* Craigie House.
Loom, 274 ff., 282, 295
Lorenzetti (lōr-ĕn-zĕt′-tē), Ambrogio

(ăm-brō'-jō) (Madonna), 208 ff., 227, 229, 322
Lotus, 162, 164, 197
Lumber, 22
Lustre, 118
Luxor (lŭk'-sôr; lŏŏk'-sôr), 49 note

Machine Age, 43
Machinery, 22, 273
Madder root, 288
Madonna (Lorenzetti), 208 ff., 227, 322
Maiden, Bronze, 165 ff.
Maitreya (mī-trā'-yå), 164 f.
Man with the Glove (Titian), 236 ff.
Man-Eagle (Hopi), 312
Manufacture, 22, 273
Manuscripts, 243, 258
Maps: Athens, 33; Egypt, 44; Istanbul (Constantinople), 60; Italy, 209; Navajo and Hopi reservations, 292; Rome, 54
Marble, 2, 26 note, 38, 53, 63, 66, 108, 144, 158 note, 175 note
Margin, 206, 254, 256, 270, 321
Mass, 9, 12, 17, 33, 40, 94, 143, 147, 169, 171, 172, 174, 298, 313
Materials. See Alabaster; Alloys; Berries; Brass; Brick; Bronze; Carbon; Cedar; Cement; Chalk; Cinnabar; Clay; Concrete; Copper; Cotton; Diorite; Dyes; Earth; Egg; Enamels; Fibers; Glass; Glue; Gold; Gravel; Gum; Gum arabic; Honey; Indigo; Ink; Inlay; Iron; Ivory; Jewels; Lacquer; Lapis lazuli; Lead; Leather; Lime; Limestone; Linen; Lumber; Madder root; Marble; Metal; Minerals; Mucilage; Oil; Paint; Paper; Pigment; Piping; Plaster; Plaster of Paris; Porphyry; Reed; Rice (paper); Rock; Sand; Sandstone; Silver; Size; Skins; Soap; Soot; Steel; Stone; Stucco; Sugar; Threads; Tile; Timber; Tin; Tones; Travertine; Tufa; Varnish; Wax; Wire; Wood; Wool; Words
Medallion, 80, 255; window, 89, 90
Medici (mĕd'-ĭ-chē) Vase, 301 f.
Medium, 145, 146, 321
Melody, 2, 320, 321, 322
Meštrović (mĕs'-trō-vĭch), Ivan, 171 ff.
Metal, 44, 61, 66, 87, 168, 324, 325

Metope (mĕt'-ō-pē), 41, 42, 174
Michelangelo (mī'-kĕl-ăn'-jĕ-lō), 97 ff., 146, 147, 154 ff., 182 ff., 240, 324
Michelson (mī'-kĕl-sŏn), A. A., 327
Minarets, 60 note, 109, 111, 112
Minerals, 22
Miniatures, 254, 258
Miracle of Saint Mark (Tintoretto), 223 ff., 229
Moby Dick, 264 f.
Modeling, painting, 183, 185, 186, 237, 241; sculpture, 145, 160, 164
Moldings, 94
Monochrome, 178
Monotony, 44, 51, 320, 323, 324
Mosaic, 60 note, 61, 66, 67, 68, 73
Mosque, 32 note, 60 note, 61
Motif, 100, 149, 156, 157, 200, 202, 218, 237, 282, 289, 290, 293, 294, 302, 305, 316
Movement, 4, 17, 19, 24, 66, 155, 156, 175, 234, 286, 289, 303, 316
Mucilage, 191
Music, 1 f., 7, 47 f., 63, 64, 76, 166, 188, 194, 207, 240, 264, 285, 318, 322

Navajo (năv'-å-hō) blanket, 294, 318, 320 f., 326 f.
Nave, 70, 72 ff., 96
Nebraska State Capitol, 14, 41, 101 ff., 143, 150; plan, 105
New Sacristy, 154, 156
Nine Dragon Scroll (Chinese), 232 ff.
Northeaster (Homer), 232
Nude, Greek, 166

Obelisks, 45, 46 ff.
Obi (ō'-bē), Japanese, 285, 286
Oil painting, 182, 186 ff., 225, 227
Organization, 114, 166, 201, 216, 220, 231, 236 f., 298, 301, 315
Originality, 39, 109
Ornament, 40, 41

Painting, direct, 186; indirect, 225
Palmette, 286
Panathenaic (păn-ăth-ê-nā'-ĭk) Procession, 41.
Paneling, 118, 119, 120, 220, 221
Pantheon (păn'-thē-ŏn), 94
Paper, 118, 207, 244, 250, 255
Papyrus (på-pī'-rŭs), 244
Parchment, 244
Parthenon (pär'-thê-nŏn), 13, 14, 32 ff., 63, 82, 83, 102, 111, 115, 142,

158 ff., 174, 199, 216, 230, 323; frieze, 40, 41, 175 ff., 219 note, 221; plan, 37

Patio, 130

Pattern, 6, 40, 41, 126, 201, 218, 240, 278, 280, 285, 312

Pediment, 38, 41, 42

Pen, 245, 247; strokes, 245

Pendentives, 67, 81, 82

Persian Animal Carpet, 288, 294, 303, 321, 327; Jar, 301; Miniature, 180, 204; Romances, 205, 253 ff.

Personality, 5, 15, 17, 34, 76, 109, 112, 166, 238, 240

Peruvian (pê-rōō′-vĭ-ɑn) textiles, 280, 281 ff.

Pharaoh, 46 f., 49, 51, 62, 154

Pheidias (fī′-dĭ-ɑs), 158 note

Picasso (pē-käs′-sô), Pablo (Harle-quin), 199 ff., 218, 229, 230

Piers, 29, 30, 31, 65

Pigment, 146 note, 182, 185, 186, 187, 191, 196, 200, 207, 274, 279

Pilaster (pĭ-lăs′-têr), 98, 99

Pile, 277 ff., 287

Piping, 146

Pitcher, 299 f., 304 ff.

Plain cloth weave, 277

Plane, 24, 151, 152, 159, 160, 175, 177, 217, 307, 316

Plaster, 121, 182 ff., 195

Plaster of Paris, 184

Plinth, 149

Porcelain, 299, 314

Porphyry, 144

Portrait, 153, 166, 170, 236 ff.

Potter's wheel, 296 f., 299

Pottery, 298 ff.

Powel House, 117 ff., 127

Principles, 141, 179, 319, 320, 322, 325

Printing, 248 ff.

Profile, 175, 176, 197

Proportion, 10, 11, 24, 40, 73, 86, 90, 103, 131, 147, 171, 213, 222, 239, 249, 256, 298, 304 ff., 309, 313, 315, 319, 324–25

Psalter, 257

Purpose, 9, 10, 31, 38, 324. See Function.

Pylon (pī′-lŏn) Temple, Egypt, 44 ff., 153, 326

Pyramid, 101, 109, 110, 149, 219; form, 10

Quill, 245, 247, 249

Rai (rä), Ray. See Rhages.

Ramesseum (răm-ê-sē′-ŭm), 50 note

Rectangle, 66, 156, 221

Red-figured ware, 306

Reed, 196, 244, 324

Relief, 51, 104, 141, 150, 174 ff., 186

Religion, 38, 39, 49, 62, 67, 76, 84, 107, 147, 153, 161, 164

Rembrandt van Rijn (rěm′-bränt vän rīn), 228 ff.

Renoir (rěn′-wär), 203, 231

Rep, 276

Repetition, 51, 71, 115, 149, 155, 200, 305

Rhages (rä′-jěs) jar, 300 ff., 308

Rhythm, 4, 12, 17 ff., 20, 24, 25, 31, 40, 61, 66, 68, 72, 100, 101, 159, 168, 173, 175, 199, 212, 231, 234, 272, 280, 282, 285, 286, 289–90, 314, 316

Rib vaulting, 85; ribs, 84 f., 96, 100

Rice (paper), 121, 122, 250

Rock, 30

Roofing, 28, 56, 57, 65, 85

Roofing stones, 48, 50

Royal Portal (Chartres), 83, 84

Rugs, Persian, 287 ff., 304

Saint Francis. See Death of Saint Francis.

Saint Jerome as Cardinal (El Greco), 238 ff.

Saint Paul's Without the Walls, 68 ff.

Saint Peter's, 97 ff., 105, 106, 107, 109, 110, 114, 133, 156; plan, 98

Sand, 129

Sandburg, Carl, 322

Sandstone, 144; red, 108

Santa Maria del Fiore (sàn-ta mɑ̀-rē′-ɑ̀ děl fĭ-ō′-rě), 92, 95; plan, 96

Santa Maria in Cosmedin (cŏs′-mä-dĭn), 72, 73, 152

Santa Sophia (sô-fē′-ɑ̀) 60 ff., 84, 90 ff., 96, 105, 114, 231, 240, 256; plan, 64

Sarcophagus, 157

Satin weave, 276 ff.

Scale, 23, 53, 56, 57, 63, 256, 264

Screens, 120, 121, 125

Scroll (Chinese), 232 ff.; book, 249 ff.

Serica (sär′-i-kɑ̀). See Silk fabrics.

Serifs (sěr′-ĭfs), 248, 249

Setting, climatic, 10, 41; geographic, 10, 52, 74 ff., 105, 127 ff.

Shed, 275

Shuttle, 276, 279

Sienese (sē-ĕn-ēz′) Madonna. *See* Lorenzetti.

Signature, guild, 80, 87

Silhouette, 5 note, 68, 101, 121, 170, 171, 172, 211, 224, 307

Silk fabrics, 53, 122, 284 ff.

Silver, 48, 66, 108, 180

Silver point, 180

Simplification, 154, 170, 279

Sistine (sĭs′-tēn) Chapel, 183

Site, 69, 141, 143, 148, 161

Size, 184

Skins, 244

Skyscraper, 4, 7, 10, 15, 18, 20, 21 ff., 43, 44, 51, 114, 115, 149, 231, 318

Slip, 301

Soap, 207

Solidity, 50, 98, 103

Soot, 191

Space, 53, 56, 61, 64, 75, 90, 171, 190, 213, 216, 222, 224, 226, 230 ff., 307

Sphere, 11, 98

Spiraling, 155, 158, 289, 303

Spire, 74, 75, 76 note, 81, 96

Square, 63, 66, 74, 110, 172

Stability, 4, 30, 31, 56, 85, 103, 142, 143, 219

Stairway, 116

Steel, 12, 20 f., 22, 51, 114, 146 note

Step pattern, 293, 294, 320, 326

Stone, 12, 21, 27–28, 50–51, 84–85, 126–27, 129, 141, 144, 146–47, 151, 155, 158, 177, 321

Stone-carving, 154

Stoneware, 315 note, 316 note

Story of Two Lovers, 263

Street Boys, Egypt, 198

Strength, 12, 18, 168, 326

Stucco, 2, 118, 127, 130

Subject matter, 67, 104, 141, 146, 166, 171, 219

Subordination, 110, 153, 156, 211

Sugar, 207

Sunflowers (Van Gogh), 186 f.

Swiss Chalet (shà-lā′), 13, 14, 16

Symbolism, 90, 108, 110, 153, 164, 181, 233, 272 f., 293, 294

Tactile sensation, 2

Taj Mahall (täj mȧ-häl′), 15, 106 ff., 125, 133, 164; plan, 106

Tapestry, 276, 281 ff.

Tasse de Chocolat (shȯ′-kȯ-lä) (Renoir), 203

Technical processes. *See* Bronze-casting; Chinese painting; Cire-perdue; Clay modeling; Fresco; Glassworking; Glazing; Gouache; Inlay; Mosaic; Oil painting; Pottery; Stone-carving; Tempera; Water color; Weaving; Wood-carving; Woodcut

Telephone Building (New York), 23

Tempera (tĕm′-pȧ-rä) painting, 182, 184 ff., 228

Temple. *See* Pylon Temple; Parthenon.

Terrace figure. *See* Step pattern.

Tesserae (tĕs′-ĕr-ē), 66, 67

Textiles, 272 ff., 325

Texture, 2, 12, 66, 88, 112, 127, 131, 152, 184, 187, 241, 255, 271, 272, 277, 280, 288, 289, 299, 313, 315, 316, 324

Theodora (thē-ȯ-dō′-rȧ), 62 ff.; mosaic, 67

Theotocopuli (the-ȯ-tȯ-kȯ′-pu-lē), Domenico (dȯ-mā′-nē-kō) (Saint Jerome as Cardinal), 238 ff., 241

Theseus (thē′-sūs; thē′-sē-ŭs) Cup, 307, 308

Threads, 146 note, 274

Three Figures (Parthenon), 158 ff.

Thrust, 13, 142, 160

Tile, 24, 29, 121, 127, 130, 205, 207, 208

Timber, 28

Tin, 53

Tintoretto (tĭn-tō-ret′-tō) (Miracle of Saint Mark), 223 ff., 229

Titian (tĭsh′-ȧn), 186 note; Man with the Glove, 236 ff., 239, 241

Tivoli (tĭv′-ȯ-lĭ). *See* Villa d'Este.

Tomb of Giuliano (jōō-lĭ-än′-ō) de Medici (de mĕd′-i-chē). *See* Day.

Tomb of Nakht (näkt) and Tawi (tä′-wē), 194 ff., 201, 203, 206, 215

Tonality, 88, 184, 225

Tones, 146 note, 176, 188, 193, 225, 274

Tower, 74, 81, 82, 92, 94, 101, 102, 324

Transept, 86,

Travertine, 26 note, 29, 30, 71

Triangle, 157, 200, 201, 218, 237, 238, 315

Triglyph (trī′-glĭf), 41, 42

Tufa, 26 note

Tulip wood, 120

Twill weave, 276, 278
Type, 244
Type-face, 248 ff.

Underpainting, 186, 226
Unit shapes, 200, 218
Unity, 4, 6, 14, 31, 71, 73, 98, 103, 109, 114, 122, 125, 129, 130–31, 156, 159, 172, 203, 216, 219, 240, 259, 263, 301, 305, 313, 319, 326
Unmerciful Servant (Rembrandt), 228 ff.

Variations, 4, 24, 283
Variety, 18, 24, 58, 71, 73, 100, 170, 172, 175, 200, 262, 263, 282, 319, 320, 327
Varnish, 185
Vassall-Craigie-Longfellow House. See Craigie House.
Vaults. See Barrel vault; Groin vault; Rib vaulting.
Velasquez (vā-läs'-kěth), Diego (dē-ā'-gō) (Infanta Marguerita), 240 f.
Vellum, 244
Velvet, 2, 272, 279
Vertical line, 12, 19, 20, 21, 25, 40, 73, 81, 90, 91, 95, 99, 100, 102, 103, 111, 114, 115, 157, 172, 176, 180, 201, 216, 221, 231, 239, 323
Villa d'Este (vīl'-la d'ěs'-tě), 127 ff.; plan, 128
Village Road (Cézanne), 230 ff.
Virgin. See Madonna.
Volume, 9 note, 10 ff., 31, 51, 53, 60, 103, 107, 141, 150, 152, 155; rec-

tangular, 11, 12, 17, 24, 33, 57, 61, 65, 68, 72, 74, 101, 114, 152, 172

Wagner (väg'-ner) (Tristan and Isolde) (trǐs'-tän and ǐ-sôl'-dà), 240
Warp, 274
Washington, 135 ff.
Water color painting, 182, 187 f.
Wax, 67, 145
Weave sword, 275
Weaving, 274 ff.
Wedging, 298
Weft, 274
White House (Washington), 137, 138
Whitney, Gertrude V., 149 note
Window, 16, 19, 61, 65, 66, 68, 79 ff., 86 ff., 103, 112, 243, 324
Window of the Virgin (Chartres), 42, 89 f.
Winter Horsetail, 24
Wire, 146
Wood, 120, 121, 144, 146 note
Wood block, 257
Wood-carving, 144
Woodcut, 262 ff., 270
Woof. See Warp.
Wool, 288
Words, 146 note, 274, 321
Wright, Frank Lloyd, 21
Writing, 245 ff.

Young Girl (painting), 6, 7; (photograph), 6

Zigzag, 194, 206, 239, 294, 320, 326
Zodiac (Chartres), 83
Zoning law, 23, 135